CW00546565

# UNDERFIRE

## The Dramatic Life of a London Fireman

Ray Chilton

First published 2006

Published by
Jeremy Mills Publishing Limited
The Red House
22 Occupation Road
Lindley
Huddersfield, HD3 3BD

www.jeremymillspublishing.co.uk

Layout and design © Jeremy Mills Publishing Limited
Text © Ray Chilton

ISBN 978-1905217-18-2

Front cover image by kind permission of Martin Lloyd-Elliott.

Dedicated to Christopher James Kirby
17th September 1975–6th April 2002

'There may be a wonderful completeness
in a life that lasted only a few years'.

Dean W.R. Inge 1860–1954

# CONTENTS

# PREFACE

The author was a London Fire Fireman for over 30 years. This is part of a letter from the men who served with him:

'Our Station Officer, Ray Chilton, is set to retire following a long and colourful career. Ray joined the Fire Brigade in 1968 serving at Battersea, Westminster, Kensington, Manchester Square, Paddington and Soho as both a fireman and in the junior officer ranks.

In 1975 he was commended for his actions at The Worsley Court Hotel where seven people, including a colleague, tragically died. He was further awarded The Queen's Commendation for Brave Conduct in 1976 for the same incident.

In 1984 he was promoted to Station Officer and posted to Soho Fire Station where he has served ever since. Ray has been in charge of many serious incidents on our ground, including the Oxford Circus Tube fire for which he was further commended, the Aldwych bus bomb, a serious fire at The Royal Academy of Art, and incidents on every street, alley and avenue in the West End.

He is one of the longest serving Station Officers in the Brigade and is respected by everyone for his knowledge, friendship, his fire-manship, his management style and his demeanour when dealing with whatever situation arises in the line of duty.

He has worked in Soho for most of his fire brigade life and perhaps one day he will put it all down in writing.

A true London Fireman.'

# INTRODUCTION

I am a simple man of little schooling with only one story to tell. I was a London Fireman for over 30 years. The story is about what I did and how I felt about my profession. My friends have encouraged me to put it into words. They tell me that people from all walks of life should know about real firemen. My firemen friends say that other firemen would be interested because it is a story about them. At times it is a grim, gritty story, a mixture of heartache and pain with its fair share of humour.

My aim is not to write a complicated historical account of the London Fire Brigade, nor do I want to get bogged down with detailed descriptions of fire service equipment, but sometimes my firemen friends will have to bear with me while I explain the bones of the job. I'm afraid there are some boring bits where I have to translate the 'firelingo' just to make the story clear as it proceeds.

This is my one and only chance to relate exactly what it was like being a fireman, and why we should hold them in such great esteem – to explain exactly what is at the heart of a group of people who only really come to the attention of the public at times of great conflagration, or when there is some kind of employment conflict.

Since retiring, I cannot stop reflecting on all the things that happened to me and maybe this will help to exorcise the ghosts that still haunt me. I keep thinking that if I don't make a record of it, somehow it will all have been a waste of time. I don't want it abandoned and left orbiting around inside my head. I don't want to lie on my death-bed and ask myself, 'What the hell was that all about?'

Anyone who does a job for a long time and has allowed it to become a substantial part of their life, must have such feelings and memories. Only, you could call it fortunate or unfortunate, but my story includes eighteen years as a Station Officer at one of the busiest fire stations in the world. I could not prevent Soho Fire Station from becoming part of my life, as there was no way it could be ignored. It won't roll over and lay down. It has such a powerful draw that it forces its way into your being and, as I am finding now, it's hard to shake-off.

In essence this is a story about me. It's about how I feel about my life in the Fire Brigade. It is not just an opportunity to snipe at the rights and wrongs of the job. I just want to say how important I held my pride and self-esteem. I care very much what the important people to me think, and I have a great affection for my fellow firemen. Not all of them, but the great majority of the people I have worked with, have meant a great deal. I am grateful for their friendship and trust.

I could exaggerate and say that I loved my job, but that was not the case; it was a fantastic experience that was full of excitement, humour and danger. I enjoyed most of it, but as for the rest, I just bit the bullet and got on with it. My bond was with Soho Fire Station and the firemen whose humour, dedication and ingenuity made the place exceptional.

I would also like to make it clear from the start that I will use the word fireman throughout my story. I am not ignoring the fact that there are women in the fire service, but as I have only worked with three women on a regular basis, it would unnecessarily complicate the writing by constantly differentiating between the sexes. I hate the word firefighter! I started out as fireman and as far as I'm concerned that's what I want to be called.

I will also change or leave out the names of anyone where I have anything to say that is even slightly detrimental.

It has been difficult deciding whether to tell my story or keep it to myself. After all, I know that there have been far more capable officers who served their time and have not divulged their secrets. I still look back at those men in awe, men that I admired as I was gaining my experience, who have taken their achievements with them into retirement. Sometimes I feel as though I may be betraying some code of secrecy; that I shouldn't let on. On the other hand, if we all keep it secret then we do ourselves a disservice. So here goes, 'stand from under' you unsung heroes!

*Chapter 1*

## THE START OF IT ALL

As you leave Clapham Junction railway station, heading for Victoria, if you look to your left you will see a very strange building. It looks like a helter-skelter but without the slide around the outside and certainly no coconut mats! It has openings that look like windows without glass. This is the drill tower at Battersea Fire Station, now covered with mobile phone masts.

The last time I passed this sight I was on my way to collect my personal belongings and mementos from my place of work. Soho Fire Station. 'My Station'.

That was not where it all began; it started at my first station, which was K23 Battersea where I was posted from training school in 1968.

I didn't have any life-long ambition to be a fireman. A friend of mine gave me the idea to join. He was fed up with his job but he could not get in because he was too short. This was 1967 and as I was to get married the next year it seemed like a good idea to get a secure job with some prospects. It would have been nice to have the word fireman on my marriage certificate, but as I got married to Eleanor a month before joining the Fire Brigade, my occupation went down as 'plumber's mate'. In those days plumbers were not the nouveau-riche they are now. It was a hard, dirty job that didn't pay that well. Much the same as the Fire Brigade!

I had left school at 15 without any qualifications. I had a string of jobs, which weren't going to lead to much. I had not thought about joining any of the services and certainly had no idea of how to become a fireman. I visited my local station, which was Sutton in Surrey. This was a new station, at that time having moved from the centre of Sutton to its present site out on the by-pass. I had my first introduction to the job by an old Leading Fireman who showed me around the station, told me a bit about the job and gave me the application forms.

In those days, if you were remotely acceptable, you went to Southwark Training School where you were required to carry out physical tests. These involved carrying a man of similar size and weight over a measured distance using a fireman's lift. Then you had to wind up the extension mechanism of an escape ladder. Next was a written exam. If you passed all of these you went on to have a medical. Then you had to wait while your personal details were checked. There was no way you would be employed if you had any form of criminal record. If you passed the medical there was an interview. Then, if everything was up to scratch, you were sent a start date.

Southwark Training School was built about 116 years ago in Southwark Bridge Road. Firstly, it was the headquarters of the Metropolitan Fire Brigade. It still houses Southwark Fire Station and Winchester House. Before being developed, this was the site of a pleasure gardens known as Finches Grotto – a smaller version of the famous Vauxhall Gardens, which was only walking distance away. Eventually the enterprise went bankrupt and a workhouse was built on the land. When I was there, part of the workhouse was still being used as classrooms. When the workhouse days came to an end the local MP bought the land and built a home for himself, Winchester House. In 1866 the entire site (and its buildings) were bought by the Metropolitan Board of Works who went on to build a headquarters for The Metropolitan Fire Brigade. From 1874 Winchester House was home to the Chief Officer, Eyre Massey Shaw. It was home to successive Chief Officers up until 1937 when the present HQ was opened at Albert Embankment. The Chief Officer's accommodation moved to Lambeth but Winchester House was used to house officers during the war. The old HQ was badly bombed and was demolished in 1969.

I can remember my first day at training school, 5th August 1968; it was like the first day at school. I felt completely bewildered. I did not know what was going on. Here I was, dumped in an alien land being bombarded with a strange language.

I found myself attached to a squad of about 16 men under the watchful eye of an instructor. Station Officer 'Ben' Gunn was a man who had the ability to get the best out of a group of young men from different backgrounds and his skills were something to be admired. This great man had served in the brigade since 1944 when he was able to join the National Fire Service by exaggerating his age. He was only 14 and said that he was 15!

The first thing they did with us was to send us up an escape ladder three floors to the roof, get off the ladder and walk around a flat area. What was this strange thing called an escape? Up until now escape meant get away! It would have been better if this was done during the acceptance process as a couple of recruits found they couldn't stand heights! So before the training started our numbers were reduced, and they had to go back begging to their previous employers.

This was even before we had a uniform. It was the last hoop in the selection – could you stand heights. Next we were taken to Stores and Clothing at headquarters to get our uniforms. This consisted of fireboots, tunics, leggings, two sets of denim overall trousers and jackets plus three shirts. These shirts had detachable collars – you had to buy your own collar studs. You got an undress uniform which was a double-breasted blue suit with shiny buttons and two pairs of shoes. All off the peg. Later, when you got to a station you were fitted for a made-to-measure undress uniform. On your head you wore a beret, which had to be in place whenever you left a building and entered the drill yard. If an instructor caught you without your beret there was hell to pay.

Leggings or over trousers were made from black plastic and were two separate pieces like cowboys chaps! You had to find a way of holding them up. A local cobbler did a good trade attaching a combination of split rings and snap hooks to your own leather belt to which the leggings could be clipped. We had to keep these leggings shined by using boot polish. One pair of shoes had to be bulled-up to a fine shine while the other pair was for everyday use.

I had to get used to the discipline. Some of the men in my squad had come out of the forces and knew what to expect, but it was all a surprise to me. Squad drill and being shouted at were new to me.

Training school would have been described as brutal in these days of equal opportunities and correctness. The instructors had to be obeyed, most were good-natured but there were a few really hard bastards. Now I know what they were up to but names like Clohessy, Snarey and Clarkson send a shiver down my spine! This wasn't civvy street; you had to learn to obey orders immediately and without question. If you didn't get it right you were sworn at. I can remember being called a 'scrote' and 'little shag', nothing too offensive but not language you could get away with nowadays. These expressions were used to convince you that as a recruit you were a very low form of human life. You were also punished by having to complete physical tasks. We were made to run up ladders or run from whatever part of the yard you had made your mistake and touch the blue doors of the equipment store. As you had to learn how to get up ladders quickly and safely, and some of us were not as fit as we should have been; this wasn't a bad thing.

We had to keep our uniform immaculate, which was not that easy as you constantly had to get it dry after being soaked on the training ground. On Friday afternoons we had to clean our quarters. Once your instructor decided it was clean we were allowed to leave. This was all to prepare us for station life where the firemen still cleaned the stations. Now there is no such thing as station work, and except for certain areas, the stations are cleaned by contractors.

At the end of every day you were knackered but I don't think I have ever felt fitter. I enjoyed the fireground training. This was how we learnt how to use the equipment and mostly consisted of running around and getting soaked. Not being particularly academic I struggled with the classroom studies. I also ran the risk of falling asleep. The classroom was bearable in the mornings but in the afternoon the old eyelids used to drop. I kept at it and with the help of my new wife, who tested me at home, I did get to grips with it all.

I made some good friends there, but it was impossible to keep in touch once you were posted to different areas on different watches.

We learnt how to use the equipment, how to look after it and how to test it for safe use. We also learnt how to pump water, tie knots and how to handle ladders safely. There were five types of ladder all made from wood; the 50ft escape, the 30ft extension ladder, the first floor ladder, scaling ladders and hook ladders. None of which are still in use and have all been replaced with metal ladders or completely dispensed with. Not only did we have to learn how to use them we had to learn their dimensions and weights.

The 50ft escape was a heavy extending ladder, which could also be elevated or depressed. It was manoeuvred by four men and mounted on a carriage. It was rolled along on what are best described as wagon wheels. It had to be counter balanced in order to get it on and off the fire engine. It was very heavy and needed a lot of effort to get into position, and then it had to be wound up by hand.

Long before there were organised Fire Brigades in London, these escapes were stationed at many locations in the more populated areas. They would be looked after by Conductors. These were men of great courage, some of whom became famous in their own right. They would shelter from the weather in sentry boxes. Locals would run to report a fire and then help to manhandle the escape through the streets leaving the rescues to the Conductor. Later they were transported on any vehicle capable of bearing the weight.

In about 1983 the escapes were all replaced with the 13.5 metre Lacon ladder. This is a sturdy metal extension ladder and became known as the '135'. The Brigade had gone metric by then. It also had to be handled by four men and we all had to be retrained in its use. Long props are permanently secured to the top of the main extension. When the ladder is in use, the end of the props are rested on the ground which makes the ladder more stable and stops it bouncing when it's being climbed.

The old extension ladder was a two-piece wooden ladder that could be used above the first floor and was 30ft long. The first floor ladder was a utility ladder used for low-level work. It could also be tied using a line by a prescribed combination of knots to the top of the escape so you could reach the fifth floor. The scaling ladders were short and could be shipped together either to go up or go down and were principally for use in confined spaces, such as getting down into basements when the stairs had been burnt away.

The hook ladder, although not as complicated as the escape, was the most difficult ladder to use. It was about the same length as a first floor ladder but was lighter and had a 2ft retractable bill or hook. It could be used singularly or by two men in various configurations to climb a building by passing the ladder upwards and hooking on to window ledges. Was it scary to use? Yes it was and it deserved a lot of respect. There was no safety equipment – if you fell off that was it.

The squad lost another man at this stage. He had joined straight from the army but the dreaded hook ladder got the better of him. He was sitting petrified on a sill and the instructors had to go up the internal staircase and prise him loose. It was a shame as he was a lovely bloke, full of confidence and humour.

At first you were trained at low levels but eventually you went over the top of the eight-storey training tower. The scariest part of the drill was the 'parapet mount'. You had to get on to the ladder after standing upright on the top floor, bending over, grabbing the horns of the ladder, turning and reaching down with your foot to step on to it, then swing out and proceed down.

Standing eight floors up, with bowels quivering, on a wooden sill less than 12 inches wide with nothing to hold on to, then bending over, not crouching, trying to avoid looking down at the ant-like instructor who you knew was going to give you all kinds of stick if you fouled-up. Mind you, if you fouled-up a bollocking would have been the least of your worries; you would have no worries at all!

Below the third floor the ladder was thrown around with flair and confidence. The higher you went the stiffer and more restricted your movements became. You could hear a sigh of relief when the third floor was reached on the way back down.

When fire brigades first came into existence most of the officers were recruited from the Navy and the Thames boatmen. Consequently, a lot of the terms and commands have originated from naval origin. So, except for a few alterations, does the rank structure. For instance, the whole of a station's daily activity is recorded in a log-book. Before more sophisticated instrumentation, the speed of a ship was measured by floating a log attached to a knotted rope and the distance run out in a certain time would be the measure of the ship's speed. Hence knots to measure speed and to keep a record of the distance travelled, these readings would be recorded in the logbook.

When equipment is ready to be raised from the ground, by persons working above, the order 'haul aloft' is shouted. Oppositely, 'haul away' is used, but if anything is to be dropped from above, 'stand from under' must be shouted.

Another obscure shout is 'well'. This is used when a ladder is being manoeuvred and reaches its desired position. When cannons aboard ships were being lined up to fire, 'well' was shouted when they were on target.

The working routines are also structured around those of a ship at sea. The term 'watch' is the length of time a particular group of men were on duty and responsible for the safety of the ship. In the Fire Brigade it refers to a group personnel who are always on duty together for a particular shift. At one time there were only two watches; Red and Blue. As employment conditions improved, a third watch was created – the White Watch. In these more enlightened times another colour would probably have been chosen. These colours originate from the 17th century when similarly the British fleet was split into three squadrons. Much later on a fourth Green Watch came into being and our hours were further reduced to 42.

A watch works a tour of duty consisting of two day shifts of nine hours then two night shifts of 15 hours worked around a six-week cycle and the tours move on by one day each week. On any given day all the stations in London are manned by the same colour watch. If needed, you can work out what days you will be working forever more and if you stay in the same place you could work with the same people for your whole career. This is how trust and friendships are built.

Any form of rope is called a 'line'. On the subject of lines; as part of its standard stowage, each fire engine carries a minimum of four lines; two for general use, a breathing apparatus guide line and a lowering line. The lowering line ends in two running loops, one is the standing part of the line and the other is spliced into the main line and is identified by a Turks Head knot. (A knot resembling a turban and usually made at the end of a line as a stopper. Some firemen who were a little over particular would make these knots on their axes to stop them from slipping from their hands while working.) The spliced-in leg needs to be marked because when lowering a person from an upper floor, the standing part is placed around the person's chest and the spliced-in part around their knees. If the spliced part should fail, the person will still be held by the standing part and will not fall. Practising this drill was even scarier than hook ladders. If you were the person to be lowered you were entirely dependent on the two men who were doing the lowering. Once the line was attached you were bundled onto the sill on, say, the fourth floor of the drill tower and there was always a terrifying moment when you went over the sill before the strain was fully taken-up. From there on, one man with the line passing under his foot and pushed hard against the outside wall began to pass the line from hand to hand lowering away. He was helped by another man who would share the weight and the quivering body would be lowered to the ground.

Other expressions, which are still in daily use and describe modern day activities, originate from the days of brass helmets and horse drawn steamers.

When the steamers were ready for action, to help get them rolling they stood on a purpose made slope called the 'run'. Nowadays 'on or off the run' denotes the status of a fire engine and its equipment and whether or not it is available to attend emergencies. When the steamers were dispatched into action the Victorian firemen used to shout, 'Out she goes'. That shout can still be heard to this day at Soho, 'Get them out!'.

It wasn't until I was at a station that I really appreciated how good it was at training school; I enjoyed the fact that it was busy and structured. I must admit that station life was a bit of an anti-climax. Once at the station you soon found out that it was not as exciting as you were led to believe. I was expecting fires every day and brave rescues and it's just not like that. I also enjoyed the camaraderie of the training squad, because we were all at the same level and there was not the pecking order of the watch at the fire station. You were the new boy; the snotty-nosed junior buck who was, in those days, quite frankly treated like shit.

Anyway, if you got through all this training, learnt all the theory, and learnt how to tie about 20 different knots you eventually you reached the pass-out. A few didn't make it; some resigned, others were dismissed or 'back squadded' (given more time to achieve the standard by being sent back to another squad who were further back down the line). One of the squad was very close to failing completely because he could not raise his voice. He could shout but he couldn't speak loud enough to make himself clear when we were being trained to use the radio telephones carried on each fire engine.

You could invite your family to see the pass-out, which was observed by senior officers. It took place at Lambeth, the headquarters of the whole brigade. The pass-out involved participating in a fireground exercise and showing your expertise on the dreaded hook ladder. Everything went well for me until a senior officer thought that he had seen me do something wrong on the hook ladder. He thought that at one stage I had let go of the ladder with both hands! I had to demonstrate to him and the gathered throng that I was doing this properly. Silly old duffer! If he had only known that the last thing I would ever do is let go of the ladder; my knuckles stayed white whenever I had to touch the thing!

Next came the piss-up. The instructors went out with the squad for a night on the town and after promising to be on your best behaviour you were allowed to stay overnight at the training school. I cannot remember much about the night but I do remember that we ended up at the Sunset Strip, Dean Street, Soho. I also remember that I was robbed of my wallet. It was impossible for me to foresee, thirty-five years later, on my last day in the Fire Brigade, that I would end up in the same place. I did not lose my wallet this time but I did, courtesy of the management, get a personal little show by three naked ladies who planted kisses on my poor old bald head!

So, back to the past. Not all the squad behaved themselves. During the night one of the men misbehaved; I can't bring myself to say what he did but he must have been very drunk. He was found out and dismissed. Yes, after all that work he was chucked out. It was like that back then – no compassion, no second chances.

I recently met a man who told me that he had been a fireman and had joined in the 1950s. After he had served about ten years at the old Cannon Street Station he was told that he was being transferred to Clerkenwell and he did not want to go. He foolishly put it in writing that he would rather resign than go to Clerkenwell. (Well who wouldn't?) So they said, 'Well off you go'. Being a bit headstrong that was what he did, there and then, and because all his clothes belonged to them, he had to borrow stuff to get home. He regretted it for the rest of his life; he was 65 when I met him; he would have been retired for ten years getting his pension, but he was still working.

That was it for training school, or so I thought – if everything had gone well you were taken to your posting to drop off your gear.

We lived in South London and I was given K23 Battersea, the heart of South West London. Not a bad posting, I was told that it would be busy.

It was a White Watch day duty when I was dropped off. I was introduced to the station by Sub. Officer Alan Tarrant. (The title comes from, Substantive Rank. A permanent rank in the armed forces.) Was this the real Fire Brigade? The Station Officer, Tom Swift, the man in charge, wore a collarless white shirt, thick fire trousers and was the biggest man I'd ever met. He had steely grey, close-cropped hair and looked like a prize fighter – what was I getting myself into? Did I have to be as tough as this man? After the introductions and a quick look round you got changed into your going home clothes and made your own way home.

Not realising the effect a young attractive woman in a mini-skirt would have on the firemen, I had arranged to meet Eleanor outside the station to go home. Although this was the swinging sixties there was not much excitement in Este Road.

So now that you're a fireman, of sorts, all you have to do is to wait sleeplessly and apprehensively for the first day at your first fire station.

*Chapter 2*

# BATTERSEA: GATEWAY TO THE SOUTH

Battersea is an area with only one discernable border; its northern most edge is marked by the banks of the Thames. The name comes from Badrics Island as the original site was surrounded by water or marshland. In 1968 it was a bustling inner city borough undergoing massive redevelopment; tower blocks were replacing the rows of terraced houses. The main shopping areas, Clapham Junction and the Northcote Road remained unchanged retaining a confused form of Victorian charm. There was quite a bit of industry, mostly along the Thames, including Price's Candle Factory, Gartons Glucose Works and Nine Elms Gas Works. The emissions from these processes combined to give the borough a distinct and rather unpleasant smell.

The fire station is situated in Este Road, just off Falcon Road. It is not a particularly interesting building. It had three appliance bays for the pump escape, pump and a foam tender. All the accommodation was upstairs and there were Brigade flats on the second floor. These flats were a hangover from the past when firemen lived above their workplace and were now rented to fire brigade families unconnected to the station.

There are two main types of fire engines. Some stations have both types, some only have one and others have the two plus what is called a special, which is designed for a specific task. All the regular fire engines are called pumps, which just means that they have an inboard pump and are capable of increasing the pressure of any water which may enter the pump from a hydrant or open water and then expel the water.

They are then categorised by the type of ladders they carry and the incidents that they are designed to attend. Back then a pump escape carried the 50ft escape ladder; mostly it attended calls on its own ground and was used for firefighting and the rescue of persons. The pump carries a variety of ladders, but its main ladder is a 30ft extension ladder – it is the 'workhorse' of the Brigade. Apart from attending calls on its own ground, it makes up the laid down attendance on neighbouring grounds, goes on relief to major fires and is more likely to deal with the special services like car crashes and small fires like rubbish in the street – in fact anything.

Then there are the specials, the most common of which is the turntable ladder (TL). Its most essential task is to use its 100ft ladder to reach persons trapped in high buildings. It can also be used as a staircase to transport men and equipment and as a water tower. When it is required as a water tower it is supplied with water by another pump, which is restricted totally to that task. It carries a special 100ft length of hose permanently attached to the ladder with a monitor at the head. The monitor is a hand operated, manoeuvrable, metal attachment used to direct water on to a fire from a height. It is usually used as the last resort when it is too dangerous to work inside and the building is at the risk of being reduced a burning shell.

To confuse matters even more, collectively all fire engines, whatever type, are referred to as appliances – got all that? Good! In much later times the American habit of calling all fire engines 'trucks' entered the vocabulary.

The special at Battersea was a foam tender; it only went on calls where a large quantity of foam might be required. Basically, any fire that could involve bulk flammable fuel like oil or petrol. It could also lay down a blanket of foam to prevent the ignition of fuel, for example, around a crashed aircraft. It carried a vast quantity of foam compound, which when mixed with water, generated an even greater amount of foul smelling foam. The worst job you could be given was cleaning out the foam store at the back of the yard; the stink stayed on your hands for days. I cannot remember all the exact ingredients but I know it had contained a certain amount of dried turkey blood!

You can only understand that first day and the first few months if you have gone through it yourself. Once I eventually came to be responsible for new boys, I used to look at them with the understanding that they did not know what was going on or what was being said. I would see only a confused, glazed expression and know that they were struggling to comprehend. I always made a point of telling the new boys that I was their best friend in the Fire Brigade and that if they needed any advice or reassurance that they were to speak to me. There has to be somebody to turn to, somebody to put them right.

How was I to behave on that first day? What happens when the bells ring for the first time? Just trying to follow the daily routines was difficult and even though the usual practice is to put the new boy under the wing of a responsible old hand, he can't be there all the time. Training school didn't prepare me for this – the extraordinary and bewildering day-to-day life at a fire station.

The first roll call. Roll call is taken at every change of watch, which is at 0900hrs and 1800hrs. The day watch or the night watch is booked on duty, told their duties for the shift and the other watch is dismissed. Where does the new boy stand? Usually at the end of the line. Nobody makes the effort to make you feel at ease, why? Because everybody was once a new boy, get used to it! Your name is called out and you're told that you are riding the pump escape. Yes, now I know which fire engine I am to ride but where do I sit? This was just the beginning of learning the importance of fire station etiquette. Know your place! Red Watch Battersea was only 11 in number including me. They were a mixture of ages and lengths of service. As time went by I found that they were a good bunch. As soon as I realised my place in the pecking order – at the bottom (there was no use in fighting it) – I started to get recognised as part of the watch.

At that time there were only three sets of breathing apparatus (BA) at a station, all carried on the pump. As the pump escape was usually first on the scene, the men riding it were expected to enter smoke logged buildings without the aid of breathing apparatus. Of course now, almost overnight, I was superhuman and suddenly, I had changed from a plumber's mate into a man who was able to breathe noxious atmospheres. You soon find out that the old expression 'smoke eater' used to describe a fireman whose lungs seemed impervious to thick, black acrid smoke applied to nobody. The human lungs were not designed to absorb thick acrid smoke!

In 1968 you still had veterans of the blitz. There were two real 'old sweats' on the watch: Leading Fireman Tommy Hayford and Fireman Bert Machin.

I used to see the Leading Fireman (Lfm), who lived close enough so that he could walk to the station, arrive at work wearing a tweed sports jacket over his uniform shirt and trousers. You would not see much of him for the rest of the shift. Lfm. Hayford always rode in charge of the foam tender, which did not go out much but, when it did it usually had go long distances, so a minute or so delay in turnout was not that important. Consequently the crew didn't respond to the bells. If the foam tender was required the dutyman would go and get Tom from the office or give him a gentle shake from his bed. My memory may be fading but

I can't remember much more about him except that it was obvious to even me, the new boy, that this man deserved a great deal of respect. A tough looking man, another prizefighter with a broken nose and a shaved head, who had survived the blitz. He did all the routine work in the office and was not to be disturbed unnecessarily by a little shag. He did get occasional visitors to the station who would ring the front door bell and Tom would talk to them in hushed tones. It was said that he belonged to a tough Battersea family who were not to be crossed and he lent small-time local builders money to get jobs started.

Albert Machin was a wonderful man. He was the Mess Manager. For the uninitiated, the watch mess manager is an operational fireman who food shops for the rest of the watch and, at most stations, cooks at times when there is no cook at the station. For this he gets a few hours over-time added to his wages. Albert was the old-fashioned kind of mess man-ager; mince, mash and peas one night and peas, mince and mash the next night! None of that foreign muck. He had a vast repertoire of old music hall songs that he would sing or whistle most of the time and was never expected to do too much other than cook and drive. He used to sleep in the breathing apparatus room, on the table used to service the sets, and got gently shaken if he was needed to drive the foam tender. He was such a popular man that his son, Vic, who joined the Brigade and was sta-tioned at B21 Lambeth for a long as anyone can remember, was never called by his own name but was simply known as Bert!

At this time the London Fire Brigade was organised in small divisions from 'A' to 'L' and numbered from 21 upwards depending on the num-ber of stations in a Division. Number 21 was normally the headquarters and each Division had its own management structure, which was headed by a Divisional Commander. The Divisions started with 'A' right in the centre and moved outwards and upwards in the alphabet towards the suburbs.

The three Station Officers in charge of each watch had all served and been promoted from the prestigious 'A' Division. The man in charge of the Red Watch was called Eric Jordan and I never really got to know him. As a new boy I was not even allowed to look at the Station Officer let alone speak to him. All the Station Officers who are in charge of watches get called 'Guvnor' or 'Guv', but being of very lowly status I had to call him 'Sir'. At some mystic point I would be allowed to call him 'Guv'. He kept himself separate from the men for most of the time. Firemen can be hurtful creatures and his nickname was 'Rudolph' on account of his red nose.

This was a time when the separation of the officers on the stations was much more noticeable than it is now. Or maybe it was because there was such a great difference in our ages, but it made me aware when I was in the position of authority that I would be open and communicative with the youngsters.

The Sub. Officer was the second ranking officer and could take charge when the Station Officer was absent. Len Walker was a much more interesting man. He never had clean hands and seemed to find great difficulty in keeping tidy, but he knew everything and was much more able to relate to the men. He ended up as a Station Officer himself and served for many years at Plaistow in East London. He had a horde of sons and was always getting phone calls from his wife to come and rescue her from their antics. The rest of the watch were an even mix and we all seemed to get along; a couple became special friends whom I saw outside work and one of whom is still a permanent fixture.

At that time Battersea was an area of substantial redevelopment – rows of terraced houses were being demolished to make way for the tower blocks and the housing estates that are there now. Consequently, we had to deal with fires in derelict premises on a regular basis, mostly at night and it was really hard work. Running out hose over piles of broken houses and after extinguishing the fires, under-running to drain the hose and making it up into a roll again was exhausting. The hose was unlined and absorbed water so that after it had been used it doubled in weight. Modern hose is rubber lined and has a tough rubber outer case so this problem no longer exists. The hose became covered in grit, which in turn transferred to your hands or any other part of you that it happened to touch. You got cold and wet and in the winter your hands became cracked and sore. We were not issued with gloves. Red rubberised gardening gloves were carried on the fire engines but they were useless and if you happened to get too near to the fire; they would melt onto you hands. Therefore we didn't risk wearing them very often. The leggings kept your legs dry but your backside was left exposed and of course you could not help but get wet.

If you did happen to get some sleep during all this firefighting you were still called at 0645hrs. After a cup of tea it was down into the yard to lay dirty hose out in the yard, scrub it clean then hoist it up the drill tower to drain and dry. First you had to fill the hose with water to test for leaks, separate any lengths that were damaged and get them sent for repair. We also had to clean the fire engines before breakfast, which was served at 0800hrs. If it was raining we had to wash the fire engines every time they returned to the station, day or night. Your uniform also had to be cleaned and dried so that it could be worn on your next duty. Every fire station has a drying room where you can find uniforms that have been lost for years!

Likewise, every station had a cook, usually a local old dear who would come in at about 0700hrs to prepare breakfast for the night watch. Then at 1100hrs we had 'stand easy', more tea and a cheese and onion sandwich. Then a cooked, two-course lunch. The cook's official going home time was 1430hrs but it was usually accepted that they went as soon as the wash-up was out of the way. There was more tea at another stand easy at 1530hrs, then at 1700hrs it was teatime in the old fashioned sense – a sit down with Albert preparing slices of bread and jam. Cut into triangles mind you!

There is a wealth of stories about station cooks, worth a whole chapter, but there was not much to tell about Daisy – only that she had several teeth missing, she liked a laugh, swore worse than the rest us and used to fake embarrassment when she had to walk through the dormitory of sleeping men to get to the kitchen. The older hands that knew her well would lure her towards their beds with the promise of light-hearted romance.

Much of station life was pretty mundane, occasional training, station cleaning and volleyball played in the yard. I really thought that firemen should be putting their skills to a better purpose than cleaning toilets and scrubbing stairs. Later, once the Brigade employed contract cleaners, how I wished we could have gone back to those days. Once the station was cleaned, the Station Officer would inspect our work; if it wasn't up to standard you did it until it was. Once a month we cleaned all the windows and Saturday was scrub-out day. The fire engines had a super-clean inside and out and the appliance room floor was scrubbed. The scrub-out usually ended in a soaking for someone and a game of hockey using a block of soap as a puck. The Brigade provided bars of pink carbolic soap, which were ideal for everything other than washing and there is no better stick than a bass broom!

Another nice thing that happened on a Saturday was a free tray of cakes from the local baker. All the station bought their daily bread from him and as he closed early on a Saturday any cakes left over were brought to the station by his little round son. He was excited by the fire engines and wanted to be a firemen. Fourteen years later I had a short round Leading Fireman working with me who was always partial to a nice cake!

I had to learn the skills of looking after the watchroom. The watchroom is where the teleprinter is located; one man is appointed as dutyman each shift and it is his job to receive the calls and record by hand all the changes and calls in the station logbook. The entries in this book have to be correct as it can be used as a legal document. Before the advent of the teleprinter, calls came into the station via telephone. Some stations were connected directly to the automatic fire alarms of important premises and to call boxes in the street which all had to be tested. So the role of dutyman was complicated and as he had to stay awake all night, this was called a wakeful watch. We still have to adopt this procedure if there is a communication breakdown and stations cannot receive calls in the normal way. Sometimes the dutyman would fall asleep at the desk resting on his arms and, if a call came through, his arms would be numb and they would struggle to pick-up the phone. One of my old mates who had been at a quiet station out in the sticks told me that they used to put a shop dummy in the watchroom and the dutyman would sleep on a mattress hidden by the desk. This was to fool any senior officer who happened to pass by.

It was also the dutyman's job to answer the phones, the front door bell and the running call telephone. The running call telephone is located outside every station in a glass fronted box and when the door is opened the station call bells ring, the caller can then speak to Control and give details of any emergency. Additionally, the dutyman has to get to the box and try and take the details while the caller is speaking.

When an emergency call came into the station in the normal way by teleprinter, via the area control, the printer bell would sound preceding the call bells actuating. These bells sound throughout the station; they were loud and quite startling to a newcomer. During daylight hours they made your heart pound but this was nothing when compared to the 0200hrs call when your whole body shot through the roof! It was said that because of all these shocks to the heart, very few firemen lived long enough to make the most of their pensions. That clanging bell and the jerk-reaction that followed, started the process of getting out of bed, running to the sliding pole, getting on the truck then rigging. This was stressful enough for the firemen in the back but if you were driving it was increased twofold. Some drivers handled it well but in others you could sense that for a few minutes they were operating on autopilot. A lady acquaintance of mine could not understand how we could get up and go out without having a pee, cleaning our teeth and combing our hair! It wasn't until the 90s that the bells were replaced by a more gentle electronic call system that sounded like a 'Hi-Di-Hi' xylophone, which caused less of a jolt and nowadays some stations are roused very soothingly by a recorded, female voice.

At first my watchroom duties were carried out under the supervision of an experienced fireman. When the Officer in Charge felt that you were capable of doing it on your own you had to sit a written and oral examination. At Battersea this exam was conducted by an ex-Auxiliary Fire Service lady. The AFS was another thing that was left over from the war. Now this was a tough old boot that stood no nonsense from new boys. While the exam was in progress, the watch tried to distract you by appearing at the watchroom window undetected and trying to make you laugh.

The first night on your own sleeping in the watchroom was traditionally an occasion to put the wind up the new boy. I had been warned to expect this and they did get me. Spiders lowered onto your face in the dark, strange ghostly sounds outside the watchroom window, that sort of thing. The new boy was expected to tolerate all this stuff – it was par for the course and it was no good reacting against it. Harassment was not a word that had been invented; bullying and initiations were the accepted thing, but if you stood up for yourself and if there was no malice, it soon passed, you were accepted and it was all forgotten about. In my case, boot polish and genitals come to mind!

I wasn't the only one to get the piss taken. I soon found out that everybody gets it from time to time. One night we had a driver in from a station out in the sticks. When bedtime came around he took off his trousers to sleep. We all went to bed fully clothed in readiness with our unlaced shoes on the floor. Once he was asleep, his trousers were slid away and his legs were tied up with sail makers. This was made from thin, hairy string used for all kinds around the station. Eventually you'll get sick of all the naval analogies! The first I knew of this was when the bells went down and he was hopping around the dorm trying to get into his trousers. He had to run to the trucks and drive in his underwear, much to the dismay of the Station Officer and the amusement of the blokes!

I hadn't been there for very long before I was volunteered to be part of the pump competition team. There were two forms of drill carried out as fast as possible. They were against the clock and competed against other stations. It was a big do. Divisional finals, leading on to the big one – the Brigade finals held at Lambeth HQ. Battersea Red Watch didn't get past the Divisional finals but it was great fun, like being back at training school.

The first drill entailed two men running-out hose, setting into a hydrant and getting a water supply. The drill was over when a target was knocked down with a jet of water. The other drill involved getting the escape ladder off the appliance, pitching and extending to a drill tower and getting a jet to work against the clock. The whole affair was a great moral booster, encouraging teamwork and fitness. But the Brigade eventually put a stop to it because they considered that the additional risk to physical safety was not viable; men were getting injured unnecessarily, going off sick and this then placed a burden on the finances. Volleyball, the traditional game played at stations to increase fitness, met a similar fate for the same reasons and was banned for many years but has since been reinstated.

What was my first job? A rubbish fire behind a block of flats in the Wandsworth Road. I got out of the fire engine in a complete panic and fell over; I blamed it on the newness of my leather-soled fireboots!

I soon learnt that in the real world of the fire station things move at a much slower and in a less regimented way than at training school. I performed a little better on the second; a car fire in Battersea High Street. When we arrived we were met by a ball of flames in the middle of the road; it was a Reliant Robin. Once the fire was out all that was left was the metal parts; the fibre-glass shell had completely disappeared.

There were lots of fires in domestic properties. Houses were still heated with coal fires and a lot more people smoked, so there were fires caused by careless disposal of smoking materials and sparks from fires. We also dealt with a lot of chimney fires, which are a rarity these days. Putting out chimney fires was a skill on its own and if you didn't do it correctly you caused more damage than the actual fire.

I went to the biggest post-war fire at Fords, Dagenham. Battersea to Dagenham on the bell. It was an actual hand bell and no blue flashing lights! This was the last fire that I can remember when 100 pumps were needed to extinguish it. If you were called late on to a major fire you knew that all you would be doing was making-up hose. At major fires a special, called a hose layer, is used and the hose has a larger diameter than that carried on a normal fire engine and, of course, it is twice as hard to make-up and three times as heavy.

There is not a lot of greenery in Battersea except for Battersea Park. This borders the Thames and was once common fields later used for labourers housing. The site of attempted Royal assassinations, duels amongst the gentry and the infamous Red House Tavern, a house of ill repute, which attracted the low-life of London. During the 1800s it was developed into  pleasure gardens and in 1951 the Festival of Britain Gardens were laid out and this included a fun fair with a big dipper.

The big dipper is not there now – it was the biggest fire I actually attended on home ground. The fire was discovered in the early hours of the morning and by the time we got there the big dipper was alight from end to end. It was a very strange sight and seemed to be completely out of place; it should have been at the seaside. This fantastic wooden structure ablaze and sending sparks high into the night sky. To get the fire out was just a matter of getting water to the site and spraying it around. There were lots of statues spread about the area and they were covered with smouldering debris. It all took on the appearance of the set of some biblical epic after the Romans had ransacked the city.

I vividly remember two separate fires at the same address in Elverton Street, just off Battersea High Street. There is a bit of background to tell about this. These fires were started deliberately in a dwelling above an empty shop. The occupier was a local villain who had accidentally killed a young woman while driving under the influence. He served a period of time but not enough for her family and they were out for revenge. One night after the pubs had closed they started a fire in the entrance hall. We rescued him the first time so the next week they had another go!

When we arrived the first time the fire was going quite well. It was our job to enter the premises and search for any persons involved. This was my first rescue. We found the man in bed up on the second floor. The place was really smoke logged but we managed to manhandle his insensible body down the narrow staircase. We should have taken him down feet first but he went down head first with money falling out of his pockets and rolling down the stairs. On reaching fresh air I suddenly found that I was left with the casualty. Albert Machin, who was pump operating, told me that I had to resuscitate this individual. Training for this is totally different from reality. Under Albert's guidance I started mouth to mouth. I had never had the desire to put my mouth over another man's, especially one stinking of beer and smoke! Fortunately he soon came round coughing and spluttering a mouthful of abuse. Suffering from smoke inhalation, he was removed to a waiting ambulance. The next week the same thing happened, only this time he was conscious and was able to alert us to his location by throwing a bottle of tomato ketchup out of the window. This struck one of the firemen and smashed on his helmet and, of course, he thought he had blood dripping down his tunic. The man was pulled from the building, the fire was put out and, for the Fire Brigade, that was end of story.

I went to fires in factories, shops, in fact, everywhere including the railways. Clapham Junction is one the biggest railway intersections in England. With all the railway lines on the ground there were many occasions in the summer when the embankments caught fire. This was always hard work; firstly reaching the locations and then getting water to the fires.

It is complicated to list all the types of incident the Fire Brigade deals with – car fires, road traffic accidents, persons shut in lifts, persons locked in or out of premises and floodings. The best way to categorise the incidents is to say that we deal with anything that causes public distress. We also deal with suffering animals. I once had to attend an unhappy Great Dane with its leg trapped in some railings. It had tried to jump the railings but had caught its foot in the hooped top of the railings and must have been in agony. The owner was there and held the dog while we released him. Getting assistance with animals is always hard as the RSPCA can only attend at normal road speed and there are not that many inspectors.

I can't remember whether I really enjoyed my new job or not. I can say that it was unique – the shift work, working at weekends when your friends were out enjoying themselves. Was it my job for life? I had my doubts.

## Chapter 3

# ECCLES ROAD, SW11

In July 1969 during a day shift, the pump was away from the station doing breathing apparatus training and the pump escape's crew were alone in the station when a call came in – fire, Eccles Road, Battersea. I can't remember the exact time. There was a crew of four riding the escape; this included the Sub. Officer in charge. Eccles Road is not far from the station and it seemed as though we were there in no time. When the appliance entered the road turning from Lavender Hill and you could see the fire from the end of the street.

There was a crowd gathering opposite a terraced house with bay windows at ground- and first-floor levels, the fire was coming out of the ground floor window up the face of the house and back into the first floor. In the crowd of people outside was a mother screaming frantically that her baby was inside, upstairs in a bedroom. The heart is pumping already but that sent it into overdrive. The great burst of adrenalin that tells you this is it. Now you have to put your head over the parapet and be counted.

When I look back over thirty years as a fireman and experiencing some really difficult and dangerous fires, it was a piddling little fire, but at that time it was the most severe I had ever come across. We firemen were desperate; there were only four of us and the nearest assistance was coming from Wandsworth. So it was going to be a long time before we got any help. The mother was hysterical, and even if we could have got any more information out of her, there wasn't time to ask. We had to get into that blazing house; was the baby at the back or the front of the house?

The hosereels were off. There wasn't time to find a hydrant and get a jet. Peter Vallis and Sub. Officer Walker slipped a first floor ladder and Peter played the hosereel on the Sub. Officer while he tried to get into the first floor. Bob Barrett and I took the other hosereel and tried to get up the stairs from the hall, but the heat was too intense. Remember, we had no breathing apparatus. Suddenly, the fire came down the stairs to meet us. Bob fell backwards onto me and we tumbled back down the stairs.

Although shaken and winded, we had to get out and find another way to get to the baby.

When we got outside I saw Peter helping the Sub. Officer, whose leggings were on fire. I grabbed a hook ladder from the fire engine and went through the house next door to the back yard. I used the ladder to get on top of the dividing wall. On top of the wall, standing on one leg, I managed to reach the sill of the back bedroom window. I managed to smash the glass with my axe, then pull myself across and up into the window. (I was only a slip of a thing back then!) As I got inside I was met by the BA crew from Wandsworth, who were able to lift the baby from its cot and take it outside. It was unhurt, but if the bedroom door had been open it would have been a different story. Everybody was safe, but the Sub. Officer needed a new pair of leggings!

Mother and child were reunited but their home was wrecked. The fire had been started accidentally by an elder son in the ground floor front room and this was completely burnt-out. There was no such thing as a fire investigation team who could come up with the cause of the fire and help out the officer in charge. Anyway, none of this was my concern; it was my duty to make sure the fire was out, make-up any equipment we had used and ensure we had all the equipment in order to be ready for the next call before going back to the station.

The aftermath of a fire is a sensitive, miserable time, especially when it is someone's home. They might not even be present – only to return and find the possessions of a lifetime reduced to cinders. You have to help them cope with that. Somehow it is even worse when people come home to the aftermath. In some cases there was nothing left and they had nowhere to live.

A while after Eccles Road – I don't know how it happened – we were all recommended for our bravery and received an Area Commander's Commendation. I now know that the officer in charge of the incident – the Station Officer from Wandsworth – would have completed a report detailing any meritous conduct. This would then have been considered by a more senior officer who would propose that some award should be made. Later, this was something I was able to do for men under my supervision who had done something that was beyond the normal call of duty. It gave me a great deal of pleasure to recommend my men for anything, be it for awards or for promotion.

We were all summoned to the headquarters of Southern Command, which was Croydon Fire Station. The largest station in the command full of, what looked to me, gnarled old firemen. The Area Commander shook hands and photos were taken. I still have that letter of congratulations among my treasures.

It may be that my memories are fading, but I am sure that I didn't know anything about any developments in the Brigade. Neither was I encouraged to learn and improve. Nowadays, all new boys have a structured development programme to follow. Not that I had promotion in mind, but learning more might have made the job more interesting. When I became an Officer I made a conscious effort to include everyone, and inform them of everything that was happening in the Brigade that concerned them and the station. I would have regular sit-downs with the blokes and encourage any potential officers – although my regular first day duty team briefings invariably deteriorated into hilarity. The hounds would be waiting for the first slip of the tongue and that was it!

After about two years I became very disenchanted. I had to do a second job to keep the wolf from the door so I was hardly at home, always working. It was about this time that I started to think that the Fire Brigade was not what it was all cracked up to be. I have to admit that I didn't like the discipline and I didn't like the influence it had on my way of life.

Eleanor and I had bought a house in Maidstone. A lot of firemen moved out of London to the Medway towns. Property was cheaper and, on a low wage, it was all we could afford. What with both of us working in London, the shift work, travelling, and my second job, we didn't see much of each other. If I was away, Eleanor couldn't get to the railway station, so on those days she had to live out of a suitcase staying at her mum's place. We realised that we had to change our lifestyle or face the consequences of a messed-up marriage. I was still only 22 and quite frankly a bit immature, but I had to get my priorities right so I handed in my notice.

Work imposed so much on home life that the Fire Brigade took over and became the main part. We worked a 56hr week – two day shifts, two night shifts and two days off. You came off duty at 0900hrs on your first leave day and had to travel home, which could take anything from an hour upwards. Then you had one and a half days off. If your wife had to work, you were really only together on the weekends when you were not working, and they only came around every six weeks. And the money was miserable. The mortgage came to a massive £40 and I was lucky to clear £100 per month, even with the mess manager's allowance included. (There had been a mess-room revolt and Albert's catering skills were voted out, so I had become the mess manager.) All the part-time work messed it up even more, but you had to do it to survive.

So I resigned, and Eleanor transferred her job to Maidstone. There wasn't much work around but I got a job in a local factory, which was horrible. I really cannot believe that I let it go; if I had stayed I would have retired aged 50 on a full pension! We should have found another way around it. But there it was; I had to earn a certain amount to keep up with the mortgage. It was only then that I began to realise how good the Fire Brigade had been, but it was not until it, and my circumstances, changed that I could even start to think about rejoining. I had just about enough time to forget about the bad bits I suppose.

If the job I was doing had been better I might never have thought about it, and if Peter Vallis from Battersea had not come to see me and told me about the changes, I might never have gone back. Even though the money had got better they still couldn't get people to join, so to make it more attractive, they were paying full fares from home to work. Our first child had just been born so Eleanor was at home and I couldn't wait to get back.

It would be better; of course it would!

## Chapter 4

## BACK TO THE FRONT

Now would be a good time to talk a little more about my family; a very private and precious thing. I will get no thanks from Eleanor by saying too much. A stable home life is essential to keep you on the straight and narrow, and it keeps reliable people reliable. Eleanor, known to all as El, and my two daughters, Teresa and Liz, are the foundation of it all. The refuge from the storm. If it wasn't for El, I think I would be walking the streets – living on Special Brew and baked beans straight out of the can!

1974, the year of the 'M' reg's and the Wombles. That's what they called the 1974 intake. The hours had been reduced and all the Brigades had to increase their manpower to keep the same level of fire cover. There are those that will say that they took anyone but us 'M' reg's know better. Look how many have survived their 30 years to 2004.

After going through a reduced selection process, I reported to Southwark Training School on 8th April 1974. We were known as the 'retreads'. Some were returning to London after working in county brigades; one man had returned from the Brigade in Australia. A squad of six, and that was also the number of days that we spent training. We did everything: all the drills that the drivers were familiar with, and if you were qualified in breathing apparatus you did that as well. I had neither qualification so I did a lot of self-study and going home early.

When our induction was complete our instructor said 'Right, where do you want to go?' I thought this was great; normally you are sent to a station – no choice involved. I thought that now I was living in Maidstone I would go to the nearest station with a bit of life, and asked for Lewisham in South East London. When my posting came back it was far away Paddington in North London! Just where I did not want to go. I had left because the Brigade took up too much of my time, and now I was going to be travelling even further. I whinged and whined; I even got to see the training school commandant. Commandant, indeed, that was what he was called! But no joy, they wouldn't have it. It was pointed out that it was either Paddington or the job centre. Anyone with any experience was needed at the inner London stations.

So, reluctantly I packed my gear and went to A21 Paddington. I'm sorry but it is not a nice station. A great big, ugly, concrete mausoleum. On the outside it's as cold and unwelcoming as the inside is anonymous. The ground is great and is the home of some of the hardest fought fires, but the station was not for me. Even at the busiest stations you spend a lot of time cooped up twiddling your thumbs. It makes it all the more tolerable if your surroundings are amenable. There is no peace there; the traffic noise from the Westway and the railway sounds from Paddington Rail Station combine to bash your ears at all times day and night.

In 1974 the watch strength was 36. Too many to get to know anyone. Two fire engines, a turntable ladder and an emergency tender were attached to the station. This was my first experience of the emergency tender (ET). It was like a medium-sized coach and carried all the equipment to deal with heavy rescue. Jacks, spreaders, winches and cutting equipment were just part of the gear it carried. The ET men were looked on as the crème de la crème – the most experienced and highly trained men in the Brigade.

The area staff office was located there with the breathing apparatus, control vehicle and all the general purpose vans. These all needed drivers and operators. The mess room was massive with seating for at least 40 men. The kitchen needed two cooks, and various assistants were provided from the watch in order to feed all the staff. Oh, and the senior officers; they were everywhere and they all had car drivers who also needed accommodation and sustenance. The car drivers were old boys in reach of the end and they all seemed more than a bit crazy. I once made the mistake of walking into their dormitory when they were asleep. It was like a black hole with the walls going in and out with the snoring! Some of the senior officers had flats above the station where they and their families lived rent-free as part of the job!

With all those appliances there was little peace from the call bells, in and out, in and out. Not that I minded it being busy, but this was crazy. It was a madhouse!

Getting from Maidstone to Paddington proved to be a nightmare. The main line rail service from home to Victoria was not like it is now. Then you had to get from Victoria to Warwick Avenue by underground. You could never make your connections. As it was a busy station you often entailed overtime; that is, you were out on a shout after the normal finishing times and I was getting home after 2100hrs. This was just what

I had wanted to avoid, so at the first opportunity I spoke to the officer in charge about my problems. The Station Officer, Neil Wallington, was very understanding and helpful; he did not want me being there if I was unhappy and said that he would try to get me transferred. I was to meet Neil many times over the proceeding years, and he always impressed me as being an honest and considerate Guvnor. Now he is an authority on everything Fire Brigade and has written many books on the subject.

Don't get me wrong, I did enjoy it there; the watch were fantastic – a lot of senior men who had been there since the station opened in 1970, and had previously worked at the old Edgware Road station. But I could not put my heart and soul into it. I couldn't let it all go wrong again for the sake of the family. Thank God I was soon given a move to A25 Westminster.

*Chapter 5*

# THE QUEEN'S FIRE BRIGADE

With the Queen renting a modest place just around the corner, what else could the men of Westminster be called? The ground is amazing; it contains many of the nation's most important buildings. Government buildings, the Home Office, Downing Street and the Ministry of Defence. All those anonymous-looking buildings in Whitehall that contain the people and institutions that are at the hub of the nation. The list of risks is endless, including Buckingham Palace and the Houses of Parliament. It also has a large area of multiple-occupant residential properties. There are large council housing estates and some of the most expensive private properties in London. It is also a massive tourist and travel terminus with Victoria Railway and coach stations.

To cater for all these travellers, there are streets full of bed and breakfast type hotels. Small hotels with transient residents are a constant fire risk and some of the most difficult fires have happened in these buildings. These hotels are complicated buildings and when they are full of people who are unfamiliar with their surroundings, it is a recipe for disaster. These are the type of hotels where groups of visiting foreign and British students are likely to stay.

It was a smaller, old London station where I was to spend six contented years developing a more wide-ranging knowledge of all things Fire Brigade, and realising that this was it – for life.

Since those days, the station has since been completely renovated. While I was stationed there, although it was a sad, old-fashioned building, it did feel more like a real fire station. Everything was cramped. The dormitory, the mess room and the TV room were all on top of each other and sometimes it was very hard to live together. Some men are very inconsiderate and are incapable of being quiet at any time. This was one of the reasons that encouraged me to go for promotion. You got your own room, or at least shared with another, and there was no point in disturbing your roommate. But, as I was to find out later on when I returned to Paddington, four junior officers shared a room. At Soho, just the two leading firemen shared. It meant that it didn't matter which fire engine you were riding; the nights were constantly disturbed by either you or your fellow firemen going out on calls. This wasn't a problem if all the trucks went out at the same time, as you were required to respond to the call bells, whatever truck is being dispatched. But you were disturbed again if you were not required when your colleagues returned. My long-term roommate at Soho was a smoker and after every call, no matter the time, he would roll-up and smoke, sitting on the bed.

As no other emergency service is allowed to sleep while on duty, I ought to explain the reasons behind this practice. The official Brigade Order states that you are allowed to rest between midnight and 0645hrs when the station bells ring and the men are expected to get ready for work. Well, this word 'resting' means different things to different men and different stations. They provide beds, and how can you lay on your bed for seven hours without nodding off? This practice is at least 150 years old and dates from when the firemen spent 24 hours, seven days a week on duty and all for a pittance; well at least the hours have changed!

Nowadays, the long 15-hour night shift has a lot to do with it. Although the 56-hour week I experienced has gone, that long night shift still exists. The management has always been happy because it is cost effective. Longer hours, less men, less to pay out in wages. And who really cares what firemen do on duty as long as the people are saved and the fires are put out? Any objections to this practice only come into question when wage negotiations come around, but if you were able to calculate the advantages to the employers, I am sure that over the years they have had the best end of the deal.

Every time the employers start talking about conditions of service, the rumour starts that the beds are going. That would be a problem to a lot of firemen – those who rely on getting a few hours sleep at the station to allow them to do their secondary job during the day. In most cases, part-time work is a necessity. I won't harp on about low pay, but a young married man with children can find it impossible to live on a fireman's wage. Several of my firemen admitted that they were eligible to claim benefits and that part-time work was the only thing that kept them financially afloat. Until I became a Station Officer I always did something – anything from removals, to plumbing, to driving. It was essential to take the kids on holiday and buy decent presents at birthdays and Christmas. I slaved to get away on holiday each year. We started by borrowing a tent and going to the New Forest, and then by taking our own tent to Cornwall. When we got fed up with the English weather, we drove to the south of

France with our tent. Our last few wonderful family holidays were spent in a mobile home in St. Agulf, southern France. This was until the girls were too old to go away with mum and dad. That's why I did part-time work and that's why, to me, sleeping at the fire station was part of life. It was something that happened from the beginning; it was something that was part of the job. I never considered it to be fiddle or a 'Spanish Practice'.

Back to the 'Minster' as it is affectionately called. The station is located in Horseferry Road, SW1. At the river end of the road was a horse-ferry. It was a Thames crossing point before Lambeth Bridge was built. Horseferry Road also contains a Magistrates Court, The Coroner's Court and Westminster Hospital. The station is situated on the bend in the road opposite Greycoat School and next to Strutton Ground, the oldest surviving street market in London. The station yard backed onto a social club and was once surrounded by blocks of mansion flats, which have since been demolished. There was living accommodation above the station – flats for fire brigade families and single men's rooms. The night-time bedroom noises that could be heard from upstairs were another source of disturbance and amusement. It was rumoured that the odd off-duty firemen did some visiting upstairs when husbands were away on duty, but I cannot be sure of that.

My six years saw a lot of changes in the Brigade. There was a reduction in hours whereby we were granted rota leave. We worked the same shift: two days followed by two nights then two leave days. The reduction was made by having extra days tagged onto normal leave. Not all the firemen were attentive to their rotas, and it was a great laugh when they turned up when they were supposed to be on leave. No one would let on but there were a few knowing looks behind their backs. They only found out on roll call when their name was not called out; instead it was announced that they were on leave, accompanied by howls and hoots of laughter!

Then came the Green Watch, and another shift was formed to bring us down to a 42hr week. These changes all came about after the 1977 strike. What an awful time that was. Nine weeks without pay, no financial help, El and the two girls to support. I can remember vividly putting on my undress uniform with the watch and walking out the doors to line up outside. I thought it would last about 10 minutes, considering how important we were to the safety of the nation, but there we stayed. There was no phone call, no emergency teleprinter message saying 'alright,

alright get back to work, a deal has been done'. I felt the same in 2003 on the first evening of the strike; again that call never came. We stood out in front of Soho Fire Station; all of the station personnel came to work that evening just to walk out. As it turned out we sacrificed so much in what became a futile gesture. I told my men that whatever happened we must stick together. If someone needed money, we will all help out, but if we go out together, we stay together and return together. Thank God that's what happened, although they are now a very bitter bunch of men, although at the same time, still prepared to do what is expected of them.

At the beginning of the first strike we all went to the station on Red Watch duties, as dedicated to the picketing as the firefighting. After a time, when we realised that this wasn't going to be over in a few days, we split the watch in half and picketed for one day and one night. That way all the boys from Kent could travel together in one car.

It was miserable but the good old Londoners brought us food and drink, and contributed to the strike fund. They even turned up with wood for the brazier. It was essential that we stuck it out but picket duty was mind numbing. The nights were the worst when the streets were empty. After a time we took to sleeping in the station.

The high points were limited, but one evening we were approached by a representative of another union. He told us that his union was holding a conference at a hotel around the corner, and would someone come and talk to them about the firemen's cause and collect some money. I was nominated. It was either St. Ermine's or St. James's Hotel and I was expecting a small group of people sitting around a table. Suddenly I was on a stage facing about 150 delegates! Fortunately they quickly started to ask me questions, which made it easier. The bucket was passed around; I was refreshed and went back to the picket line.

The White Watch at Westminster voted as a group not to go on strike and refused to follow the National yes vote. Consequently, the station became the centre of argument. Firemen turned up from all over London to show their disgust and it became quite violent. Eventually the Brigade told these men that they should stay at home and phone HQ daily, stating that they were willing to work. So they stayed at home during the whole strike and got paid. Gradually, one by one, they joined the strike until there were just five who stuck it out. The irony of this was that the five men who stuck it out were all scallywags – the type that took the piss out of the job and were all take. When we returned to work they carried on as if nothing had happened. Eventually all but one left the brigade for one reason or another – good job.

This is the only occupation where employees pay their own fares to go to work, have their jobs done by somebody else, and are still expected to risk life and limb by answering calls to desperate emergencies from the picket line and not get paid when they are on strike – it beggars belief. We have three sets of bosses to appease: the senior management of the Brigade, the Joint Council of Local Government and the Government. Is it any wonder that we get nowhere with our efforts to improve pay and conditions?

An added complication to me being on strike the first time was that we were in the process of moving house. By foul or fair means, and with the help of friends and family, we kept our heads above water. We got through the strike and moved from Maidstone to Croydon. We had decided to move back closer to London; at the time I just could not see me driving 40 miles up the A20 for the next 25 years.

There's just one more thing I want to get off my chest concerning strikes and industrial action. I always felt underpaid but that was something that I accepted; it went with the job. The unsocial hours were another thing that went with the job and you got on with it. What I did object to was the lack of appreciation from my employers. When there is a major disaster, we are a fine bunch, the salt of the earth. Just see how the esteem drops when we ask for more money. When a fireman or a nurse or a paramedic actually reaches the stage where they are prepared to take industrial action, or withdraw his or her labour, it is a massive decision – it goes against all that you stand for. It is not just a call for more pay; it is akin to a cry for help, a cry for appreciation, and the best way to show real appreciation is by giving a decent living wage.

When we returned to work after the '77 strike nobody would do higher duties; that meant the Brigade were acutely short of officers. Prior to the strike, it was hard work getting into Westminster's office, such was the competition for promotion between three or four individuals, me included. I had passed the written and practical exams for the next rank up, Leading Fireman, and I wanted to get moving. After about six months we started acting-up again, and then began the long road to achieve my target – to be a Station Officer by the time I was 35.

Why did I want to be a Station Officer? I've already given one reason: I wanted my own room. Another reason was to end up with the best pension I could. It wasn't until later that I found that I liked the responsibility, and after having served under a few dodgy officers, I just thought that I could do a better job.

A lot of officer-ship is luc;, you hear of things that go wrong at a fire or a station and know that could so easily have been me. There are so many things that can go wrong that are out of your control and, in a lot of cases, the officer in charge just becomes a scapegoat for something that was essentially unpreventable. For that reason I made a point of never criticising another man's fire unless I was there to see it at first hand.

Unfortunately, reputations can build or fall on just that one mistake which cannot be hushed-up. The decisions of the officer in charge at the start of an incident are so crucial, and any mistakes are magnified throughout the whole emergency. I was lucky, I think. I avoided making too many mistakes; well, at least none that anyone took any notice of, and none that I didn't have the ability to cover up. It helps if you have established some respect, and the men you work with are prepared to give you a little leeway. You can very easily lose all credibility and respect by being impatient and making stupid mistakes. This is why it should always be the case that promotion is a gradual process, allowing the young and enthusiastic to develop into experienced officers with the ability to handle and control even the most difficult and complicated incidents. Even then, luck still plays its part.

The Fire Brigade needs people who will take on the responsibility of running a fire station and taking control at incidents, but they don't train you properly to carry out these responsibilities. You take exams, you are interviewed and are expected to know your job inside-out; but I have only been on one training course that set out to help me to manage correctly. This course was so well prepared by the London Fire Brigade that at the end of the course, we were given a certificate to confirm that we had been successful. Only problem was that there was a certificate for one bloke who never even turned up!

The role of the officer-in-charge is multi-faceted, where one minute you can be completing the petty cash return, or teaching someone else how to do it, and the next you are supervising a serious fire. The Brigade relies on the individual having the ability, competency and authority – most of which is self-taught and gathered through experience – not to make mistakes that could so easily result in the most tragic of circumstances. Apart from the varied decisions you are expected to make on the fireground, you have to be an administrator, a personnel manager and a counsellor. Added to these responsibilities, you have to consider equal opportunities, racial differences, the rules and regulations of the Brigade, the laws of the land, and your duty to the general public. Oh, it was an easy job – well worth 30 grand a year and the unsocial hours.

During those first few years at Westminster I qualified in the use of breathing apparatus and became a driver. The breathing apparatus which the Brigade used then was a self-contained oxygen set. The Proto breathing apparatus was complicated and had a long duration. It was uncomfortable – you had to wear a nose clip and the mouth-piece which was inserted into the mouth caused you to bite down, and after a time this made your teeth and jaw ache. It was also another layer to be worn over your uniform, increasing your body temperature. They were also noisy. I remember being called to a gas-filled flat where an old lady was in residence. You had to put on the apparatus to enter and therefore you didn't know whether or not there was gas present. We got into this flat and began searching for the old lady who suddenly sat up in bed and became hysterical at the sight of two monsters with tubes coming out of their mouths and making strange hissing noises while stumbling about in the dark! Poor old girl, if the gas doesn't get you the firemen will!

Later on, the brigade went over to compressed air breathing apparatus which was a fair bit lighter and more comfortable to wear, but didn't last as long.

I liked driving the fire engines. In those days they had manual crash gearboxes and were hard to drive. No power steering either. It really was a case of man against machine and the blokes in the back used to have a great laugh with a new driver.

Once you had passed the test and as you had only been taught to drive a lorry, the officer in charge of the station was responsible for ensuring that you learnt how to drive a fire engine. At first you would drive only in non-emergency situations. You would drive back from calls after swapping with the experienced driver. Then, if a call was received over the radio, you had to pull over and swap back. It was on these drives that the blokes in the back would put a foot through from the back cab and stop the gear lever from moving from one gear to another, making the driver really crunch the gears!

When the OIC finally decided that you were competent enough to drive on emergencies, you were allowed to drive the pump, which is normally the second appliance to leave the station and follow the pump escape. Also, by this time you should have learnt the area which a station covers – the ground. If you hadn't, as soon as you started driving it was essential that you did, as driving on calls and not knowing where you were going is a nightmare. All stations have route cards but the OIC has to follow these as you proceed. Not good at a time when concentration should be uppermost. A lot of new drivers make up their own alphabetical route books and, until you were familiar with the ground, a quick look at the book and at the map in the watchroom was necessary.

A great cheer always goes up when you get your first shout as a driver. The adrenaline is pumping no matter what the call entails. One of the main routes away from the Minster was to turn right out of the station, left into Rochester Row and forward until you reached Vauxhall Bridge Road. At this junction there used to be a public lavatory in the middle of the road, right on a set of traffic lights. There was always congestion at this point and you always had to decide which side of the road you should use to get through this junction quickly and safely. At the same time you had to get down into second gear, the hardest manoeuvre with a crash gearbox. You had to come out of third, get the revs right then back across the 'H' to find second. Even in non-emergency driving, you had to concentrate, but on a shout you hoped you would do it cleanly, as the crew were always waiting for the crunch.

It was while driving a fire engine whilst stationed at Westminster that I had a very bad experience. It still worries me and, even after all this time, I cannot satisfy my conscience that what happened could have been avoided. It still haunts me, but if I am to tell the whole story I can't just tell the good bits.

It happened on the 7th November 1978. I was driving the pump heading for Eccleston Street, SW1 on a call to a fire. I was involved in a serious collision at the traffic lights which control the junction of Buckingham Palace Road and Eccleston Bridge. This junction is horrendously busy since it is very close to Victoria Railway Station, which is the busiest travel terminus in London – double-decker buses, coaches, cabs and a multitude of pedestrians all in a dash to make their travel connections.

I had reported for duty early for a night shift. I relieved the day shift bloke driving the pump, did my daily checks on the fire engine and got ready for roll call. Colin Searle was my Guvnor and he was also riding early. The pump escape was not in the station so the pump turned-out on its own.

I approached the junction with blue lights on and sirens sounding. Your line of sight to the right is restricted by a continuous high wall that is the back of Victoria Railway Station. The traffic lights were at red against me but the traffic had stopped to allow me to pass through. I did not know and could not see that on the far side of a double decker bus a Mini was approaching the junction. As I passed the front of the bus, the Mini, moving at speed, was there, right in front of me and I struck it side-on.

The painful details of the accident are not the reason for me raising the subject; it is to emphasise the confusion that still exists over emergency vehicle drivers and traffic lights. What happened led me to being charged and to appear at Horseferry Magistrates Court, and then sent for trial at Newington Butts. What was going on? If I had not been driving a fire engine none of this would have happened. It felt so unjust. I felt as though the Fire Brigade should have been in the dock, not me. Then the local press got their teeth into me; how did they get to know?

The Fire Brigade were less than helpful. Accidents at red traffic lights were a hot potato. The Advice and Counselling section were not what they are today and I felt completely isolated. At the Magistrates Court a senior officer was appointed to assist me; a lot of help he was. While I was waiting to appear, standing out like a sore thumb, he was off speaking to a long lost mate! How I wished that Colin were there instead.

I was represented by solicitors appointed by the insurers of the Brigade. I can just about remember being interviewed at their offices in the Inner Temple. After the magistrates, next came my appearance at the Inner London Sessions. That's all a blur. In reality I was standing in the dock like a criminal. I can remember Colin speaking for me and I was found not guilty. It had a lot to do with the fact that the driver of the car had his radio on very loud and could not have heard the two-tone horns. There were several witnesses that stated that I had slowed down and was driving with caution as I approached the lights.

It is only self-esteem that spurs a fireman to become a driver. Drivers didn't get anything extra for their qualifications. This originates from a complicated issue concerning the qualified fireman's pay. After four years' service, and if you pass certain tests, you go on to a higher rate of pay. When this increase in pay was first negotiated, one of the conditions of its payment was that you had to be a driver. The problem was that the Brigade could not provide enough driving courses. So you just had to state that you were prepared to become a driver and wait until a course became available.

Now the Brigade say that only those who agreed to drive are receiving their additional money under false pretences. But who can blame them? It doesn't take four years to discover that the additional responsibility is just not worth the aggravation. The heavy goods vehicle qualification is a good one to have, but not only are you responsible for ensuring that the fire engine is roadworthy, you are also responsible for the safety of the crew and that of the public. If you do have an accident of any kind, even if it is not your fault, there is a certain stigma attached, so why take it on?

Why are traffic lights a hot potato? The law states that the driver of an emergency vehicle while driving to an emergency can treat red lights as a give-way. He has to ensure that the audible warning horns are sounding and that he has blue lights flashing. But if an accident occurs, or if the driver causes any vehicle to crash, he can be at fault and has to face the consequences. This seems preposterous. What if the drivers obeyed all the traffic regulations when driving to an emergency? Just consider how long it would take to get through the 20 or so set of lights in Oxford Street! The driver is faced with saving a life or sitting waiting for traffic lights to change, just because he could be prosecuted if an accident should occur.

Additionally, until recently, when the Brigade decided to take action, drivers who were involved in accidents could even have their private car insurance affected by admitting that you had had any kind of accident in the last three years.

The drivers were always shit upon. There is always a shortage throughout the Brigade and therefore they get the most standbys. (A standby is what happens when another station has a shortage of essential manpower and a station with an excess is ordered to send an individual to fill the gap.)

At one time some bright spark thought that it would be a good idea for appliances that needed servicing to be taken to workshops the night before. If you worked in the central area there was no point in taking them during the evening rush, so drivers would have wait to take them during their stand-down period. They would then try to get back to the station, sometimes late at night, facing the dangers of travelling on public transport while in uniform.

This whole episode made me think seriously about my future. I considered coming off driving, I seriously thought about packing it all in again. If it were not for El and Colin and feeling that if I did those things, I would be admitting that it was my fault. So in my usual stubborn way, I kept at it.

*Chapter 6*

# THE WORSLEY COURT HOTEL

Meanwhile, life at Westminster went on as usual. Firemen and officers arrived and moved on. Head down, I was trying to learn the job of an officer with the best Sub. Officer anyone could want. Ron Morris knew almost everything, but he could not pass the Station Officer's exam to gain the promotion that he so rightly deserved. However, he helped me a great deal; not only in a practical way but he also set an excellent example. He was what a proper officer should be: efficient, good with the men, competent on the fireground, smart and tidy and full of wit. He would always get his work done and still have time to show this new boy how to do the office work.

One evening he was taking us for training out in the yard. There was a small underground space where we could simulate a sewer rescue.

Sewer-men occasionally have accidents underground and the Brigade has a procedure to deal with such incidents. This procedure can be adapted and can be used to control any kind of underground rescue. Muggins here was acting as the person trapped. You had to act as though you were really unconscious and not assist your rescuers. Ron made the point that if another fireman was in difficulty, everything, other than the rescue of persons, should cease to get your colleague to safety. It was hard work getting me out of that hole but it was a success, and of course we had a good laugh into the bargain. Drill was finished, 'wash hands' time, and then supper.

I suppose everybody reaches a milestone in their lives when things change from drifting along, taking everything as it comes, to actually thinking and preparing for the future. That night was mine. Overnight I realised that I could no longer swan around. Life is too precious and can be ripped away in an instant.

That night was Friday 13th December 1974. I was on duty in the watchroom and riding the back of the pump escape. It was one of *those* nights. Friday nights always seemed the busiest and we had been in and out all night. Much later that night, as I was making my bed up in the watchroom, a demon was setting light to a hotel on Paddington's ground. A kitchen porter called Edward Mansfield lit several fires around the

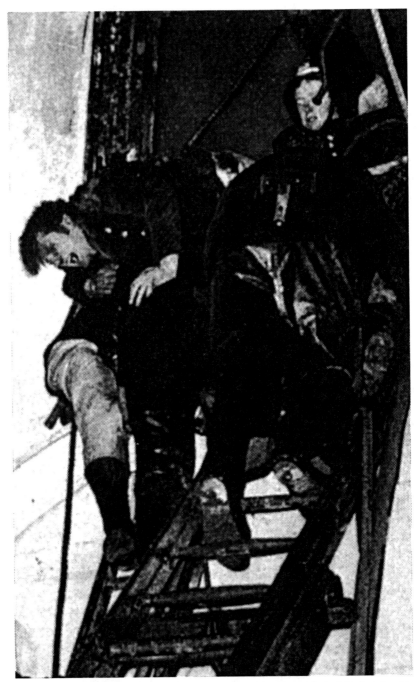

The Worsley Court Hotel. The first casualty is released and rescued. (*The London Evening Standard*, 1974)

building in an act of revenge. He was caught, tried for the manslaughter of seven people and gaoled for life.

The hotel was the Worsley Court, Clifton Gardens, W9. The first call came into Paddington's watchroom at 0341hrs. Both of Westminster's appliances were ordered-on when it developed into a 15-pump fire. I already knew that something big was going on as control appliances and senior officers' cars were passing the station coming from Lambeth HQ. Lambeth Bridge and the Horseferry Road is the direct route to that part of North West London.

When Westminster's trucks arrived at the scene, flames were leaping from the upper windows and the whole atmosphere was laden with smoke – it was so thick that you could barely see across the road. There were fire appliances everywhere and the street was a mass of hose. Ladders were pitched to the front of eight interconnecting terraced houses; three of them were five storeys with attic rooms in the roof space.

Many heroic rescues had already been carried out at the front of the building. People had been removed from the roof using the turntable ladder. A particularly brave and precarious rescue using a first-floor ladder tied to an escape had been made in deteriorating conditions. There were so many people needing rescue that the firemen had been awestruck at the shear scale of their task; it was frightening. Ambulances were ferrying the dead and injured to hospital. Even at this hour police had to control hordes of onlookers.

The whole of the old 'A' Division were there except for A23 Euston. A man who was later to mean a lot to me, Station Officer John 'Shiner' Wright, was standing on his forecourt watching the trucks rush by, but he was never called. Euston's trucks were left in position for the duration. Well, somebody had to remain in reserve to look after the rest of the West End. He remained very bitter about that, and in later years I could easily wind him up by reminding him of that night.

All the crews were working really hard, and we were told to take an extension ladder to the rear as there were still people awaiting rescue. The old wooden Dewhurst extension ladder was a heavy old thing. We had to manhandle it across a couple of garden fences to reach the back of the hotel. There were no more rescues but a lot of firefighting to be done. I remember standing on a staircase landing at the rear, unable to proceed as the staircase was burnt away. I was there with an Assistant Chief Officer, Taffy Watkins.

At this point I have to say that in these days, due to improvements in command and control, I would not have been on my own away from my crew. It is now policy that, other than in exceptional circumstances, crews stay together.

Standing on that landing in such exulted company, I could see through to the front of the hotel and could make out firemen moving about in the smoke, and I thought that I could see my Guvnor, Colin Searle. I decided that it was a waste of time being at the back of the building and made my way around to the front.

Once at the front, I was standing at the foot of an escape ladder helping to pass hose up the ladder. Suddenly there was a great crash from above, and we were showered with sparks and smouldering embers. The air was full of sparks and dust; I looked up and saw that part of the roof and the floor below it had collapsed. Instinctively, I started to climb the ladder in a state of apprehension. I didn't know why I was going upwards. At one stage I had to stop and shelter from the falling debris. I knew I had to get to the top of the ladder but I didn't know what I was going to do, or what I might find. Behind me on the ladder was a fireman from Soho, Eric Hall, known to all as 'Nobby'. He was moving a bit faster than me and when my legs were not moving voluntarily, he shouted 'Come on, Ray'.

When somebody does something heroic, people say that he acted without any thought for his own safety. That was the first thing I thought of! As I'm going up the ladder, the rest of the building could fall down on me! There were two floors of unsupported brickwork above me. 'What the fuck was I doing here?' was the major thought that went through my mind!

When I started this job I made a promise to El, and on the few occasions where I have been in extreme danger, it always comes back to me. I promised her that I would get through this unscathed. I really wanted to remain in one piece.

So there I was, about to become a reluctant hero. I had to do my duty but at the same time, when it was all over, I wanted to go home in one piece.

I got to the head of the ladder on the third floor of this Victorian hotel, where a crazed arsonist had had his evil way and there was nowhere to go. The smoke-obscured room ahead of me was filled with burning, smouldering timber. There was no way I could have known that, buried under all this, were four firemen.

Nobby was backing-up on the ladder but I didn't want to step into the room. I couldn't see what was in front and I wasn't sure the floor would hold me if I stepped inside. I stepped off the ladder and stood on the windowsill trying to make out the conditions ahead of me. All the time the smoke was burning my eyes and choking my lungs. My duty soon became apparent; I could see a white fire helmet half showing in the rubble beneath my feet. A Station Officer was wedged against the front outside wall, buried by fallen timbers and rubble. There was a long section of floor joist on top of his shoulder. and I tried to lift this off him but it was impossible; it was held fast by other timbers. This was eventually lifted using a turntable ladder as a crane.

As soon as the trapped man was aware that we were there, he spoke and, although I couldn't see his face, I realised that it was my Guvnor. Nobby and I had to get into the room. With the words of Ron Morris ringing in my ears: 'Drop everything and get your mates out', we had to get Colin out of this awful mess. At first we dug with our hands and later with tools. We started to remove the timbers and rubble that were trapping him. At one stage Colin said, 'Come on you bastards, get me out of here.' His head was visible by then; he looked up, saw it was me, and in a completely relaxed voice said, 'Oh, hello Ray.' It was so preposterous: there he was at death's door and still able to respond. It had only been a few minutes; we were making some headway, and then I heard the groaning of another man buried even deeper right next to Colin.

Meanwhile, I could make out voices at the rear of the room but could not make out what was going on. Our ears and eyes were in disbelief. Not realising I had moved further into the room, I was now standing on the other man. He was buried so deep that I still could not see him. Not wearing gloves, the hot timbers were singeing my hands.

Eventually, four men made it up the ladder and were working at the front of the room. Then we were joined by the Station Officer from Paddington, Neil Wallington, who took control of the situation and realised that there wasn't space for further help. He was concerned that the floor beneath our feet was becoming unstable.

None of the men working in that room gave any consideration to the precarious nature of their surroundings. Ripping at the smouldering debris with our bare hands, we began to expose our bent and crushed colleagues. Rising like great smoke-shrouded stone monoliths, the walls on three sides of our position were unsupported and unstable. All firefighting had stopped, but the fire was still burning and tons of fragile brickwork could have toppled in on us. Fortunately I was too busy to look upwards.

I cannot remember the exact sequence of what went on in that room. Time seemed to stand still. It was really smoky and it got worse as the rescue went on. I was permanently crouched over with the smoke rising into my face, back aching, knees cut and sore. These days, we would have been wearing breathing apparatus and would have had to change cylinders or personnel every 40 minutes, but this was not a consideration; speed was of the essence, no thought of being relieved. Anyway, nobody would have left.

I was still aware that something was going on at the back of the room. I really didn't know who was there. Now I know that Ron Morris and the Leading Fireman from Westminster, Peter Lidbetter, were trying to release two more firemen. There was a lot of noise from outside but the rescue was performed with very little noise, except for the man trapped next to Colin. I was trying to dig him out and he was moaning, in a lot of pain from a back injury.

Nobby was trying to get Colin's helmet off as the chin-strap was choking him. He was talking to us the whole time, saying that he was hot. By then we had a hosereel, and water was being sprayed down into the timbers trapping him. We had to go carefully while freeing the other man, not knowing what damage had been caused to his concealed limbs – sawing and lifting timbers, removing brick by brick. As the rescue continued, minor falls of burning timbers and debris were going on all the time. In time I was able to clear the rubble, and with help from Station Officer Wallington, we managed to lift him clear. Then we managed to get him past Colin to the window. I had to be so careful where I trod. Then he was carried down the ladder by the Station Officer from Soho, Keith Hicks.

Now we were all able to concentrate on releasing Colin. Every time we moved him, he swore at me! It must have helped him to cope with the pain. Eventually, when we got him free and lifted him up, we realised why he was in such pain. All through the extrication, the fire had been eating away at his leg and back, exposing the white of his bones. All down one side he was seriously burnt. Everyone took a sharp intake, and quiet replaced our short-lived elation. He couldn't see, and we were too professional to comment on the extent of his injuries. Brave man.

He was taken to Queen Mary's Hospital, East Grinstead, which has a specialist burns unit. He had to have a lot of skin grafts but did get back to full duty. He would show off his injuries at the drop of a hat or, should I say, trousers! When I visited him in hospital, I was shocked to see the burn injuries suffered by other patients. But, typically, Colin was in good spirits; he never doubted that he would get back to work.

I only found out later that one of the two men at the back of the room had died. His name was Harry Pettit. I didn't know him, but he was a new boy at Paddington and was in the building working with Martin Walker, another good man, who was also trapped and sustained burns to his feet and legs but again, in time, got back to work.

I find it hard to describe how I feel when a fireman dies while performing his duty. I was severely affected by that night; not in a way that would make me not want to be a fireman, but it made me realise the frailty of it all.

Years later I saw two close friends, who had been hurt at separate fires, on television: one collapsing from his efforts at the height of the Kings Cross Underground fire, the other lying in a hospital bed after he had been burnt rescuing children from a hotel fire. A bolt of emotion hit me. Until then I did not appreciate how much people meant to me. I grieve at all my losses; I hope it will go away, but it never does. I never forget friends that I have lost. Every time a fireman dies I can only imagine if it were me or one of my close friends; we all think that it will never happen to us. Every time I see some horrendous incident, all I can think of is the men who have to put their hands in there and rest their eyes on the horror.

Once the two casualties were removed from the front of the building, I helped for a while at the rear but soon realised that I was useless, suffering some sort of shock and had to get out of there. Another fireman touched my shoulder saying it was time for me to get out. My whole body was hurting, my lungs heavy with smoke, shaking with the cold. Covered in muck and soaked to the bone, I needed the warmth of home: I needed my wife. So after about two hours that was a lifetime, but seemed like a moment, I was able to climb down that ladder. It was light by then and I stood at the Salvation Army canteen van trying to drink tea, but unable to keep my hand still.

I'd done my bit and got out safe!

One of Westminster's fire engines was released from the scene and we went back to the station without our Guvnor. I got washed and changed and went back into the watchroom to finish off any outstanding bookings and tidy the teleprinter. So many messages had come into the station, the paper had spilled out over the floor.

I did start to get a bit pissed-off with repeating the story to the oncoming Blue Watch.

'What's happened? Where's your Guvnor?'

Eventually the Blue Watch Station Officer, Robbie Graham, arrived. He took one look at me and took me out of the watchroom and sent me home.

There have only been a few occasions where, when I got home, the 'stiff upper-lip' would last no longer. It's always when I have not only endured the emotional shock, but am also exhausted.

Thankfully I have someone to look after me.

Back to the station. Temporary Station Officer Ron Morris was in charge and that's how it stayed until Colin returned. Ron, Peter and I received Chief Officer's Commendations for our actions at the Worsley. We went to the old County Hall to receive our awards. The ceremony was held in the afternoon. I didn't invite my family, and afterwards Ron and I just went on duty. On reflection, I wished that I had made more of it, but even then I didn't feel comfortable with the establishment. But these things don't happen very often and I should have made the most of it. If not for my sake, but for my family who never get to see their husband, their dad and their son being appreciated.

A few months later it was announced in *The London Gazette* that I had been awarded a Queen's Commendation for Brave Conduct. All the firemen working in that room were recognised with awards. Ron Morris, Peter Lidbetter and two firemen from West Hampstead, David Blair and Roger Stewart, went to Buckingham Palace to be presented with the Queen's Gallantry Medal. For Nobby Hall, Neil Wallington, Harry Pettit's wife and me, it was back to County Hall to receive the Queen's Commendation for Brave Conduct.

About a month previously I had received a letter from the Prime Minister, Harold Wilson, telling me of the award. I got nice letters from all sorts of people: from the Chief Officer to the Fire Brigade's Society. It was a proud time.

Now I was able to make up for my ignorance and take the family to the ceremony. The awards were being presented by the Lord Lieutenant of Greater London. Awards were made to people from all the services. Hearing the citations being read, detailing the bravery of men and women from the police and the armed services, was a humbling experience.

I am very proud of that little pin holding a spray of silver oak leaves. When I became a Station Officer and I had a proper uniform, I wore it all the time. I was very pleased to show that I'd got something that I didn't just get because I was able to pass an exam.

Gordon Honeycomb was writing his book 'Red Watch' about Paddington at the time of the fire, and he visited The Minster several times to hear accounts of our actions. It was funny that he always arrived at suppertime and we, being polite individuals, invited him to eat. Maybe he did not understand that the food was paid for by us and not the Fire Brigade, but he never chipped in voluntarily; perhaps he had long pockets! We also had a visit from the late Linda Lee Potter; the quality of the mess manager's cooking must have gotten around the journalistic world.

When 'Red Watch' was published in paperback, I got invited to the launch. We were on strike at the time and I took the whole picket line. We made real pigs out of ourselves. Well, we were on the breadline!

*Chapter 7*

# THE OLD MINSTER

During my six years at The Minster there were many fires and incidents. I cannot remember the sequence or the dates, but some are worthy of being recounted.

When we were ordered in the early hours to the Moorgate Underground train crash, as a relief to carry out firefighting duties, I sat in the back of the pump, and I can remember that I really didn't want this one. During the previous day's morning rush hour, a train packed with commuters had crashed at 30mph into a dead end tunnel. Forty-three died, 34 were seriously injured and hundreds received treatment. My apprehension had to do with the fact that I knew that all the live casualties had been removed and now it was the turn of the dead. The street outside the station was full of the usual fire appliances, but with the addition of the undertaker's vehicles.

Straight away we were issued with face-masks and given salt tablets. The rescue operation had already been in progress for 15 hours and it would take several painstaking days to reach the front of the train. As there were no trains moving, there were no through drafts, and the heat down on the platform was debilitating. It was like working inside an oven in firegear; the temperature was 120 degrees. The heat was accelerating the decomposition of the bodies, so it didn't smell too good either. As the emergency tender men were hot cutting the crushed metal, they were setting light to seating that was compacted into the metal. It was our job to put out these fires. Every so often everything went silent, as yet another body was located. The medical teams stepped in and did their work, and then we had to help extricate and remove. We were only down there for one four-hour stint, but our emergency tender crews worked in shifts around the clock to the bitter end. The job wasn't finished until they finally reached the driver. We Londoners are so lucky to have such men looking after our wellbeing.

The Red Watch also picked up the bomb at the Houses of Commons. I had to get off the bus and walk past my mates who were at the job of the year. I had been standing by at Soho. I must have just walked out of the station when the bomb exploded. I was sitting on a bus that wasn't moving, returning to the Minster after the night duty. You couldn't park at Soho as the yard was so small. Standing-by at Soho was like being a fish out of water. The blokes' language had a sprinkling of slang all of their own. This playing with words was something you only got used to by being there for a long time and knowing the origins of the sayings.

I also attended the worst road traffic accident of my career from Westminster. Again, in the early hours of the morning, we were called to an RTA at Pimlico Road Junction, Buckingham Palace Road, SW1. This junction has since been altered. A car overloaded with kids returning from a concert at Wembley had turned right too early onto the wrong side of the dual carriageway, and gone head-on into a dustcart. The kids in the front were trapped and the rest were flung out and spread across the road. It was a shitty job and one that I try to forget, but horror seems to cause a photographic memory.

We had a cracking job in an upstairs flat in Claverton Street, SW1. The first and second floors were involved; they were both blazing. We had to fight our way upstairs, and as we were getting into the flat, we realised that something was flying about inside the room. I've always been a bit frightened of birds. All of a sudden I heard a shout as a window shattered: 'Get that fuckin' parrot!' and Polly made a dash for safety. When the lady occupant returned to her devastated home, she was only interested in the whereabouts of her parrot. She said at the top of her voice, 'Where's my fuckin' parrot!'

This became a popular response around the station whenever any form of bird was mentioned. Another funny thing happened at this fire. The place was burnt out; literally. Firemen, for some reason, after they have had a lung full of smoke, light up a fag. Well, even the kitchen table was burnt to the floor, but this lady handed the boys an ashtray! There are some strange people hidden away in SW1!

None stranger than the man who called us to his flat complaining of a smell of burning. The man was a well-kept seventy-year-old and all round the walls were photographs of him in various states of undress in erotic poses. Once we had satisfied his mind of the smell of burning, he proudly gave us a tour of these pictures. In one he was dressed as a cowboy wearing chaps but no trousers!

A regular part of our training was the carry-down. It was thought to be essential that you were capable of carrying a fireman of similar build down the length of a 50ft escape ladder. There were after-effects to this drill; your legs ached for days. The man being carried wore a safety harness called an Everest Device, which would lock if the line passing through it went too fast. If you fell or dropped him, he would be suspended in midair. It was very unusual to do a carry-down in anger but I got one. I was in the wrong place at the wrong time, and I had to carry-down an elderly woman from a second-floor window. It is much easier to take people down the internal stairs, but the smoke was too thick for this old lady and she was already overcome. The escape was pitched to a second-floor window. In preparation to carry-down, you had to get to the head of the ladder and stand with your head just above the windowsill with your right arm held skywards. The person is passed out and manoeuvred over your shoulders with your right arm between their legs. You can then walk down the ladder carrying the person in a fireman's lift. Fortunately, this poor old lady could only have been about six or seven stone, no comparison to a thirteen-stone fireman. I was finding it easy until about half way down her bladder emptied down my neck! When I reached the ground, at least I had an excuse to pass her to another fireman who did the mouth to mouth. Amazingly, after a stay in hospital, this lady made a full recovery. She must have been about 100!

The Minster makes up the 'predetermined attendance' on Soho's ground (every address in London has a laid down attendance; this consists of the quantity and the type of fire engine and from what station it is to be ordered). As Soho had many more calls than us, we were often able to nick a few jobs when they were busy elsewhere. As I was to find out later, this was something that regularly happened. Soho's firemen would be dealing with something mundane while other fire stations were getting the excitement.

One Saturday morning we were called to a fire in a bank, Pall Mall, SW1. It was going like the clappers, but banks are hard places to get into. So by the time we gained entry, the fire was bottled-up and the temperature was incredible. We had a new boy on the watch; this was not his first fire but was the most serious. The OIC told me to rig in BA and take the new boy inside. New boy wanted to go first, so I let him. We were taking in a line of hose and got to a point where he came to a standstill in front of me. It's hard to make yourself understood while wearing a facemask, but I got through to him and encouraged him in 'firelingo' to move forward. He grabbed me and pushed me in front, and then I realised why we were not moving. It was so hot that his ears were blistering and now so were mine. It's never easy trying to find your way around in thick smoke; it's disorientating and frightening.

Another job that has stuck in my mind was another Soho fire in Pall Mall at the RAC Club. It was a real classic. Smoke and flames were rolling up the face of the building, high above one of the most dramatic streets in London. When we arrived, the Soho men were already inside and hose was being hauled up the outside of the building to the floor below the fire, which was situated a room in the roof. I never actually got inside while the fire was raging; I was out in the street getting water and equipment up to the crews fighting the fire.

It's all a matter of teamwork, and unfortunately it's usually the drivers who get left outside doing the donkey-work. When I finally got inside and upstairs to where the fire had started, I entered a galleried room on the mezzanine level. I looked down on a man lying on the floor in the centre of the room, who had been so severely burnt that his skull had cracked open. I could clearly see his brain with a blob of blood right in the centre. You can't choose the images that get stored away; horror makes its mark again.

Early one summer evening we were called to a man collapsed in a basement in Winchester Street, W1. This turned out to be a real heart-breaker. It still gives me goose pimples. You may think you have become hardened to the rigours of the job, but that wasn't to say that a sad scene had no effect. A young builder had been left alone to clear up at a house that was being refurbished. We found him lying shirtless, down in the basement area. He had been shovelling up mortar and had cut through the live cable of the cement mixer and had been electrocuted. It was the only pump that was called, so there were only four of us. We tried for what seemed like forever to revive him, and were still trying right up until the ambulance arriving. The paramedics took over but with no success. A young man, far from his home, died all-alone in a wet basement.

A vision and a memory that has never left me.

The most bizarre incident I attended while at Westminster was a call to a fire at The Cut on Lambeth's ground – another of our 'take calls'. Lambeth's appliances were in attendance. They had entered the premises and we followed the hosereel upstairs to a flat on the first floor.

There was no smoke and no fire but there was an awful smell. All the firemen were standing around an armchair. Slumped in the chair was a large elderly lady who had either died while sitting in front of an electric fire or had caught her clothing alight by sitting too near the fire. Most of the body was blackened and the flesh on the lower part of the body had been burnt away. This had happened over a long period of time, and the fire had burnt itself out. This was a ghastly sight; only one of the incidents I attended where people had set themselves alight, either accidentally or deliberately.

In another incident we were called to, a woman had poured petrol over herself outside the Houses of Parliament. She was dead before we arrived and there was little for us to do but cover the body and wait for its removal. This must have been some kind of political protest, but how would anyone know what it was about?

The third instance happened one morning. It was at the end of our second night shift and a Blue Watch bloke was riding with us. Colin Searle was in charge and I was driving. The call came in at about 0830hrs to a fire in a children's playground, Abbey Orchard Street, SW1. The residential dwellings in this area are mostly old Peabody Trust tenements. They were usually constructed around a square of common ground with a playground in the centre.

A young man, for whatever reason, had gone into this playground, poured paraffin over his clothing and set himself alight. He was wearing a quilted blue nylon anorak with the hood pulled up tight around his head.

As we were called to a fire on open ground, only one pump is ordered and we were expecting to see a rubbish fire. The hosereel was taken in and there was just a ball of flame that was hard to make out at first, but Colin Searle knew what he was about and had control of the situation.

This poor tortured soul was lying on his back so severely burnt that where his genitals should have been there was just a blackened hole, and the nylon material of his anorak had fused to his skin. He was still conscious and was asking us why it hurt so much.

It was a rotten coincidence. The Blue Watch man who was riding with us was Patsy McGill, a nice man. He had grown up in the area and actually knew this man. We tried to make the casualty as comfortable as possible until the ambulance arrived. Sometimes the reassuring sound of an ambulance approaching is as much of a relief to the firemen as the casualty. He was eventually removed and taken to the specialist burns unit at Roehampton Hospital, but unfortunately died.

I was still cracking-on, trying to get promotion. I was taking a lot more notice of how the experienced officers were dealing with the various incidents. One of the more important duties of the OIC is to send messages. Messages fall into three categories: Assistance, Informative and Stop.

The origin of the stop message comes from Victorian times, when London was a much smaller city and only had 13 fire stations. If there was a serious fire, all the local stations would attend and reinforcements were sent from all the stations in the shape of a single man. This man would have to set off at a brisk walk wearing his firegear with his helmet under his arm – can you believe it? At each station he passed he would call in to find out if he had been stopped. If he had, he could walk back to his station; if not he had to keep going. Nowadays, if the OIC, on arrival at an incident, judges that the appliances that are in attendance or that are already on their way are sufficient to deal with the incident, he can send a stop message. This message can also be sent once a more serious fire is eventually under control.

If, however, he feels that he needs additional appliances, he has to send an assistance or make-up message stating how many and what type of appliances he requires. If an assistance message is sent or if the incident is to be protracted, he must also send an informative message. The informative message should include the location and the extent of the fire/incident and what actions he is taking. This message is important as it lets Control know the situation, and plans can be made to move appliances to cover the stations involved, and Control can pass this information to any senior officer who may be required to attend.

Correctly constructed messages are not only important for operational efficiency, but they are essential for your reputation. If you make a mess of your messages, your mistakes are broadcast all over the Brigade's radio system. If you do make a mistake, you will also get a call from an officer at Control when you return to the station, asking you for a correction, which is even more embarrassing. Then the corrected message will again be broadcast to all via the teleprinter.

To me, it was a matter of pride that I got my messages correct. So, therefore, I was very interested in what Colin would send concerning this man who had set himself alight, who was severely burned, but still alive. Every message in those days was worded. Nowadays, routine messages are coded so that you can just send a number, but you still have to know how to construct a worded message. Usually the OIC will get his driver to send the messages, and that is the way I began to pick up the skill.

Colin sent his stop: 'Small fire in Street – Hosereel', then his informative: 'Ambulance required for person suffering from severe burns'. I stored that away just in case I was ever in charge of anything similar but, happily, I never had to use it.

In 1980 the fourth watch was formed – the Green Watch. Colin Searle was selected to be in charge and, as part of the deal, he was able to take some of the Red Watch with him. He took me, which I suppose was a bit of a compliment, and Steve Coleman. Steve began his service at Westminster in 1974 when he was just 18, and we were to work together several times over the coming years. As the Brigade had managed to increase its manpower, the rest of the watch was made up from existing Westminster men from other watches and some new boys. That was it; just more of the same but with a different bunch of blackguards!

The old Red Watch had changed over the years and my best Sub. Officer, Ron Morris, had moved on and had gone to Soho Reds and then on to the Greens. We all thought that he was mad to be going to a much busier station at his time of life!

This change made me renew my efforts to get on. In those days the initial written promotional exams had little to do with the Fire Brigade. I was frequently reminded by my White Watch that I had passed these exams, when all you had to know was how to make jam and hem curtains! However, you also had to undergo a practical test where you did have to demonstrate fireground skills. Now I had to concentrate on gaining the skills needed to become an officer – being in charge of an appliance, attending and dealing with minor incidents and doing the routine office work.

The next stage in the promotion procedure was an interview, where you were questioned by a Board of Senior Officers. They tested you on your knowledge of operational matters and on how you would deal with problems and tasks around the station.

It always improved your chances if you had the qualifications for the next rank, and you had undertaken temporary promotion at other stations. So I started to study for the Subs exam and had my name added to the Divisional list of those who were willing to act-up at other stations. My first period was with the Green Watch at Soho. Back with Ron Morris. I didn't get the Soho bug then; that came later!

Soho Fire station, in addition to the usual pump escape and pump, had a TL known colloquially as the 'ladders'. I had no experience with this appliance and had to learn the basics very quickly, as on the first night on duty I was riding in charge. There were two Leading Firemen and we shared the duties; one shift on the pump and one shift on the ladders.

I'm not kidding when I say that it was a shock to the system. I had gone from a station where it was busy, but there were only about 2000 shouts per year, to a station with about 8000! Both the pump and the TL were incredibly busy. As Soho's ground is surrounded by other busy stations, they were in and out all the time. There were many occasions when the TL went out on its first call of the shift and did not make it back until the end. Or, worse still, you just got back to the station, sat down to eat your dried-up food and out you would go again.

The ladders are based strategically at few stations. They are part of the initial attendance on all calls in an 'A' risk area. As all the inner London stations were 'A' risk, it attended not only all the calls on its home ground, it also went to most of the calls on the surrounding grounds. Areas are categorised from 'A' risk – densely populated with high buildings, through to 'D' – the countryside. There are a specific number of appliances for each level and laid-down times for the appliances to arrive at incidents.

At that time, the ladders were not as sophisticated as they are now. They were uncomfortable – cold in the winter and the cab became overheated in summer. You always had to rig in your fire gear for every call; by the end of the shift you were knackered. It was like being wrapped in a blanket inside a sauna.

I had further spells of acting-up at Euston and Paddington. This was the only way to learn your trade. It was always difficult at first but you just had to operate on the principle of keeping your eyes wide open and your mouth shut tight. As you were the new boy, wherever you went there was nothing to be gained from making waves. It was a case of keep your head down; let the others make the mistakes and try to learn from them. The OIC of the watch you were temporarily attached to was supposed to do a report on you before you left; they never did, but eventually I got my interview. If successful, you were placed on a promotion panel and as soon as a vacancy arose, once you were top of the list, you were offered a job. If you refused a posting, you went back to the bottom and waited.

I accepted a posting to Red Watch, Kensington. After the usual leaving piss-up, I said cheerio to my mates on the Green Watch, said goodbye to the old Minster and set off to try to become an officer.

*Chapter 8*

# KENSINGTON: THE ROYAL BOROUGH

The less said about my time at Kensington the better. I was there for 10 months, and a combination of hardly any action and a difficult management situation made it miserable. I got on with most of the blokes. They were reasonable, and the junior officers were experienced, but some of the blokes were mean bastards. The Station Officer didn't help; with hardly any effort, he was wrecking the place. He had been sent there directly after the strike, when the men were at their most bitter, and as far as I could see it was still rumbling downhill.

It wasn't actually anarchy, but not far off. The Sub. Officer was the area union rep. The Guvnor showed weakness in all aspects of his job. Everything had changed since the strike. London had voted to stay out, but the rest of the country wanted to accept the deal and get back to work. I'm sure that some of the blokes got so used to it that they actually liked being on strike.

It just goes to show the detrimental effect a weak and inefficient officer can have on a group of men. Firemen need to be led; they need to be confident in their leader, and that leader has to show them respect whenever it is due. He has to uphold the discipline. If not, you will find that the stronger individuals of a watch will all become leaders. This can have disastrous effects on the fireground, and the other aspects of the job start to slip into anarchy.

I have my own theory as to why Kensington was so miserable. Sunlight never entered the building. The yard is always in complete shadow until late in the afternoon, when one small corner gets a shard of sunlight. Seriously, the station is situated in a side road adjoining one of the busiest roads in London. It has a ground full of residential properties, and the potential to be a very busy station, but hardly anything ever happens.

The pump and the ladders were out a lot on other stations' grounds. I was happy to spend most of my time riding in charge of the ladders away from the mayhem. It was ironic riding the ladders as number one. There you were; you could have none or very little knowledge of the technicalities of the appliance, but were supposedly in charge. Whereas the man sitting next to you driving the thing, with its considerable intricacy at his fingertips, was the expert. Over the years, the TLs have developed into sophisticated machines and a training course goes with each model. As they are so complicated, they often go wrong and a spare has go on the run; these operators have be able to adapt to each appliance or a suitable stand-by driver has to be sought. Another major headache with the TL is that they all should carry a small but essential amount of equipment wherever it goes. When a spare comes in, this is always missing, and the poor old Leading Fireman has to scour the Brigade to find it.

The best thing about being on the ladders is that you go far and wide to all kinds of incidents, adding to your experience, and it makes for exciting times. One minute you're going to a fire with the sole purpose of rescue, the next a person is threatening to jump, then to some major fire to be used as a water tower, spraying water down onto the flames from above.

The most unusual shout I attended was to a prisoner making a rooftop protest at Wormwood Scrubs. The man was high up, ripping slates off the roof and throwing them down at his pursuers. We could only provide access to the roof; I wasn't allowed to get involved. We had been told to stay in the cab as the appliance was being driven through the maze of prison blocks. Why? I soon found out. We started to hear objects striking the TL. Excrement wrapped in newspaper was being thrown from the windows.

Usually, as the ladders augment the attendance on other stations' grounds, you arrive at the incidents last. The ladders are essentially a rescue appliance and carry very little fire-fighting equipment. It rarely ever happens that the ladders pick up a job on their own. One day, Brian Mills was driving. Brian became a long-term friend. He was to work with me at Soho as a Leading Fireman. That was once he got his finger out and realised his potential. I received a call to a fire in Elvaston Place, SW7. On arrival, we were on our own with smoke belching from a third floor flat. Neighbours were standing outside and they told me that there was a man inside. We had to get on with it. As was usual, Brian was getting the ladders to work and extending it to the third floor. I had to work without water. I climbed the ladders, got into the room, and as luck would have it, found the man straight away crouching near the open window. He was still conscious, and I was able to get him onto the ladder and assist him down to safety. While this was going on, the remainder of the attendance arrived. They rigged in BA, took in a hosereel and another was taken up the ladders, which were still in position, and the fire was soon under control.

An ambulance had been ordered and the man, who was suffering from smoke inhalation and shock, was removed to hospital.

Another incident which was out of the ordinary took place at a very exclusive address off the Brompton Road. The house involved belonged to Princess Lee Raziwell. It was a serious fire and the place was gutted.

Everybody working inside was hot, wet from damping down and cutting away. This is done when the fire is out, just to ensure that there are no remaining hot spots which are likely to cause the fire to re-ignite. In walked the Princess accompanied by a couple of police officers. Honestly, in she walked wearing a fur coat and Wellington boots. Now, remember that we're up on the second floor in a room which I presume was her bedroom and it was a blackened shell. She starts creating, 'Where's my jewellery!'

If something like this happens, the OIC of the incident is not allowed to let anyone leave the incident, and any appliances that have left have to be called back via the radio. The police, if they are not there already, have to be called to investigate.

Once the fire was completely out, we were all searched. The trucks were searched, and even the soles of our boots were inspected. Nothing was found, so I suppose the jewellery was still inside, mixed up with the remains of the room. Again, I suppose the police had to sift through the rubble to find the missing gems.

On 10th July 1980 the Red Watch had just started their night shift, and were ordered as a relief to Alexandra Palace. This was a thirty-pump fire. We were ordered to proceed on the bell. Normally, reliefs are ordered to be at the incident at a specified time and travel at normal road speeds. It was obvious that we were not going just to clear-up, but to fight the fire. Kensington to Hornsey is a long way to go on the bell. This was a particularly difficult fire as the water supply was poor. Water had to be relayed from pump to pump uphill to the Palace. The water supply was also intermittent and would fail without notice, then return with no warning. It was because of this, and the fact that a lot of the firefighting was taking place outside on the slopes around the building, that I took a tumble down a steep grassy bank. Don't laugh! I was not badly hurt but it did give me an excuse to take a few days sick with a bad back. I really didn't want to go to work.

I don't want to talk about the things that went on at Kensington, but as I have already said, it was not how I expected a fire station to be. My sickness record reached its worst level. I didn't want to go to work, and could not wait to get out. I heard that one of the Leading Firemen at White Watch Soho was being promoted, so I confirmed it with him and put in for a transfer. I was successful, and, although I had made a couple of good friends at Kensington, I escaped under the shadow of darkness without looking back and with no regrets. As they used to say, 'Have kit bag, will travel'.

## Chapter 9

# SOHO: THE FIRST TIME

When we moved from Maidstone to Croydon I decided that I would start cycling to work. I had been quite keen as a teenager, and as I was reasonably fit I bought a bike and got on with it. It was a great way of commuting – cheaper than public transport and quicker than the car. It was about a 30 mile round journey. It got a bit hard riding home after a busy night and sometimes the weather got to me, but just to be able to get on the bike and not sit in traffic or wait for a train outweighed any disadvantage.

I had already shifted my gear to Soho by car so I could cycle in on my first night. Because of the way the shifts work, I knew a lot of the Reds and Greens, but was unfamiliar with the Whites and Blues. So they didn't really know who I was. I was having a wash after the bike ride and felt half a dozen pairs of eyes on me. Half the watch were standing at the washroom door commenting about my lack of hair and the fact that I was getting on a bit – 33! Nothing I hadn't heard before and it was quite light-hearted, but I knew I was already being tested – let's see if he bites!

They turned out to be, mostly, a great bunch. They worked like dogs on the fireground and were great fun around the station, and they stuck together against the common enemy – the Guvnor.

I had the greatest of respect for this man. Everyone who has worked at Soho will know of him and the unfortunate, cruel nature of his downfall, but it would not be fair for outsiders to form any opinions from my words. Most of what happened was unsubstantiated. It was just unfortunate that he was in charge during the most notorious discipline case the Brigade had ever had to deal with and became the fall guy.

He had a reputation of being a bit of a maverick. He was good on the fireground. He was wise to what he could and couldn't do, but most of all, if he did make a mistake he knew how it could be concealed. He had striking pale blue 'Dirty Harry' eyes and would stare directly into yours daring you to look away. The blokes were alert to this and would go to great lengths to make you laugh when he had you under the stare. They would climb ladders to look over him, try to catch your eyes from behind him and even climb outside to look through a first-floor window just to make you laugh!

One night he came into the Leading Fireman's room. I was in bed and really just wanted to go to sleep. It must have been after midnight because he would search the places where the men would sleep and tip you out if it was before midnight. Anyway, he was at the door and the blokes were outside standing on the window ledge at first-floor level, out of his sight, just staring at me. He was talking about wine – a favourite subject – and I'm wetting myself trying not to laugh. While this is going on, the whole world and his brother are passing by in Shaftsbury Avenue.

The Guvnor had a very rigid attitude towards the men. I know now that past experience had made him like this. He showed no favouritism, even towards the good blokes on the watch. He was like this because he was able to foresee the consequences if he showed any sign of weakness. His example taught me to look at every situation and say to myself, 'If I allow this to happen, what could be the worst outcome?' He once advised me to save a copy of every piece of paper that included my name. This turned out to be invaluable advice, and my red lever arch file has got me out of a few scrapes with wayward personnel and difficult senior officers. It was great to say, 'Look, it's here in writing'.

On the rare occasion, he would look in at the station when I was doing his job. It made me feel like the new boy all over again! He was so confident and self-assured.

Although he did communicate with the men, I cannot remember a time when he sat down and ate with us. He would send out for food and eat breakfast out at a café after the shift was over. He would not stand for any misbehaviour, but he was seriously let down by some of the men and senior management. I think that he got to a stage where he thought he was fighting a losing battle. I also think that even though some of the men were more than a bit lively, he still had affection for them. As I was to find out later on, even the most wayward of individuals – as long as they don't let you down in their duties as a fireman – manage to wangle a way into your heart.

The White Watch was formed when the horrendous work hours – endured by the two original watches – were reduced. As it was made up of personnel from the original watches, it was said that it was established with all the rejects: the bad boys. Therefore, they were called the 'Bastard Whites!' Even though the transformation had happened years previously, some of the Whites at Soho were trying to live up to that title a little too seriously. The majority were decent, hardworking, reliable blokes, and some others were being influenced by a couple of really bad men.

The worst influence on the men's behaviour was drink. Drinking before coming on duty, and in some cases while on duty, was quite normal. At one time this practice was even encouraged by the Brigade. There had been a tradition of allowing drinking on stations; again, a leftover from the naval influence. Bars were allowed on stations. County Brigades still have them, but only for the use of off-duty personnel and they're treated like a social club.

Ever since I had been in the Brigade, we used to have a pint in the evenings. It was just something that happened. At Battersea you took your turn in going to the off-licence, and at Soho you went next door to the pub and brought back a tray of drinks. There seemed to be nothing wrong with this. It only came home to me while on a call. The appliance I was riding was involved in a minor road accident. The police had to be called, and they noticed that the Fire Brigade driver smelt of drink. This was pre-breathalyser, and I believe that the OIC managed to convince the police that he had only had one drink so they took no further action. This was not just a practice involving the men; senior officers would turn up to fires smelling of drink.

Eventually, the Brigade got round to banning alcohol on stations. But, in their usual lily-livered way, it took years to get any form of procedure to back up their newly-found temperance. The poor old OIC still had to make a judgement with no real back up. 'No individual should report for duty under the influence of drink or drugs'. That was how the order was worded. But what if you had a couple of glasses of wine with your lunch and then later went into work for a night shift? You would smell of drink but how could he tell if you had one drink or five? Was the man who had a social pint with his mates before a night duty under the influence or was it just one pint on his breath?

If you thought that they were under the influence you had to prove it, and we had no means to do that. You could call in a senior officer to back up your suspicions, but it was possible that it could take hours for him to get to the station.

I know that the OIC of the White Watch was trying to deal with a serious problem. Some of the men didn't go home during the day. When they were between night shifts, they went to the pub. Was this a problem peculiar to Soho? I don't think so. I know it happened all over the Brigade. It was just that it is so much more available in Soho. Walk out the door of the fire station at any time of the day or night and it was all there – anything you wanted within 100 yards in any direction.

I also know that one night he tried to run three men who were the worst for wear and they got away with it. He got them all the way to a discipline hearing and they were let off. They came back to the station, caps tipped to the back of their heads with the attitude that they could get away with anything. So therefore, who could blame him for finding it hard to keep on fighting? In the end it was him who ended up with egg on his face. Afterwards, he was the man who still had to try and manage the situation with the offending individuals who believed they were now invincible.

By the way, at one time a friend of mine went into pub management and his first pub was The Avenue next door to the fire station. He's a cab driver now. He and his wife lasted one shell-shocked and sleepless week due to the constant noise of the fire engines turning-out. The Palace Theatre opposite the station can only put on musicals, due to the sirens which you can still hear even when the cast and orchestra are going full blast!

Anyway, back to the Bastard Whites. As I said, the Guvnor had a solid Fire Brigade background. He was a wise and canny officer. I believe that it was because he was so smart that he did make some jealous enemies from higher up the management chain. I know of one incident where he got front-page publicity; some might consider he brought the Brigade into disrepute. From there on he was a target and a trap was set.

The incident in question has been well documented and was just typical of what can happen in Soho.

The Whites were called to a fire at the Sundowner nightclub in Charing Cross Road. They knew the premises as they had already attended several small fires. On this particular night there was a launch party for the film version of 'Tommy'. Involved in the party were all sorts of stage acts, including a fire-eater, a snake charmer and trick sharp-shooter. The place was full of tipsy celebrities. Even as I write this, and even though I have all this experience of working in Soho, I still find it hard to believe, let alone make the story sound credible.

The fire-eater had set light to the snake charmer's basket and the drapes; the gunslinger had accidentally shot the DJ in the neck and the whole place was in uproar. Oh, and the snake had escaped! The firemen did their bit, but because the police were there and a crime had been committed, they were not allowed to leave. This was when it all went bad. Drunken starlets were dragging the firemen onto the dance floor and the photographs appeared on the front of the worst Sunday newspapers. The Station Officer managed to divert all criticism and that, I believe, planted the seed that led to his downfall.

This was all history by the time I arrived. As I was now a proper Leading Fireman, I had to establish myself on the watch, and for reasons of self-esteem, do my job correctly. I stayed there for just under a year and for the most part it was great. I still look back and think that the Leading Fireman's job at Soho was the best. I like work and I was so busy. I attended more calls and did more reports of fires and all types of incidents than I had done in all the preceding years. The Leading Fireman is not really one of the officers and not really one of the men. It was my job to carry out the Guvnor's instructions and he made sure that I did all the unpopular tasks. Although I found it hard at the time, I knew what he was doing and I was grateful. If we did get a bit of sleep on a night duty, he would always be the first one out of bed and he would come and find me to get the men up. Not that he wasn't capable of doing this himself, he was just putting me to the test. Getting the men out of bed is no fun!

At every station in London the teleprinter would start-up at 0645hrs, and a bell would ring throughout the station. This was the wake-up call but nobody takes any notice. Then at 0700hrs, control would test the fire bells. It was the dutyman's job to oversee this test and it was also his responsibility to see that the test lasted the shortest time possible. The slumbering masses would still be scratching in their pits. It was then that muggins had to go round and try to get some movement. I tried every-thing, but the bastards would never move. At one time I resorted to blow-ing an old cavalry bugle. I would go around the station blowing tuneless blasts. Now this did get some results. They got up, only to give me a bucket of cold water!

At first, when it was my sole responsibility to get them out of bed, I would courageously enter the dormitory and give a shout. Later when a tannoy system was installed, I decided that piped music to suit the mood of the station would be a little gentler and perhaps achieve some move-ment. It started out with a little Russian folk music, but it soon became a tradition where I was expected to come up with something original every morning. From disco to 'Okalahoma', from Gilbert and Sullivan to James Brown. Louis Prima and Louis Jordan went down well, and Sunday always had a religious theme. 'Five Little Fishes' by the Zion Travellers became an institution.

Another example of his way of making a man out of me really got my goat. When I presented a fire report for his approval, if something was incorrect, instead of putting a line through the offending word he would cross out the whole report so that I had to complete the whole thing again! We must have been the only station in the world that still typed fire reports!

It wasn't serious stuff all the time. Even in the office we were up for a laugh. The Guvnor was a smoker; everything – roll-ups, tailor-mades and even, at times, a pipe. He always had a box of Swan Vesta matches and us Leading Firemen would turn the inside of the match box upside-down so that when he opened them they fell onto the floor. We also used to put match heads in his pipe and hide, waiting for them to explode and hear him curse the blokes. 'Not us Guvnor, how could you think such a thing?'

I had passed the Sub. Officer's written exam and was trying to prepare for the practical. This entailed getting the men out into the yard and supervising their training. It was no fun for any of us. It was just a matter of remembering instructions that had to be detailed to the men. The Whites were never hard to get out for drill, but there were problems. The yard at the old Soho was so small that you could only just fit in one appliance. The other problem was that I was unable to keep a straight face. I would always start laughing and the whole exercise would fall apart. It was all so unreal; there you were training in this matchbox-sized yard with the door open to the street, and thousands of people were walking by going to the theatre! What a place!

Against all odds, I did pass. I had a good interview and I was offered the Red Watch at Manchester Square. There was no problem with this but I didn't want to leave Soho. In the normal case, I would have moved on with no hesitation, but I had to think long and hard about leaving. Later on, for the same reason, I had the same difficulty in persuading young men under my supervision to go for promotion.

Before my interview and before the Guvnor had written my promotion report, he sat me down and asked me what I wanted. If I wanted the promotion he would recommend me, but if I wanted to stay he would be happy for me to stay as his Leading Fireman. Eventually I realised that I did have to go, but it was always possible that I could get back.

Yes, I did have the Soho bug! I caught it on that very first night on duty. On that very night another man started work at Soho straight from training school. He was detailed to ride the pump sitting next to me. You don't have to wait too long for your first ever shout at Soho. Ten minutes on duty and out you go!

I can't remember what all the shouts were, but in the early hours we were called to a fire in public lavatories, St Christopher's Place, off Oxford Street. While we were on our way, I heard Euston and Manchester Square on the appliance radio booking in at another address on our ground. On our shout, smoke was drifting out of the toilets in the middle of the square. It wasn't thick smoke, so I went in with the Guvnor and we found someone living in there! An old man dressed in what looked like a night-shirt had lit the fire to keep warm. The Guvnor asked him, 'What are you doing in here?' The old man in a very refined accent said, 'I might ask you what you are doing in here,' as if we were trespassing in his home. The Guvnor was not a man to stand for any nonsense and in fireman's talk he 'fucked him off sharpish'.

The other incident was a far more serious affair. On that job the officer in charge had already called for assistance and reported that people were involved. It was about the time the Vietnamese Boat People were arriving in London and a few turf wars were breaking out.

A petrol bomb had been thrown into the front window of a terraced house in Gossfield Street, W1, and the fire had whipped up the stairs. It was alight from bottom to top. One of the firemen from Euston did some real heroic stuff getting two people down the escape. It was a really tough rescue. He was a great big strong bastard, but nevertheless getting two people down at the same time was a bit greedy!

It is usual that after a serious fire, the OIC of the incident will ask for the local pump to attend at a predetermined time to ensure that the fire is completely out. In this case, Soho's pump was called, not just to inspect the premises but to help remove a body. Some poor soul had perished in a bedroom on the top floor. This was obviously a crime; and when the police had finished their investigation, it was time to get the body out to the undertaker's van.

This was the first time that I had had to do this, and like everyone else I was apprehensive as we went upstairs. It's one thing seeing a burnt body, but it's wholly different when you have to handle one. The Guvnor, the driver, the new boy on his first night, and me.

The Guvnor, in his usual brash way, said, 'Come on, new boy, in you go.' The body was crouched on the floor with his head towards the window, wedged between the bed and the wall. There was very little space, and the only way to move the body was to drag it backwards. There was nothing for it; it had to be done and the new boy had to show willing. Poor boy; he grabbed the body by its most accessible part, a foot, and pulled. He must have been shitting himself as he fell back with a handful of skin! This wasn't going to work but I managed to get to the front of the body and lift it by the shoulders while new boy got him around the waist and we managed to shuffle out into the hall. We were then able to wrap him in a salvage sheet (a heavy gauge black plastic sheet) and get him downstairs. No body bags in those days.

For poor new boy it must have been hard enough just being there, but having to handle a dead body on your first night was certainly his baptism of fire.

The first real night at my first real fire station. It did not stop there; it just went on and on. Little fires, bigger fires; nothing massive but always interesting. Honestly, there was never a dull moment.

I needed no further convincing, but one Sunday morning after another busy Saturday night, I was getting ready to do my office work when I heard a noise outside. It was always a great sight to see the troops exercising their horses in the early morning, on the empty streets of the West End. So when I heard the sound of horses' hooves out in Shaftesbury Avenue, I looked out expecting to see the cavalry. Instead it was a pair of white chargers, pulling a chariot driven by a centurion!

It brought home the saying that if you stand in Shaftesbury Avenue for long enough, the whole world would pass you by. Another nail in my coffin. There and then my ambition was confirmed: Station Officer before 35 and somehow being stationed at Soho.

The Guvnor recommended me for promotion. I had a good interview and found myself being offered the Subs job on the Red Watch at Manchester Square.

But before I left, I did a short period of acting-up, and as a Temporary Sub. Officer, I was in charge of the station. It was during this period that

I picked up the first serious fire where I was in charge. It was in the middle of summer. It was always weird turning out at that time of year; it was about 0330hrs and already light. We were called to a fire in The George public house in Wardour Street. As you turn right from Shaftesbury Avenue into Wardour Street and as you get past the junction with Old Compton Street, you can see the length of the road. Half way up, smoke was billowing out of the upstairs windows.

It turned out to be one room well alight on the second floor. There was no one around to give me any information, but I knew that most of the pubs in the West End had staff in residence. The blokes were getting on with their duties: gaining entry, laying out hose, finding a street hydrant and getting rigged in BA. Soon after they got the door open, a man burst out of the smoke and into the street. He told us that there were still two people upstairs. I was then able to get a message sent: 'Make pumps 4, persons reported'. Once that message was sent it gives the OIC a bit of time to make sure that the incident is proceeding to plan and that all the safety precautions are in place. All the time I'm not only thinking about what I'm doing, but what should I do next? The good thing is that although you are responsible for all that's happening, the blokes just get on with it and you only have to ensure that they are doing it safely.

They were off up the stairs wearing BA, pulling the hosereel and I had to make sure that they have had their entry recorded. We have a BA entry procedure that has to be closely observed. Each BA set has a removable tally that is filled in by the wearer when he takes it over. This tally, and its information, is attached to a BA control board and the man appointed to be the control officer has to work out the time that the wearers are allowed inside the building. It is then his responsibility to inform the OIC when the time of whistle is nearing and the wearer's air is getting low. When the air in a BA gets low, it actuates a low-pressure warning whistle and the wearer then knows that he has approximately 10 minutes of air to allow him to get out.

All this was happening before the fire engines arrived from the next nearest station. These are called the 'take pumps' and on this occasion they were both coming from Euston.

The man in charge of Euston White Watch at that time was a man called Bob Winter. I knew him vaguely, as he had been a fireman at Battersea when I was there. He was really helpful to me. Officially, he was required to take charge of the fire, but asked me to send my messages in his name, and he followed me around asking what I was going to do, what had I already done and offering advice. This was a great learning exercise and something that I did later on with more junior officers. Far too often, once the higher-ranked officer takes over the responsibility, he will dispense with the junior's services, sending them off on another task and losing a valuable source of information.

I learnt a lot from the Guvnor. Although I wasn't 100% in agreement with his management style, it did help me develop my own. He was a good man and he set me a good example in most ways. He was always the man in charge. Everything that happened on the station was his responsibility; therefore, how he did it was up to him. I just thought that I would not do it the same way.

I left Soho with my feelings a little confused. On one hand I thought the station was a great place to work, but from the outset I hadn't been happy with some of the men.

Right from the start there had been confrontation. Soon after I started, I reported for night shift. The Station Officer was on leave, and so was the Sub. Officer. The other Leading Fireman was senior to me and acting-up as Sub. Officer in charge of the station. I was in charge of the pump escape. When we went out on our first call, it was obvious to me that I was riding with a crew who had been drinking. It was the same old story, but I knew it wasn't just a case of a couple of pints. When I got back to the station, I spoke to the man who was in charge. We decided that we were both in a difficult position. He decided to change the driver but would not take any further action. I was not happy with his decision so I got the blokes together and told them that if they ever did this again, I would not get on a fire engine with them. That would ring some bells, as the fire engine would have to come off the run, and someone would ask questions. Not that they took any notice of my threats; they thought I was a fool, but it eventually went wrong; their downfall was just waiting around the corner.

I was sorry to leave and wanted to get back. I may have kidded myself, but I thought that if I did get back, I would be able to do it on my terms and succeed.

*Chapter 10*

# THE 'SQUARE'

Manchester Square is located in Chiltern Street, W1 just north of Oxford Street. It, and the hills, are to blame for my name to be constantly misspelt! It is a lovely old station and the second oldest in the Brigade. (The oldest London station is Clerkenwell, which is also the oldest in the world.) It is a three-bay station. At one time it also had a TL but, after it was crushed when a warehouse collapsed during a fire on Euston's ground, it was not replaced.

The station was once the HQ of the old 'A' Division. Part of the station was used as the control room for this area. Above, the first floor was used as accommodation for senior officers and their families. There are some great stories of domestic strife. The men were greatly amused to hear and see these high-ranking officers berated by their wives.

There is a small single-storey building in the yard that was the gym for the now disbanded brigade boxing. While I was there, this once proud building was used as a boat store by one of the senior officers. There is also a watchtower. This was used to scan the area and pinpoint any fires. Once it had been the tallest construction in the area, but with the passing of time and the growth of London, now you cannot even see to the next street.

My new Guvnor was a difficult fish. I found it very hard to get on with him. It was as though at the start of each shift I was meeting him for the first time. We had little in common and absolutely no repartee. He made no comment about my work and I received little encouragement. I was a new Sub. Officer and would have appreciated a little guidance.

Strangely, the Square is not the busiest of places considering the area it serves. However, it is surrounded by three much more lively stations: Paddington, Euston and Soho. So it did attend many incidents off its own ground. Three of the most memorable fires that I ever attended were during my 18 months at the Square. I think they were so memorable because as a Sub. Officer, I was still able to get inside and do some fire-fighting.

The first was on 21st December 1981 at about 0830hrs in St. Stephen's Street on North Kensington's ground. I was in charge of the pump and we had just finished dealing with a call in Baker Street. We received the order over the radio, and at that moment it started snowing. Not the normal snow that falls in the centre of London; there was great lumps of it and it was settling – so much so that the conditions were getting pretty dire as we were trying to make our way to the fire.

When we got there, we were met by the Station Officer and Sub. Officer from North Kensington carrying a casualty out of the front door. They told us that there were more people inside. There was not even time to get the BA going; we just had to get inside. Halfway up the stairs laid an oriental-looking woman; she was apparently dead. We are trained to leave bodies in place unless they may be further involved in the fire. I made my way upwards to find the seat of the fire. We were only following the footsteps of the first BA crews and helping them get water on to the fire. When I reached the head of the stairs, I was told that a man had jumped into the back garden and was lying unconscious in the basement area getting covered with snow.

I grabbed a couple of blokes and we made our way outside. This man, also oriental, was in a bad way and seemed to have broken both legs. I made the decision that we had to get him out of the elements. I knew that the OIC would have ordered additional ambulances and normally we would have waited for them to arrive. But I knew that because of the inclement weather and the rush-hour traffic, they would probably be delayed. Fire engines do not carry stretchers so, in cases like this, we use a short ladder. We made the casualty comfortable and secured him to the ladder to make sure he didn't fall off. As we got outside, the ambulances were arriving. We took him to the nearest ambulance, untied the rope and left him on the ladder in the care of the paramedics.

When the fire started, the occupiers had not called the Brigade but had tried to put the fire out using a garden hose and it got out of control. The hose was still laying on the stairs when we got there, a sad reminder of their misadventure.

The next was at the Arama Hotel, Sussex Gardens on Paddington's ground. There are many small hotels in Sussex Gardens because it is close to the main line railway station. Most of them are not exactly four star, and are used by the Department of Social Security as a stopgap for the homeless. I'm sure that this was on a Sunday afternoon, as I can remember that there was not much traffic, and we got there from the Square quite quickly. The Station Officer at Paddington was another creative officer who was always likely to do the unexpected. I could hear him on the radio telling control to stand-by for a make-up message as he had seen a lot of smoke. As we arrived he did in fact make-up, and the crews from Paddington had the escape off and were involved in rescues from the upper floors. I was told that there were more people inside so, with my crew, I entered through the front door. Before we could climb the main staircase we first had to get water onto it, as it was burning under our feet. At the head of the stairs there was a skylight glazed with wired glass, and the fire was hitting it and coming back down the stairs towards us. Eventually, we reached the top landing only to find that part of it had been burnt away. One of my crew went back down to the street and brought back a ladder, which we used to bridge the gap. Now we were able to search the rooms off the main corridor. I entered the first room on the left, which was strangely smoke-free. I found a middle-aged man lying on the floor by the side of the bed. Although he was obviously dead, I tried to find a pulse, but his skin was cold I realised that there was no point in trying to resuscitate. This looked doubtful so I left him in position; if you did have to move a body, you had to make a mental note or a drawing of its exact position. I then had to inform the OIC who would call the police. These were very strange circumstances, especially as the fire had all the signs of being started deliberately. When I got home there had been a phone call to my house asking me to contact the station. They wanted me to write a hand-written report of my actions and it would be collected from my house. It seems that foul deeds had indeed been committed in that hotel. I was never asked to attend court so I suppose the case remains unsolved.

The third was on Soho's ground and was the notorious Mr Byrites in Oxford Street. As there was no Station Officer on duty at Soho, our man was in charge. It was 11th January 1982 and the call came in at 1130hrs. It developed into a 15-pump fire. At one stage the smoke was so thick it was entering the Underground and the trains were asked to pass through Oxford Circus.

It was the middle of a busy shopping day so there were thousands of onlookers. Mr Byrites was a clothing store, which was stacked from top to bottom. Every one of the four floors was a muddle of racked clothing and the smoke, which was coming out of every opening, was as black as your hat. The first crew to arrive had a jet off and were trying to get in the main front entrance, but were being beaten back.

There is a great photo taken by the Brigade Photographer of the moment when the whole of the shop facia falls to the pavement.

Every Station Officer in the Fire Brigade is destined to get a job that has all the possibilities of turning out to be his folly, and this was to be our man's. It would not go out. There we were, with the whole world watching! The fire just got away. Later on he worked his way up the ranks to become a senior officer, and I have a mate, also a senior officer, who kept a photo of Mr.Byrites in his desk draw. If ever our 'ex-man' got out of his pram, my mate would get out the photo and rub his nose in it!

When things start to go wrong, no matter what you do, it just seems to escalate. Everybody tries to put it right, but it's going downhill like a runaway train.

At the side of the shop there was an alley, which sloped downhill away from Oxford Street, and I found a door that led directly into the basement, where the seat of the fire seemed to be. I reported this to the OIC and, with his permission, made an entry. We were already wearing BA, but once inside it was impossible to move; the smoke was so dense. Not only were we confronted with an area congested with racks of clothing, to make matters worse, part of the false ceiling had collapsed. It was impossible to get across the room; it was getting hotter and we had to retreat. Just as we were about to exit, I heard people working at the other side of the room. A crew from Euston had made it down the stairs and located the seat of the fire, which was in the electrical intake room. This room, which should have been kept clear, was stuffed with clothing that had fuelled the fire.

The smoke damage throughout the building was phenomenal. Racks and piles of smouldering clothing, mostly denim, were stacked ceiling high. It all had to be turned over and extinguished. We were exhausted. There were rows of steaming firemen out in Oxford Street, either taking a break or changing their compressed air cylinders in order to go back inside. The building was still upright, just about, but it could have so easily have become another car park.

While I was at the Square I attended day release in order to pass the Station Officer's Exam. This was a pig of an exam; there was so much to learn. The only way I could make it go in was parrot fashion, by writing out Q&A cards and trying to memorise it all. I even recorded the data to audiotapes and listened to them day and night. You would see me in the car playing the tapes and answering the questions out loud.

Our man left soon after that and was replaced by a very different man. Peter Osbourne was great – good on the fireground and the font of all knowledge. I knew him from the White Watch at Knightsbridge. He taught me that another responsibility of the Station Officer is to maintain the morale of the watch. His style of management certainly lifted the men at Manchester Square. He encouraged me to go to the Fire Service College and motivated my promotional studies.

I sat the exam and passed four of the papers and marginally failed one. This meant that I achieved what is called a referral, and meant that the next year I would only have to re-sit the failed paper. When I showed Peter my results, he saw that I had only marginally failed this paper. His take on the subject was that it was not marginally failed it was more marginally studied. He was right, as he usually was.

It was at about this time that I was offered the Sub. Officer's job at Paddington. Peter encouraged me to take it on, saying that it would help with my promotion. I was sorry to leave the Square, but it was a case of onwards and upwards.

*Chapter 11*

# THE FLAGSHIP

Paddington was still the area HQ and it was one of the busiest stations in the brigade. Some of the Red Watch I worked with when I re-enrolled were still there, although the establishment had been greatly reduced. Just three appliances; pump escape pump, and TL. The emergency tender had been moved to Euston and the HQ staff had been reduced.

The Station Officer liked his own way and seemed to know his way around a fire, but he was a little progressive; he didn't always do it by the book. The two excellent old Leading Firemen were the best – great characters, wells of information and capable of much lamp-swinging. Ernie Arthurs and Norman Wooldridge in another time would both have been in charge of their own stations.

This move came about as a bit of a consolation. I had known that there was a long period of temporary promotion at Knightsbridge. As I was the most qualified Sub. Officer in the 'A' Division I should have got the job, but I was overlooked. I had a bit of a go about it and this was their way of placation. Anyway, it was not that important and if I had ideas of being at my new base station for very long, they were short-lived. I was soon off doing temporary promotion, slotting into vacancies at other stations where things had either gone wrong, or were looking like going that way.

My first stint was at Chelsea. I knew little about Chelsea except that it was the quietest station in the area. As I have already said, these temporary posting are always difficult, even more so when you are in charge. The previous Station Officer, whom I knew as a fireman at Westminster, had been promoted, causing the vacancy. I had a slight problem with the Sub. Officer, as he was expecting to get the temporary and was a bit put out. We soon got over that and eventually got on quite well.

Back then, the station was quite modern and situated right on the fashionable Kings Road, but it was unpopular, and in the words of Elvis Costello, 'Nobody wants to go to Chelsea'. Senior men were always transferring and, consequently, the majority of the watch was made up with recruits.

The Red Watch just needed a little direction. They needed to be shown that somebody cared that they developed into good firemen. My principle that a busy watch is a happy watch was just the ticket, and after they got over the shock, I was able to make the most of their enthusiasm.

All firemen really want to do is fight fires, be brave and get their noses full of soot. If that doesn't happen on a regular basis, you have to pretend. So, training played a big part in our daily routine. My methods must have worked because they bought me a present when I left: two cycling tops – that never happened before!

There was only one good job at Chelsea. I was still learning and still getting away with it by the skin of my teeth. It was a big terraced house in Belgrave Square. Now these are great big four or five-storey terraced houses. It was lunchtime, and the top floor and mansard roof was well alight. Painters had been burning-off, went off to lunch and came back to million pounds worth of damage! You should have seen their faces! The spread of the fire had been greatly accelerated due to high winds, and the fact that the painters had left the windows open creating wind tunnels. We were very lucky at this one; we lost water on the top floor because the hose burst. There were dramatic stories of the hose burning through, but as I've gotten older and wiser, the less likely this seems. We did, of course, get a lot of water damage. Some water damage to the lower floors is inevitable. We carry a supply of tarpaulins and normally try to sheet up as quickly as possible, but the sudden volume of water from a burst hose was just too much to cope with.

My six months came to an end. Back to Paddington and back down to Sub. Officer. You miss the money and the responsibility. One day you are in charge, your own boss; the next you feel like a spare prick.

It wasn't too long before I was out again. I was asked to go to Green Watch, Kensington – an offer I accepted without much enthusiasm, especially as this time I was informed that there were difficulties there. The Station Officer had been removed. Something had gone wrong at a fire; the inquisition had made a visit and found all sorts of problems, so he was out.

There wasn't even a regular Sub. Officer, but to help me out they gave me a man that I knew. He was a straightforward bloke who had the added benefit of being a martial arts expert, although I did hope that I wouldn't have to call on that part of his expertise! I decided that all I could do was try to steady the ship and attempt to maintain some sort of authority. I didn't know any of the Green Watch, so I just had to make a fresh start.

I've always found that it is better to deal with individuals face to face. Only if I felt that I needed to stamp my authority, would I give out some instructions that I expected everyone to follow. I would then observe and have a go at any individual who wasn't going along with my rules.

I have always liked a tidy appliance room. I like to see all the uniforms on the fire engines, not hanging on the doors or on the floor. When I first joined you had to fold your tunic in a particular way, and store it in your place in the rear cab, with your helmet on top. Things have gotten more and more relaxed over the years, but I did insist on boots and overtrousers being on the fire engine, not on the floor.

I have found that most of the blokes are happy to go along with me but, if there were any who did not, it gave me the chance to speak to them individually. This also gave me the chance to check if they had marked their boots with their name. This is another thing that the Brigade insists on – all items of uniform must be personally marked. I only had one who resisted and even he gave up when he realised that there was no way I would give in. I was also lucky in that the senior officer in charge of the area had given me his backing.

Far too often officers will try to enforce some sort of discipline by being harsh with the group instead of the individual, just because they are incapable of dishing out a bollocking face to face. I didn't find it easy but I just thought that it was the right way. I had to bite the bullet and get on with it. I think that in the end you got the bloke's respect by being fair, honest and up front. Another principle of mine was to sort out everything by the end of the shift, and not to go off duty with any problems in the balance.

I was only there for a month (thank God) and I was packing my bags, back to Paddington. Being the area HQ, there were always senior officers roaming around, so you had to be seen to be doing it all correctly all of the time. One day I was out in the yard supervising a bit of training and a staff officer came over to me and asked me to report to the Divisional Commander. I was riding in charge of an appliance, so I had to get that taken off the run, get changed and knock on the Commander's door – all the time wondering what's going on.

Alan Jones was a tall, distinguished-looking man who looked like an officer. He was well spoken, amenable and a man that you couldn't help but respect. He asked me to sit down, and told me that something dreadful had gone on concerning the White Watch at Soho. The Station Officer and some of the Watch had been suspended.

He had to be careful in what he said and that he could not give me the full details. As he was responsible for the whole area, even he was part of the investigation. He asked me to take over the watch. He thought, as I was familiar with the station and the watch, that I would be best for the job.

I tried to find out what had happened, but the phones were constantly busy. I discovered later on that the station had been shut down: no calls, no nothing. I did manage to find out that it had something to do with a female firefighter who had been posted there after I had left. I must have been leading a charmed life; if I had stayed there I would have certainly been in the middle of the affair.

This was the first case of sexual harassment in the fire service. It developed into the biggest discipline case the Brigade had ever dealt with, and its repercussions have affected the Brigade's equal opportunities policy ever since. It should have made anyone, with any sense, aware that harassment and bullying were definitely things of the past.

When I reported for my first duty on 6th May 1984 I found that not only had some of the watch been suspended on full pay, but two had been summarily dismissed. I had never heard of anything like this before. It was not only the White Watch that were involved: men from all the other watches and other stations were being called as witnesses. Every night and day, an inquisition of senior officers would arrive, fire engines would be taken off the run and individuals interrogated. As they did not know if they were implicated, most of the White Watch were in fear of losing their jobs.

When I first heard that a woman had been posted to White Watch I was astounded. It was the last place in the world that I would have sent a woman. She was one of the first women to be enrolled in the Brigade and it was rumoured that this was the Station Officer's comeuppance for the Sundowner.

Not all the blame could be aimed at the watch. The Brigade had its own case to answer. Women in the Fire Brigade were a revolution. It was the biggest change that any of us had experienced. The policy for dealing with this minefield was barely developed. I do know that the pitfalls had not been brought to firemen's attention. The Brigade was so conscious of achieving their Government targets, they were desperate to get women into stations. Where better than Soho to get a bit of publicity? – in the public's eye all the time and many of the incidents on the telly.

The problem was that not only were the women unprepared, so were the stations. Shared dormitories and no separate locker rooms meant the men had to sleep and get changed in the same space as the women. The women did get a shower/washroom that could be locked, but there was nothing to stop her from walking into a room where a man might be changing.

Women in the Fire Brigade were a development that could not be resisted. The Government had decided that, although women could not work in coal mines, they could work in the fire service. Even with the problems that could arise by shared dormitories. The whole process was handled badly.

Just imagine being female and starting work, not only in such unique surroundings, but alone with 15 men who did not really want you there. To add to all these difficulties it was generally felt that this particular woman was not physically capable. That meant that these men, even with their wicked ways, who prided themselves on the physical part of their job, were even less willing to accept the newcomer. Although in this respect, it would have been the same for a male or female.

It was still acceptable for initiations to be dished out, and these men were not about to make any exceptions. As recently as 1982, photographs of men being tied to lamp posts and left on display in the street were published in the quarterly house magazine 'London Fireman'. It was all treated as a bit of a laugh and the Brigade seemed to have no objections. The whole Brigade should have been told that the initiations, practical jokes, and even the swearing, which had always been part of the job, were now unacceptable; that the same rules, which apply to other mixed-sex work places, would be enforced with the threat of dismissal.

I can't disclose what went on, as I was not privy to the official investigation and, in reality, all I know is hearsay. I am also a bit ashamed of the individual's behaviour. Most of the watch kept out of it; some had to deal with it by just completely avoiding the woman. However, they managed to deal with it, and I'm glad that some very good men were not considered to be at fault.

Eventually the sentences were dished out. The Station Officer was reduced in rank to Leading Fireman – even though he was not directly involved, he was in charge when things happened. Not that he could have been present for every single minute. Nowhere in the official Brigade Orders does it say that the OIC has to look after any individual 24/7. I don't know if the woman even reported her grievances to him or if she went directly to the Equal Opportunities Section. I do know that although he had some strange ways, he didn't deserve this treatment, and I'm glad that not only did he get his original rank back, he retired while holding a much higher one. If this had not happened, I wonder how high he would have reached. I spoke to him much later on after he had retired. He asked me how I was getting on and did I have any thoughts about further promotion. No, I told him that this was it; this was where I wanted to stay. It was then he told me: 'That's all I ever wanted'.

Initially, one of the two men who were summarily dismissed was sacked and the other was reinstated. Later, the man who was dismissed was also reinstated after an appeal. They were both sent to other stations. I believe that the man who had been sacked had to be moved again after women's rights activists laid siege to the station. I'm not sure what level of punishment they received under the Brigade's discipline code. Four others were simply posted for being in the wrong place or saying the wrong things at the hearing.

I was left with six of the original watch and the Sub. Officer. Incidentally, one of the Leading Firemen, a decent man, was posted to the outer limits of the Brigade. His only involvement was that he tried to defend all the watch against insurmountable odds. The other Leading Fireman was a temporary, in from another station, and he was sent back to his home station.

During this time all I could do was try to run the station and look after the blokes who were not in trouble. I had now passed the remainder of the Station Officer's exam. I had an interview coming up and I had to study; oh, and try to have some kind of home life!

The other Station Officers at Soho were a great help and a source of advice. Colin Townsley, Tony Willmott and 'Turk' Manning were only too willing to give me fatherly advice. I was, after all, still a boy amongst men. It was essential for me to have someone to talk to, and get guidance from the more experienced officers who were aware of the situation.

The Station Officer's job can be very isolated and sometimes the inner sanctum of their locker room is the only place where you could find some solace. The comradeship found amongst the men on the watches extends to the Station Officer's room, where sensitive subjects can be discussed and treated with discretion and trust.

Once the dust had begun to settle, we had to set about getting the watch back up to strength. I still had all the senior blokes who were all drivers and TL operators, but we needed seven more bodies. Volunteers were asked for from other 'A' Division stations. I had no part in the selection procedure but I knew a couple, and with the best part of the 'old Whites' we had the startings of a good watch.

While the case was still in progress, I had my interview and I was successful. The Assistant Chief Officer who congratulated me on my promotion, Joe Kennedy, was a well-respected man. He offered me the White Watch at Westminster. I said that I would be happy with that, but I thought that I should stay at Soho until the case was over. He agreed and I was posted to Westminster on paper but remained attached to Soho.

When it was all over, DACO Jones came to see me and thanked me for my efforts. As there was now a vacancy at Soho, he asked me whether I would like the job or go on to Westminster. I thought about it for about a second and then began 18 years of excitement, heartache, joy and the rib-splitting humour that became my White Watch.

# Chapter 12

## SOHO: MY STATION

Well, I did it, and achieved my ambition. One year late due to me not passing the exam the first time, but by luck and circumstance, I was there – a substantive Station Officer, with white shirts and white fire helmet! I had a group of men to work with that were keen and who wanted to be at Soho. This made it easy for me to maintain my style of management from the start and try to make it a fair and happy place to work.

For the next 18 years it would stretch my capabilities to the limit; the entire gamut of emotions. I now had my own accommodation, which I shared with the officers in charge of the four watches when they were on duty. That room became my refuge at bad times, a counselling chamber and where, at times, I attempted to find some respite from the constant bombardment. It is remarkable that, when no matter how tired I was, there were times when I just couldn't sleep. I learnt very early on to try and relax after calls during the night. Get off the truck slowly; leave any office work until after 0700hrs and walk, not run, back up the stairs to my room.

The Station Officer's room forms an overhang above the front door and the passing hordes on the pavement below. It wasn't just the calls that disturbed my rest – the noise emanating from the avenue was phenomenal; from the obvious noise coming from late night revellers to the more unusual disturbances. At one time, before it became the Bank of China, the ground floor of the building opposite was an all-night convenience store and was a constant scene of conflict. Every night a bag-lady would tie her barking dog outside for several hours and every 'boy-racer-motor-car', with its sound system blaring, would park and rattle my windows while its occupants used the shop.

Where else would you hear street entertainers as diverse as a lone piper, a Chinese Elvis impersonator and a really poor trumpeter who sat on the steps of the Palace Theatre at all hours impersonating a strangled cat? In desperation I took to wearing earplugs – they didn't shut out all the noise. I never missed a call, but they did help. It's very strange but sometimes, if I was asleep, I would wake up even just before the bells went down. We had a saying, 'Don't even try to go to bed before midnight as, sure as eggs is eggs, you will be up and out at ten past'.

The ground is the best and must be the most interesting in the UK, perhaps even the world. I can imagine that there are other fire stations in similar cosmopolitan areas in other cities all over the world, but none is located in such a condensed space.

The boundaries extend from the middle of the river Thames in the south, to Kingsway in the east and Mortimer Street in the north. The western border is more complicated. Halfway down Piccadilly there is Halfmoon Street, and if you drew a line northwards towards Bond Street then doglegged into Portland Place, and then forwards to Mortimer Street, that would be about right. Within this square mile there are examples of every kind of building and enterprise. The only thing missing is any sites of major industry, that is if you exclude the rag trade.

The major risks are numerous and some are of national importance. The National Gallery, The British Museum, The National Opera House, St James's Palace, Clarence House, Somerset House, The Royal Academy of Art, a number of Government Ministries, Charing Cross Railway Station, nine Underground railway stations and numerous underground tunnels and passageways; many major hotels including The Savoy and The Ritz. Forty-five theatres and 15 multi-screen cinemas (and some dodgy single screens!); uncountable clubs, pubs, restaurants and Foreign Embassies; the major shopping areas of Regent Street and Oxford Street; Middlesex Hospital, Kings College, The Admiralty, Horseguards and St. James's Park. The list goes on, and to be added to the fabric of the buildings, there is their history. Preservation of the history is just as essential as the building.

Can you imagine what it was like when the Fire Brigades first started?

The area was one of great deprivation and riches. It was once part of a Royal Park, which was used for hunting and named after the ancient hunting cry 'So-ho!' The rookeries of St. Giles were a refuge for the desperate, as opposed to the finery of Piccadilly, Regent Street and St. James's.

At its centre is the cosmopolitan area of Soho, which is still a magnet to foreign exiles. Huguenots, Jews, Greeks, Italians and almost every other nation has found just enough space in the narrow, crowded streets to make a living. The firemen had to get their steamers and horses through these streets in a time when fire was the greatest peacetime taker of human life.

Before the London Fire Brigade there was the London Fire Engine Establishment, then The Metropolitan Fire Brigade. Shaftesbury Avenue didn't exist before 1886 but Old Compton Street did, and just to its south stood Kings Street, where there was a fire station. That was where my Victorian counterparts tended their horses, polished their steamers and shouted, 'Out she goes'. As the establishment changed, there were five fire stations that were called upon to deal with fires in the area: Old Scotland Yard, Whitefiars, Holborn, Great Marlborough Street and Chandos Street. The most famous of these was Chandos Street, where the Prince of Wales would regularly turn up to ride the fire engines. It was there that he kept a full fire-fighting uniform and he would respond to major fires in the company of the Chief Officer, the equally famous Massy Shaw.

There have been many massive fires on the ground, many of them in the theatres of the time. For instance, on the morning of 30th September 1808, Covent Garden Theatre was completely destroyed by fire. Twenty-three firemen were killed. Still, they were two-a-penny in those days! Those old theatres were tinderboxes and fire precautions were unheard of. Now they are very well protected against fire and are regularly inspected.

The most famous theatre fire destroyed the Alhambra Theatre, Leicester Square. It was discovered by a night watchman an hour after the audience had left the building. The fire soon escalated, and 25 pumps and 150 firemen were at the scene. At this time the Chief Officer decided that he should take command. (Today he would have been strutting around as soon as the TV cameras arrived.) On his way to the fire he picked up the Prince of Wales. At the height of the fire, the Prince was being attended by Assistant Superintendent Tom Ashford and was talking to a group of firemen. At this moment fragments of stone and slates fell around them. Then a whole gable end came crashing down, burying eight firemen. Ashford had been able to push the Prince out of the way. Unfortunately Ashford and one fireman were not so lucky; they later died from their injuries.

Now the plaque in Charing Cross Road, which commemorates this disaster, is passed daily and probably goes unnoticed by thousands of tourists and Londoners.

In 1921 the stations at Great Marlborough Street, Whitefriars and Old Scotland Yard were closed. Chandos Street had already been closed when Old Scotland Yard was opened.

The Fire Brigade took over the newly-vacated 126 Shaftesbury Avenue. This building had been the home of the London Salvage Corps, an organisation formed by the Insurance Companies to protect and preserve buildings that had been damaged by fire or flood. They didn't do any firefighting; their job was salvage and security. This building became not only a fire station, but provided homes for the firemen. The officers, the men and their families lived at the station. They worked a week of days then a week of nights with a 24hr shift on Sunday, which was the change-over day.

It was located between The Avenue Bar and the Shaftesbury Theatre. The theatre was the only one on this side of the avenue and it was destroyed by a bomb during 1941.

Previously, on 7th October 1940, the station had received a direct hit; several firemen were trapped and two died. Half of the six-storey building was reduced to the ground. It continued to be used as a fire station with the sliding pole outside exposed to the elements! Most of the remainder had to be demolished, leaving only the three appliance bays and a small first-floor corner section used as the office. Above the remnants of the ground floor, a prefabricated construction was assembled. This became the dormitory, snooker room and the junior officer's accommodation. The station still looked like this when I first saw it in 1974.

The Avenue Bar was still there, but where the theatre had stood was a bomb site. At the rear of the station the whole area, right back to the houses opposite in Newport Court, was another bomb site. This was being used as a car park, which was used as a bedroom for kerb-crawlers by the lovely ladies of the night. It stayed like that until 1982 when a new station was built. Now, whenever the 'old station' is mentioned, the men do a phoney 'Lord, I'm not worthy' bow to the east!

Before I left in December 1982, the poor old station fell into disrepair. There was little point in getting any maintenance as a developer had made an offer to our masters, the Greater London Council; they wanted to develop the whole block surrounded by Charing Cross Road, Newport Court, Shaftesbury Avenue and Gerrard Place. The arrangement was that if the GLC would hand over their land, a new fire station would be built free of charge! As the developers were over a barrel, the GLC architects could insist on a really high standard of building, fixtures and fittings. Once completed, it was of a higher specification than any other London fire station.

There is a plaque in the reception area which is a reminder that the new station was opened by the famous actor, Sir Ralph Richardson, on 24th August 1983. He said as part of his speech: 'There's not a man in the whole of London who would be more proud than I am to take part in any celebration to do with the London Fire Brigade. Regarded with deep love, compassion, and wishing it great joy for its nobility – I'll always be proud.'

## Chapter 13

# MEARD STREET, W1

When I returned in May 1984, the new station was fully up and running. It had just been moved further down the Avenue and was bounded on one corner by Gerrard Place. There was a service road at the other side, which led to the yard. The building on the other side of this service road stands on the site of the old station and the Avenue Bar. The Welsh Chapel on the corner of Charing Cross Road, which had stood derelict for many years, was now a nightclub. More noise!

The old station had an open area at first-floor level where we could stand and observe the varied, legal and illegal goings on in the avenue: the drug deals going down, marauding football fans, protest marches and parades.

It was a shame that it had moved. In its previous position, from the flat roof, there was a view directly into the dressing rooms of the Palace Theatre. Not that I ever took advantage of this delight! On a hot summer's evening when all the windows were open, there was often two-way conversation with the actors.

One night at about 2300hrs there was a ring on the doorbell. I answered the door to find an old lady dressed completely in black with another younger woman. At first I couldn't quite understand what she was saying. Then I fell in; the young woman was her daughter and she was offering her for 'business' to the whole station! I told her that we were closed! That was something I did when I was in charge; we are allowed one hour for lunch, normally between 1300hrs and 1400hrs. If this period is interrupted by calls it could be extended for hours. But if it was quiet and the phone went, on my instructions the dutyman would tell the callers that we were closed for lunch! Well, everyone else gets a lunchtime away from work, so why shouldn't firemen at least have a break from the phone? You should have heard the confused silence on the other end of the phone!

Apart from the three sets of big red doors, the new station looked like part of the new red brick development. Laid out over three floors, the ground floor houses the appliance bays, the watchroom, and there is a reception area decorated with framed photographs of the old station and the plaque marking the opening. The three appliance bays have automatic doors, which break down with alarming regularity, and there is a lift – a service lift that is so slow that it is only used for supplies. Upstairs to the first floor there is the main office, a few stores and the Station Officer's quarters. This comprises an office with a pull-down bed, a locker room and a washroom. Up to the second floor and you will find the mess/TV room, the kitchen, and five locker rooms, each with its own washroom, the junior officers' accommodation and the main dormitory, all with pull-down beds. By the way, the word 'mess', where we all ate, is another naval original. The old English word *mes* meant a communal dish from which comrades would eat.

I had never worked in a new fire station and, after some of the old slums, it was a pleasant experience. Most of the old stations are in a poor state and nobody wants to look after them; they usually have to wait until they are in such a poor state that they end up having a complete refurbishment every 100 years!

By now, the White Watch were getting to know each other and getting to understand me. Nothing brings you together better than a good job (or jobs), but two six-pump fires in one shift – that's bonding in the extreme!

On 5th September 1984, a call came in at about 2000hrs to the Civil Service Stores in the Strand. It was a big departmental store and was subject to major reconstruction after a 25-pump fire in 1982. It was a six-storey building with a basement and sub-basement with some of the ground floor open and taken up with builders' huts. On arrival, we were met by heavy smoke logging and a severe fire situation. The surrounding streets had to be closed because once the flames hit the concrete floor above, instead of being contained, they were whooshing out into the street and on up the building. It looked even worse as the sheeted-over scaffolding was involved.

The fire had started in one of the huts, spread to the next and was now getting through to the first floor. To add to the situation there were cylinders involved.

Acetylene cylinders are particularly hazardous when involved in fire. If they are heated, the contents start to decompose, pressure builds up and they can explode causing serious injury. They have their own operational procedure, and the first part of it is to send a message stating that cylinders are involved. Then they have to be cooled from a distance or from behind some form of protection. Usually the hose would be lashed in place. Once cooled, they have to be moved to a dam by men wearing special protective clothing. Then it had to be left submerged for 24hrs. Only then can they be declared safe and removed by contractors.

Once the fire had been extinguished, we found that there had been several seats of fire. This is an indication that the fire had been set deliberately and then the police were informed.

After I got back to the station, as I was entering the details of the call on the register of calls, I noticed that there had been seven small fires in the area. I made a call to the Fire Investigation Team and we decided that it was a high possibility that all the fires had been set by the same person. (The register of calls has now been replaced by a computerised form. At most stations it was kept in a ring binder and filled in after each call but at Soho, it was permanently in the typewriter.)

Multiple small fires were a regular occurrence at Soho; some maniac would set light to all the rubbish in the street which was awaiting collection. We would follow his trail, chasing our tails putting out the fires. As the streets are so narrow, it is not unusual for these fires to spread into shops and cars.

This was the first fire of the night and it had started just before the call to supper. The food had been dished up and now it was nicely dried out in the hotplate. But before you can even think about getting back to the charred remains of your food, all the equipment has to be cleaned and the BA has to be serviced and tested.

Every fireman keeps a chinagraph pencil in his pocket. This is used for several operational tasks where we have to write on plastic. But it is most importantly used to write your name on your dinner plate before someone quickly puts it in the hotplate when you go out.

The next fire came in at 0230hrs the next day – Meard Street, named after John Meard, a famous carpenter. It is a street of little importance and lies almost unnoticed between Wardour Street and Dean Street. It is known to all at the station as 'Shit Street'.

On a Saturday night and into Sunday morning the streets of Soho are thronging with people out for a good time. The narrow streets are congested with cars, cabs and buses. At that time, the early hours of Sunday morning, the streets were still buzzing. In any other place the Brigade in action attracts concerned onlookers, but in Soho half of the street life passes by without a blink and the other half are all over you. All of a sudden you are surrounded by the neighbourhood oddballs.

Earlier in the evening the police had been called to a disturbance out-side No. 6. The dispute involved the occupant of the first floor flat and three youths. The police had stopped and questioned the youths, but they were not detained.

At 0200hrs a transvestite who lived in the property opposite was awakened by the sound of breaking glass. They looked out of the window and saw three youths throwing a cardboard box containing bottles through the first floor window. The youths escaped on foot. At that time there was no fire. Approximately 30mins later, a passing police patrol heard an explosion and saw sheets of flames shooting from the windows and called the Brigade.

This was only my second serious fire with a white helmet. Vulcan, the Fire-God, wasn't giving me much time to settle. It was well alight. The flames were so intense they were cracking the plate glass windows of the shops opposite. The pump escape and pump were attending, and the TL was on its way, returning from an earlier call on another ground. I imme-diately called for assistance and because I was informed that there were persons unaccounted for, I also sent a 'persons reported' message.

The additional appliances were coming from Euston. Straight away, Euston's pump with a Station Officer in charge cocked-up by stopping right on the junction of Meard Street and Dean Street blocking the road. No matter how serious the fire is, or how quickly you have to get to work, it is essential that you take a few seconds to get the parking right. Not too near, not too far and leave space for any special appliance that you may need as the incident develops. I really needed the ladders but now I could not get it into position until we moved appliances and hose. To make it even more difficult, the normal traffic was backed up.

This is another problem you encounter in the narrow congested streets of Soho. Once you get four big fire engines parked anywhere, the sur-rounding streets become grid-locked, and any additional engines coming from further afield have difficulty in reaching the scene. There were many occasions when the traffic was so bad that we would have to abandon the fire engine, gather essential firefighting equipment and run to the fire.

I had some experienced men trying to get into that terraced house which turned out to be a brothel. The fire was so intense that they could not get past the second flight of stairs. Red-faced and steaming, they tumbled back down the stairs. I had already established that there were no persons involved. I had to do something that is completely out of character with London firemen: fight the fire from outside. It was just too dangerous for the men to enter. Unfortunately, we managed to reduce the building to a car park. The fire had got too strong a hold before we arrived. Nothing was left; where there was once a roof, there was only sky. The borough surveyor had to be called and he declared it an unsafe structure. It remained that way for a long time, standing as a reminder of that dramatic night shift.

I had to give a statement to the police and was called to appear at the Old Bailey. I was waiting outside the court sitting between two ladies of the night and the transvestite who was knitting! When I was called to the witness box, I didn't have to give any sort of opinion; I only had to state that there had been a fire and that I had attended.

If there was a Coroner's Court on your ground you were often asked to attend inquests to represent the Brigade and witness the hearing. There were no Fire Investigation Officers in those days. When they did come about, not only would they deal with the police, they produced expert reports which could be used in court or as part of insurance investigations.

When the Brigade realised that there should be specially-trained Fire Investigators, it made my job much easier. If the cause of the fire was not obvious or it did not stink from some kind of accelerant, these specially trained men could come up with the cause. Previously, the OIC would have made an educated guess, or put the cause down as the careless disposal of smoking materials.

During my 18 years I cannot think of a single street, place or passage that has not fallen the victim of a fire or some kind of incident. Most of the streets are named after famous landowners, actors or politicians. There are only two roads on the ground: Charing Cross and Tottenham Court. The ghosts of what happened in those streets still linger there, but there is no longer any visual evidence. The damage is soon repaired and buildings renovated. But I can remember everything that happened, and I was there at times when the actions of the Fire Brigade were vital. There are many buildings of great importance to the nation, and those that are just as important to their owners or workers, that owe a debt to my firemen and me. If it were not for our sweat, determination, compassion and professionalism, they would not be standing.

The typical construction of the buildings is such that you may see smoke issuing from a window, but to reach the seat of that fire is a different story. A lot of these buildings have been so altered over the years that the obvious point of entry will turn out to be false, and be further down the street or around the corner. You break down half a dozen doors that all lead to nowhere. This is also the case with the spread of fire.

An example of this was a fire in which I was in charge of in Dean Street, W1. In the early hours of 23rd October 1995 we were called to a fire in a restaurant. It was a good job. The whole of the ground floor eating area and the basement kitchen were damaged by fire. It had started in the kitchen and spread up a narrow flight of stairs. We were there for at least two hours. The ceiling had been pulled down; it had all been turned over and I was convinced the fire was out. I always stuck to my rule that even when you thought the fire was out you stayed there a further 30 minutes just observing.

I informed control that I would re-visit the premises three hours later at 0700hrs. As usual, we picked up a couple of early morning calls and were not able meet the appointed time before another call came over the radio to a fire in Carlisle Street, W1.

Apparently, a cleaner had arrived for work and opened up No.3 Carlisle Street and, as she did, the hallway ceiling had collapsed and revealed a roaring fire. The front door that led to the hallway and the staircase for the upper floors was only divided from the previous fire by an internal wall, which I had not considered as part of the original fire. By now, I had been a Station Officer for at least 10 years and I thought I knew what I was doing. Soho fire engines would have driven past, long after I was gone, and it would have been pointed out to the new boys that that gap in the buildings is 'Chilton's Folly!'

Fortunately I had learnt something. The restaurant was on the junction of Carlisle Street and Dean Street. My first set of messages came from Dean but I sent the second lot from Carlisle. Now unless anyone was interested enough to study a map, they would not have noticed that it was the same premises. It's a cardinal sin to have a re-ignition. It is almost guaranteed that discipline charges of neglect of duty will follow.

Although we had pulled down the false and the original ceilings, nobody noticed that in part of the room there was a third layer. I didn't often have to shout at my blokes but I did this time: … 'If you don't get that fuckin' ceiling down, the next stop will be the job centre'.

They saved me. So did the Station Officer from Manchester Square who, although in attendance, informed control that he was delayed due to heavy traffic so that he could stay longer to help me without causing suspicion. So did our Blue Watch. As we were still there at 1000hrs and we were all knackered, we just wanted to get home. I got one of the boys to ring the station on his mobile and the Blue Watch walked up the road and took over from us.

It all stayed quiet. I delayed forwarding the fire report for as long as possible in the hope that if anyone had noticed, by now they would have forgotten. It's great to have mates.

As the months and years went by, I grew more interested in the ground. I already had quite a good knowledge of the topography but I wanted to be an expert. I needed to know how to get from the station to every part of the ground. Once I had that knowledge, I started to become interested in the history.

A good way of learning the ground was by walking the streets inspecting hydrants. They are located in pits below the pavement and are a simple valve with an outlet. All fire engines carry a standpipe, which is shipped to the outlet and water is transferred by hose to the pump where the pressure can be controlled. It is the Brigade's responsibility to inspect and maintain this ancient underground system of water pipes. The local water authority has the responsibility for carrying out any repairs. At one time hydrants had to be inspected twice a year, and as usual, Soho had more than anyone else; if my memory serves me correctly there were in the region of 1,200! Regrettably, we often had to reinspect already scheduled repairs several times before the actual work was completed. It was just our luck to set into a duff one when water was needed in anger.

Nevertheless, I enjoyed being out on the ground and learning something from all the nooks and crannies. No quiet leafy lanes for us. Trying to get on with your work in the West End's busy thoroughfares invariably turned into a public relations exercise – answering the public's questions and dealing with constant requests for directions, at the same time, trying not to get them wet and preventing them from stepping into the open hydrant pits. It all added to the rich pattern.

Not only did we have to make sure the hydrant was working correctly, we had to make sure that the tablet indicating the size of the mains and the distance to the hydrant was in place. For some crazy reason some lunatic went around the ground painting them out with white paint! What was that about?

For most officers it was sufficient that everything was in place and working. But once, while standing-by at the Square, I experienced the efficiency of a certain Station Officer, Fred Alcock. This man is now long retired but still remembered with, I suspect, mixed feelings. Not only did we have to clean out the hydrant pits, but if the pit would not drain we had to pump out any residual water, and then wash the cover. Mr Alcock was unbelievable; all the firemen were scared stiff of him – he didn't relax the rules for a second.

If you drove him on a shout, you had to take your cap with you, as he insisted not only on the crew wearing helmets, but the driver wearing his cap when returning to the station. This was an established rule but was not enforced by most Guvnors. Mr Alcock would simply say, 'Put your hat on son.' No reply was expected. Anyone who served under him became known as one of 'Fred's Men'. That title meant that they were expected to maintain his standards wherever they went. Although I was wary of him and thought some of his ways superfluous, once I had my own station I realised what he was about. We all knew that if Fred was on a job, we were safe; there was no doubting that he was in charge. One of my old chums who reached the lofty heights once said to me while we were recounting memories: 'It doesn't matter Ray, none of us was as good as Fred.'

The ground is so diverse and the architecture can alter quite distinctly in a very short distance. It can also change its ambience from the peaceful and refined to downright sleazy. The hub of the nightlife in the West End is Shaftesbury Avenue. From there it spreads out in all directions to Oxford Street, Trafalgar Square, Covent Garden and Regent Street. If you stray outside those bounds, the vibrancy starts to disappear and the streets get darker and less crowded.

When I was first there, the avenue would become quiet at about 0300hrs. After that, all you heard was the occasional shouts and the scream of the taxis' brakes. Now it goes on until about 0500hrs when there is a short lull until the day workers start arriving. If you are able to get some rest, now is usually the time. The teleprinter would leap into action at 0645hrs and outside Soho was stretching and yawning, getting ready for another working day. The dustcarts and street cleaners who had been working since before midnight would be returning to their depot behind the station. Deliveries to the shops and restaurants in Chinatown would be arriving, and every day a truck would collect all the waste food from the kitchens. Not a thing to get stuck behind if you are cycling!

*Chapter 14*

## CHINATOWN

Go south and you're in Chinatown – the scene of many restaurant fires and murders. In 1982, seven men were murdered and the premises in Gerrard Street set alight. A few years later, four people died when they were locked in a vault after a robbery took place in an amusement parlour, which was then set alight.

During the summer months, at quiet times during the night, we would sit out on the flat roof at the rear of the station. You could watch the world pass through Newport Court, which was now an open public area with a pagoda in its centre. One time we were alerted by the noise of crowd chanting, and there on the pagoda was a couple engaged in the 'act' and going hammer and tong! Well, you had to look away!

Another time we heard gunshots and saw men running away from outside the King's Head leaving a dying man on the pavement. Of course, the firemen ran outside with their first aid kit and stopped the bleeding until the police and ambulance arrived.

On the Gerrard Place side of the station, there are a row of windows that overlook the street and all the restaurants. The New World restaurant is a frantically busy restaurant; it's where the Chinese have their wedding receptions. I had already witnessed a daytime shooting during one of these occasions. The bleeding guests spilled out into the street.

When you returned to the station after a call it was usual to dash up the stairs to get back to whatever you were doing prior to the call, but on your way it was always worth pausing to take a look out of the window on the first landing. (You had to keep your wits about you when you were going back up the stairs, as if you were wearing tracky bottoms, there was a likelihood of them being pulled down from behind! Never miss the chance of even more schoolboy fun!)

One night I looked out the window across to the first floor of the New World. I saw a number of men wrestling with a struggling lone man. They overpowered the man and sat him in a chair. Then they looked as though they were torturing him. I ran to the office, dialled 999 and told the police. Within minutes two squad cars blocked Gerard Place. Armed police, with weapons drawn, entered the building to save a man having an epileptic fit! Oh yes, I never lived that one down!

Gerrard Place was once called Nassau Street. At its junction with Gerrard Street, there was once a bakers called Duggans. It dated back to the 16th century. The baking was done in the basement and over the bake house at street level was a platform and the surface was heated from the ovens. A group of winos would sit on this to keep warm. On the wall behind where they sat someone had paint-sprayed the name of a band: 'The Burnt out Stars'. I should have taken a photograph of that!

My last real fire was in Chinatown. It went to six pumps at a restaurant called Won-Keys in Wardour Street. This restaurant is the equivalent of the Horse and Groom Public House in Greek Street where the landlord insults his customers. It was a Saturday lunchtime; the kitchen must have been at full blast, and the smoke was in the yard before we got the call. When it was all over and I went to drive home in my car, it was covered in droplets of grease. Every Chinese New Year it was the same; you would put on the windscreen wipers and the glass would turn into a blurry mess.

This was in the more seedy part of Wardour Street. The pedestrians hardly use the pavements and the street is one moving mass. Any road traffic moves so slowly that there is never any risk of being run over while crossing the road. Here you will find the cheaper restaurants serving all-you-can-eat buffets and a sprinkling of the more vulgar, in your face, clip joints. Now three big red fire engines were adding to the confusion. The mob was right on top of us. The firemen had to push them aside just to get the lockers open. I was always conscious that they might trip over the hose and then I would be in trouble.

Won-Keys is on five floors and the whole top floor is the kitchen. A lot of the restaurants are designed like this. It is good because the kitchen is the most likely place for a fire to start and usually fires spread upwards. While the BA crew made their way upstairs, I managed to get the TL into a good position. We were able to take hose up the ladder just in case we had to fight the fire from the roof.

The whole top floor and roof was damaged by fire, smoke and heat. The remainder of the building was damaged by smoke and water; a water main had burst, water was cascading through the building and it took ages to find the stopcock. The boys did a great job at Won-Keys, especially as the staircase leading up to the kitchen was a sea of cooking oil and grease making it a skating rink. Food was stored on the stairs – just one more hazard to add to all the other dangers. (If you saw the inside of the kitchens of half the restaurants, even those which were so called high-class, you wouldn't go again.)

At this time I thought that I was as capable as anyone in the Brigade at controlling a fire, but you would always get some senior officer taking charge who thinks he knows better than you. However, they have the advantage of time. They receive their call after I have confirmed with control that there is a serious fire and have time to think. They can listen to my messages so they know what to expect before they even arrive. The decisions I took or the plans I made at the start were done under pressure and when time was of the essence, without the luxury of hindsight.

I was always suspicious of any senior officer who was unknown to me – mainly because, if I didn't know him, he didn't know me and therefore didn't know what I was about. I dealt with the crowds, the traffic, and the habitual Soho environment on a day-to-day basis. They may never have even been to the West End! I knew that I had a good reputation – I was just a bit disappointed when it wasn't recognised.

A little further south and adjacent to Chinatown is Leicester Square. Every night of the week this becomes a sea of humanity. This is a pedestrian area and, with the exception of emergency and delivery vehicles, barriers prevent all traffic from entering the square. When we were called to the square, we would first have to open the barriers and then the trucks would have to proceed at walking pace to the address. If you had to get to work, you were continuously hampered by the lunatics – you would think that some people had never seen a fire engine. Oblivious of any kind of emergency, we were hampered by women trying to get in the fire engines and young men who just wanted to be awkward or even wanting to fight the firemen. There are many stories about the firemen having to get involved in situations where the victims of violence had to be assisted.

Apart from the various fires, floods and false alarms in the square, I was called on 17th January 1996 to assist the police. These calls can turn out to be anything and on this occasion it was to retrieve the body of a burglar, who had fallen during the course of his activities from one building onto the lower roof of another. He was positioned in the centre of a block hidden from sight and had only been seen from the back of a premises in Charing Cross Road. I could not use our TL and had to call for the attendance of another appliance, a Bronto Skylift. This is a large vehicle, which is similar to a TL but has extending booms and a cage that can carry people. The firemen put the body into an undertaker's body bag and got it as close as possible to the roof edge, manhandled the bag into the cage, and then it was lowered to the ground and taken away.

A good start to another long night shift.

*Chapter 15*

# THE VILLAGE

Go across Shaftesbury Ave., head north and you enter Soho. Parts of the area were laid out in the 14th and 15th centuries and there are an abundance of wonderful books written about the place, but I am not a historian, just a boneheaded fireman, and I could not possibly do justice to the subject without taking up the rest of this story.

Soho these days is essentially a place of business. The charm of the area when it was a small village has long gone. Now it is a maze of one-way streets lined with parking meters. Not that there are many left but, every time a traditional shop goes under because it can't afford the high rents, another sterile eating/drinking place opens. At its centre is the very colourful Berwick Street market and in every street nearby, the many businesses rub shoulders with each other – some sort of sex joint next to a dirty book shop, and a theatre next to a newsagents where you can buy papers from every country in the world. Apart from the numerous bars and pubs, there are the restaurants. There is no kind of food that cannot be found in Soho. Although most of the old cafés have been replaced by coffee shops and brassieres, there are still a couple of greasy spoons where you can get an early morning breakfast. As they open soon after the late night joints close, you can watch the dishevelled, hungover good timers try and recover with plates of egg and bacon.

When I was a teenager I used to go the jazz and music clubs like Ronnie Scott's and The Flamingo. Not even in my wildest dreams could I have known that some day I would have to go back into these places as part of my job.

The magic feeling of the doors opening and turning-out into the avenue on a busy Saturday night never failed to send shivers down the spine. I tried to act nonchalant, but it was a thrill, and it never left me. The trucks would bounce when they reached the road, then with lights flashing and sirens blaring, the drivers would weave their way through streets so congested that you would not have thought it possible. Even in these world-weary times, people will still stop and stare at the fire engines – to pull up at some incident and have an audience of hundreds makes you feel like part of the show. You would not believe the number of people who will gather to watch the firemen at work. It all adds to the adventure. Get the TL to work and they all start cheering!

There is a book written by R.M Ballantyne in 1867 called 'Fighting the Flames'. He describes what it was like going on a shout in those times. He describes the steamer's passage through the crowded streets and the obstacles they would encounter. The reactions of the people and the thrill of it all have not changed. The whole portrayal just illustrates how exciting it is, but at the same time the firemen have to stay calm, and the drivers have to drive fast, but not too fast. They have to be aware of what is all around them: the unpredictable drivers and the thousands of pedestrians.

In just one short paragraph, he describes it far better than I ever could. 'Now, good reader, if you have never seen a London fire-engine go to a fire. You have no conception of what it is; and even if you have seen it, but have not gone with it, you still have no idea of what is. To those accustomed to it, no doubt, it may be tame enough – we cannot tell; but to those who mount an engine for the first time and drive through the crowded thoroughfares of London at a tearing gallop it is probably the most exciting drive conceivable.' That should be printed in red with flames around it!

Sitting in the front of a fire engine being driven on an emergency is a unique experience. A driver who is unfamiliar to you, fresh from passing his test or a standby from another station can frighten the life out of you. Me being a driver made it even worse.

Most of my drivers were excellent, if a little eccentric. The best I have ever experienced was John Denny. He came to me from Paddington when the watch started and I can say that he never put the shits up me; I could concentrate on what I had to do and prepare in my mind for what I was to encounter. Joe and Eddy were a different kettle of fish. I would say to Eddy just after we had a near miss, 'Did you see that?'

'See what!' was his reply.

In Wardour Street there is a motorcycle parking bay where the bikes park with their front wheels facing into the kerb. 'Joe! Watch the motorbikes!'

'What motorbikes?,' as ten of them fell sideways, domino fashion!

My worst encounter with a driver was when I was at the Square. Strangely enough, that was to a fire in a Chinese restaurant in Wardour Street. On the way, the driver had two very near misses, one where a motorcyclist had to take drastic action to avoid definite damage. After the call had been dealt with, I took the driver to one side and told him that I was driving back. I had already spoken to him about his driving and this was the final straw. I took him off driving and sent him for retraining; boy, did he hate me!

Another quandary for the Soho firemen was illegally parked cars. We would be charging to a fire only to find our way blocked by some motorist whose last consideration was that a fire engine might need to get through the gap, which was now impossible. We would all have to jump out and bounce the car out of the way. This threw out another set of possibilities – damage to the car was one, and firemen getting a bad back was another. The Brigade washed its hands of this practice, but what were we to do? It never ceased to amaze me. In the early evening, drivers would be careering round the streets desperate to find a space because they had tickets for a show and the curtain was about to go up. We would find valuable motor cars almost discarded in their haste to make the performance. I would like a pound for every time I had to give directions to punters dressed to the nines with little chance of getting to the theatre on time.

We used to get a regular call to the Phoenix Theatre in Charing Cross Road. After heavy rainfall, their neon sign in Charing Cross Road was always catching light. The only way to reach the sign was with the TL. Firstly the traffic would have to be stopped. Every premise with a neon sign has an isolation switch on the outside, out of the reach of passersby. This is called the 'fireman's switch'. Once the electricity is knocked-off, then a fireman could climb the TL taking a hosereel with him. When the fire was out he would have to cut away the timber hoarding. We should have sold tickets!

Old Compton Street has always given the Fire Brigade plenty of business, and some of it was particularly unwanted. At that time, 30th April 1999, the Admiral Duncan bomb had been the worst bombing incident in London with the most loss of life and serious injury. None of the massive IRA bombs managed to kill and maim as many as a fanatical homophobe with a nail bomb.

The White Watch went off duty that day at 1800hrs. We all went home except one. When the bomb exploded at just after 1900hrs, only one was left: Fireman Robbie Ervin (2-Bob); he had just got changed and was about to leave the station.

Even before the calls came in, the Green Watch, who were on duty, were ready to roll. They heard the blast and knew it was a bomb. The trucks only had a hundred yards to drive but Robbie ran to the scene. The newspaper photographs and the television images could not show the true extent of the tragedy. Away from the cameras and inside the pub, there was carnage

We carry only very basic first aid equipment and, as the Green Watch was the first emergency service on scene, they were using tea towels and paper napkins to stem the bleeding from massive blast injuries. That night the Green Watch were heroes to a man. So was Robbie, but he has never really recovered from the incident. He was not with his usual work-mates and he was out of uniform. Afterwards we couldn't share the experience and help with the healing. If we had all been there, we would have been talking about it and that's a great reliever of stress. As for not being in uniform, that has another effect on an individual. That uniform does not only give you physical protection, it makes you a different person. You become the professional; it enables you to become, to a degree, separated from the reality. It gives you a confidence that you might not necessarily have.

I looked after Robbie as best I could in my own untrained way. After a long period of sickness, I think we almost got him back on an even keel, but how could I tell? How could I know what was going on inside his head when he was on his own?

The night after the bomb, we were back on duty. During the day our Red Watch dealt with the particularly harrowing task of removing bodies and body parts. We spent a couple of hours making the surrounding buildings safe. The eeriness of the unnaturally empty streets and the shattered glass crunching under your boots left a lasting impression.

The Brigade was invited to attend a memorial service at St. Anne's, the Soho Parish Church. Afterwards, when they walked back down Old Compton Street, all the shops and pubs emptied and they were clapped all the way back to the station.

This was not the first bomb that had been planted in order to cause injury to the gay community. On 8th November 1987, we were called to an explosion in the basement of The Golden Lion Public House in Dean Street. This is no longer a gay pub, but in 1987 it was a popular meeting place. We arrived at about the same time as the police and were sent directly to the basement. The pub was still crowded; I am no longer surprised that people stay in a place that they know is dangerous. The bar was slightly smoky and filled with the smell of cordite. Once down in the basement toilets, my first thought was that, from the state of them, I wouldn't want to use them. Then I realised that an explosion had made the mess. One cubicle had extensive damage and the walls were brown from the explosion. There were nuts, bolts, nails and screws all over the place. The police called their bomb squad. They confirmed that the bomb was poorly made using a plastic container filled with gunpowder. It was designed to cause maximum personal injury. The police eventually arrested two men for the crime.

Soho survives all its intrusions. Throughout modern times it has been the place where people go to rejoice. This is shown in all the photographs of gleeful folk celebrating the end of the world wars, then from the ravages of lunatics with bombs to gangsters with petrol bombs and rioting protesters. When any type of event takes place elsewhere in London, when it's all over, where do the crowds head? That's right, the West End and Soho. It is incredible how a few hours later it all returns to just its normal madness.

While the May Day demonstrations were going on, we counted 36 police vehicles in the Avenue. From our windows, three floors up, we could watch the demonstrators and police doing battle in *our* streets. If the Brigade has prior notice of large numbers of people, we are either restricted to calls on our own ground or taken off the run completely and stay in the station.

The north west area, to the north of Oxford Street, is the centre of the rag trade. Returning from calls to this part of the ground, we would always come back via Dean Street or Greek Street. This was a time when you could really absorb the atmosphere: the people, the sights and the smells. There would always be something happening day or night. We had to take our time because of the slow moving traffic. It was then that you were able to talk to the locals.

You would not believe the sights we saw driving back through Soho at night. The ladies love a man in uniform, and when they have had a drink they love them even more. I'm not exaggerating when I say that they would undress at the very sight of a fire engine. Women would even try to get into the fire engines trying to get into the uniforms! Hooligans would ride on the back hanging onto the ladders. That was time to repel boarders! A sight I will never forget; we were stuck in traffic on the

Avenue. A mini bus was coming towards us; as it drew level, it was full of ladies on a night out and they all mooned at us! A row of thonged backsides pressed against the windows. My helmet fell over my eyes! Mr Chilton, would you like to go back to Westminster? Not likely!

At the extreme east side of Soho is Charing Cross Road. At night, the further north east you go away from the fire station, the more deserted and darker the side streets become. The alleys and narrow streets around St. Giles are particularly threatening. St. Giles was the patron saint of lepers. St Giles in the Fields Parish Church is at the centre of the area and was once a leper hospital. That will give you some impression of how bad the area once was. The rookeries of St. Giles were lawless places, where the law had no authority. It was home to the dregs of the earth. Not that it is like that now, but there is a definite change in atmosphere at the top end of Charing Cross Road. All around Centrepoint you will see the drugged and the desolate. Centrepoint is one of the tallest buildings on the ground and is famous for the winds that whip around its base.

Andrew Borde Street was named after a doctor who was associated with the area in the 14th century. This runs anonymously past Centrepoint. We were called to a series of rubbish fires involving a piece of waste ground, which was obscured by advertising hoardings. Behind the hoardings, I found a sea of discarded syringes and needles. I don't think there is a more depressing place in the central area than the pedestrian underpass under Centrepoint.

One of the worst fires in British history started in Denmark Place, so named because of the Danish immigrants who settled there. Denmark Place is an alley behind Denmark Street (aka Tin Pan Alley).

On 14th August 1980 the Green Watch, with Station Officer 'Turk' Manning in charge, was called to a fire in a club. Two illegal drinking clubs were located in a three-storey Victorian terraced building. Earlier that night, a man had been thrown out of the club but returned to wreak his vengeance. He set light to petrol poured through the letterbox and killed 37 people. The best Sub. Officer ever, Ron Morris, led the firefighting crew into that building, which became known as 'Dante's Inferno'.

A little further east is Bloomsbury, a much more elegant area. Bedford Square appears in nearly every period film or TV drama. The British Museum can be found here. This is such a complicated building that the official custodians have to carry maps while they do their security patrols. There is also an abundance of tourist hotels which were regular calls.

In the south east, the main area of interest is Covent Garden. When I was a Leading Fireman on the White Watch, this was still a vegetable and flower market. However, when I returned, the market had gone and the new tourist area had been developed. In the past there have been two major fires involving storage rooms and tunnels beneath the market. On both occasions firemen were either killed or sustained serious injury. Underground fires are notoriously hard to extinguish. Fires in more recent times have been mostly restricted to restaurants and dwellings.

Go a little further south to the Strand (a narrow strip of land by a river) and its surrounding streets. The most spectacular and difficult fires have occurred in this location. The Savoy Theatre, The Savoy Hotel, The Strand Palace Hotel and many others have all been subjected to the ravages of fire.

During the late '80s to early '90s we had a plague of fires in the buildings hidden between the north side of the Strand and Maiden Lane. Several of these were derelict and were being used as squats. During the winter, the inhabitants would light fires inside the buildings, which soon became even more dangerous due to the holes burnt in the floors. They turned into foul places. We had to be so careful of syringes and needles, and all the other forms of human waste.

One of these fires was so serious that it delayed the opening of 'Sunset Boulevard'. Smoke from the fire at the rear of the theatre had entered the auditorium. We made the national evening news that night and I was interviewed with Andrew Lloyd Webber. Fame at last!

One quiet Sunday morning I had 'made pumps four' at a fire in the Strand. We had been called to smoke issuing from an office block. It was difficult gaining entry, and I had to get the TL to work as a staircase. This was the day of the first Countryside Alliance's protest demonstrations against the proposed ban on fox hunting, and suddenly we were right in the thick of it.

As we were trying to get to work, crowds of demonstrators, dressed in country attire, were milling around the fire engines. There was even a circus horse; the funny thing was that both the firemen and the demonstrators were treating it as though it were a normal occurrence. They were chatting to us and we to them, and all the time there is smoke pushing out of the windows four floors up. When I eventually got to see inside, I found that there was a series of rooms all set up for conferences. The place had been burgled, vandalised and set alight.

A regular call in the West End was to pavement junction pits blowing up. These pits contain electricity and telephone cables. A fire would start in one pit and spread down the cables blowing off the connecting covers the length of the street. Normally they didn't lift more than about six inches, but if the public were nearby it would be quite startling. One of our rules is that you never lift one of these covers until the electrical authority is in attendance. So we would scale the incident down, rope-off the pits and wait for the engineers to arrive. That meant that we would have to stand around the pit to prevent any danger to passers-by.

The Strand is a busy street, and in the course of an hour, hundreds of people would be walking past. Most would realise that we were not just standing there for the sake of it and go about their business. But occasionally one would stop and ask what we were doing. Not the Londoners but, more usually, someone down to see a show or a tourist. Well after being polite to the first half a dozen, the firemen start to make up the most elaborate scenarios. When the pit covers lift, they bring up all the dust from the pit. And the most creative story was that a terrorist had blown himself up and these were his remains! That got rid of the nosy parkers.

The southern-most border is eternal and can never be altered. In between the end of Horseguards and Temple Place, on the embankment, our responsibility ended midstream of the river Thames. This includes half of Waterloo Bridge and Hungerford Railway Bridge. Although the Brigade has all kinds of procedures in place to deal with incidents on the river, I never had anything really serious. Of course, there were small fires in the ships that were permanently moored and used as floating bars and restaurants. We were often called to persons who had fallen or jumped into the river from Waterloo Bridge, but these calls mostly consisted of a band of firemen with hands raised to shield their eyes, staring into the empty grey depths of the river while the fireboat circumnavigated the area: 'I see no ships!'

On one occasion we did have to manhandle a very large man who was more than a little barmy, and had got stuck in the mud at low tide. He had exhausted himself trying to get free and had to be stretchered across the mud and up a set of stairs leading up the embankment. These steps were incredibly slippery and covered with river slime. We had to attach a line to the stretcher and haul it up just to prevent firemen from falling.

Before my time, the river had already left its marks on the White Watch. In April 1980 six firemen were caught in a flash-over while fighting a serious fire on the Old Caledonian, a Victoria Steamer converted into a floating restaurant. It was a miracle that they actually survived. As it was, three received serious burns, two of whom never got back to work. Incredibly, even this became a source of amusement. The burns were mostly to the hands but one received burns to his backside – did he get some stick!

The south west of the ground is the most exclusive and most historically renowned. Pall Mall, The Mall, St. James's and Trafalgar Square have all played their part in the reputation of the nation. Whenever we were called to Cleveland House or St. James's Palace, the world and his brother were mobilised.

All the gentlemen's clubs along Pall Mall have had cause to call the Fire Brigade at some time or other – from people trapped when a heavy, ornate ceiling collapsed, to flood and to fire. Whenever an important visitor was expected at the RAC Club, two gas flambards are lit outside the main entrance, and of course the Fire Brigade gets called just to add to the ceremony.

We once sat for days in St. James's Square when the Iranian Embassy siege was in progress, just in case the inhabitants decided to set fire to the building.

Trafalgar Square is the absolute centre of London. I would say that it is a separate risk unique to itself. Just getting through the Square on an emergency call was its very own nightmare. No matter what time of day, on any day of the year, there is always something going on. From protesters making their case by climbing Nelson's Column, to peaceful political vigils, or just the day-to-day swarming mass of people and traffic.

Before Nelson Mandela was released from prison, there was a permanent protest in place outside South Africa House. In the early hours of a freezing cold winter's day, we received a call to assist the police. There was no need to go on the bell; the streets were traffic-free. When we arrived, I was met by a pencil-necked police inspector who gave me the impression that he was not a London man. He was accompanied by a couple of real coppers who were staying a safe distance in the background. The 'Free Nelson Mandela' people had lit a brazier, which was under control, and as far as I could see not causing any problems. The inspector asked me to put out the fire. I just couldn't do it. I used the excuse that the Fire Brigade was not allowed to get involved with political protests unless there was some form of risk to human life or property. If he was determined to put it out, I would show him how to use our equipment. Anxious not to lose face, he went through with the training process; his men were still keeping their distance reluctant to get involved. Unfortunately, the hosereel nozzle we were using at that time could easily be used the wrong way round, and he did it! Straight in the face and knocked his hat off! That was the end; he gave up, and made an undistinguished retreat.

There have been many major fires within the surrounds of Trafalgar Square, notably grand buildings on the corner of Whitehall and Northumberland Avenue, and in the crypt of St. Martin in the Fields.

At some stage, while in my first stint at Soho, we were called to a fire in a travel agents on the south side of the Square. This developed into a four-pump fire involving the whole of the ground floor, which was a 15m × 10m open area – no internal partitions, but the whole space was jam-packed with office machinery and desks. I was part of the first BA crew in; it was hot and the smoke was really thick. We were stumbling around knocking into everything trying to find the seat of the fire. It turned out to be a case of arson and it was starting to spread up to the first floor. Finally, after a lot of hard work and with the fire under control, the occupier arrived. Everything on the ground floor was damaged by smoke including a large stock of travel bags. We were told that we could have these bags, and for years to come you could always recognise a fireman in the West End by these brightly coloured, 'Medallion Holidays' holdalls.

I would never risk injury to the firemen unnecessarily; if there was the slightest possibility of them getting hurt in a situation where it wouldn't make a hap'peth of difference, I would pull out. So it was on a bright Sunday morning getting towards the end of another busy Saturday night shift when we were called to a man stuck in one of the famous fountains. A young man, who had obviously taken more than his fair share of the delights of the local hostelries, had climbed up and was perched in the uppermost shell of the dry fountain. He had two grinning mates standing by offering advice, not only to their mate, but also to us. At 0730hrs, and without much rest, is not the time to annoy the grumpy old bloke from whom need a favour.

'How did you get up there?'

'My mates helped me.'

'Well they can get you down!'

You should have seen the look on their faces as we pulled away back home for breakfast. There is a provision within Brigade procedure for an officer to completely eliminate a call. I sent a message stating that 'Attendance of the Brigade is inappropriate'. Then there was no need to record the call and no need to complete any form of report.

Another unusual incident that deserves recalling took place in a convenience store on the corner of Northumberland Avenue. A shop worker had been seeing in a delivery and had somehow become trapped in a doubled-up position in the electric hoist which was taking goods into the basement store. The hoist was jammed; the man thought he was going to die surrounded by slabs of Carling Black Label. After a bit of a struggle and some TLC, the man was extricated unhurt. The next day we got a letter of thanks and two of those slabs – for home consumption, of course!

The west is also a high class area. From Jermyn Street and Piccadilly, through to Bond Street, to the borders of Mayfair. Strangely enough we seemed to be busier in this part of the ground than some of the seedier, rundown parts. You would think that the more exclusive the address, the less likely you would be to get fires. I had to deal with fires in the plushest of addresses. In fact I can remember a real stinker in Aspreys, the Queen's jewellers. It's amazing the amount of damage a burnt out air conditioning unit can cause when it's left to its own devices near priceless jewellery or antiques.

On one occasion a call was received to an explosion in Bruton Street. We arrived to find the front of a furriers blown into the street with glass everywhere. The owner had tried to destroy his own business. He had placed an electric fire attached to a timer next to a butane gas cylinder. The cylinder valve had been left open. The shop had been locked and when the fire clicked on – boom! The place was devastated. Fortunately, this happened late at night and before we arrived. If we had been called for some other reason, there would have been some dead firemen. It was incredible that members of the public were not hurt. The owner got locked away for a long time – not long enough.

## Chapter 16

# STATION OFFICER – GUVNOR-STAISH

This was some of what I had to do to live up to my various titles. I have given you some idea of what it is like to be a Soho fireman. They never know what to expect during their working day. Certainly not a regular nine-to-five job. It literally is a case of love or hate. Some cannot stand it but I cannot understand why any fireman in London would not jump at the chance to work there. To me, it was worth all the travel problems getting there and all the times you finished late, got home, had some food, and got to bed just in time to go back on duty.

While I was climbing the promotion ladder, I tried my utmost to gain as much knowledge, so that I could deal with any kind of incident. The Brigade produces pages and pages of operational procedures which have to be followed when dealing with the vast variety of things that are thrown at you – although, most of the time, you can only deal with each situation as it arises. You can pass the exams, and can try and learn all there is to be learnt, but sometimes you have to act on impulse and at other times you just have to stand back and work things out. All of a sudden you find that you are the man, and the flack comes from all directions. There are so many aspects of the job. Under the umbrella of management comes: equal opportunities, welfare, discipline, station administration, building maintenance, fire safety regulations – the list goes on. All this is on top of the rollercoaster that is presented to you by the public dialling 999.

Just after I got my job, the Brigade changed its management structure. The rank above mine is Assistant Divisional Officer. There would be ADOs attached to shifts who were responsible for a group of stations and to the whole Division operationally. That meant that if I had a problem that was beyond the bounds of my responsibility, I could refer it to a particular officer. If I needed assistance on the fireground, then any of the ADOs on duty in the area would respond.

The change in structure saw the appointment of Station Commanders who have overall responsibility for a whole station with an Area operational responsibility. They work a 72hr week – forty-two hours on duty and the remainder on standby. If you lived near enough to your area to be able to respond to an emergency in a set down time, your standby time could be spent working from home. If your home address was too far away, you had to camp out either at an address provided by yourself or at quarters provided by the Brigade. In the beginning, the ADOs had to pay rent for the quarters provided by the Brigade!

This change didn't really affect me as I had only just been promoted, and therefore Station Commanders were something that had almost always been in place. Other more senior Station Officers found it difficult to accommodate what was effectively a new level of management, which encroached on their domain.

The first Station Commander at Soho was a man called Dave Reece. He had been a senior Station Officer at New Cross and I thought he was great. If he felt that something was wrong, he did something about it – he kept you on your toes. Combined with this, he was the 'dog's bollocks' on the fire ground. If I needed a bit of help, I was happy to know that he was on his way.

At the onset of Station Commanders, the Brigade was short of willing and able men to do the job. They asked all the Divisional Commanders to put forward two men to go for interviews to increase the establishment. I was still Mr Jones' blue-eyed boy, so he asked me to attend. We were to present ourselves at the old Aldersgate headquarters of the now disbanded Salvage Corps. They were so desperate. There were no selection criteria; you just had to come up with the right answers and the job was yours.

I was interviewed by a panel headed by ACO Kennedy, the same man who appointed me to Station Officer. I must have given all the right answers because right at the end of the interview he said, 'What would you say if I offered you the job of Station Commander at Plaistow?' I turned it down. 'Why?' he asked. 'There are people from all over the country who want these jobs.' I told him that whilst I was prepared to accept the extra working hours, I was not prepared to be away from home for the 36hrs at a stretch while camping out. If he offered me a job nearer home, it would be different. So, fortunately, I had a lucky escape. I think that in any circumstance, the job would have driven me round the bend.

Mr. Jones sent for me to let me know of his disappointment. He said that he hoped that I would not live to regret my decision. I didn't, and I'm pleased to say that I have often looked back to that day with relief. With what I know now, it is a horrible, lonely job and I would have always regretted not riding fire engines and not being with the blokes. When my old mate Shiner was nearing the end of his time, he thought that he ought to try it. He lasted a week and came back saying he was lonely!

My first major managerial dilemma only lasted about six years! A man was posted to me under a cloud. This man, let's call him Hazard, was the subject of a discipline case at his station. Nobody could doubt his enthusiasm or his dedication to the job. He just wasn't the sharpest knife in the drawer. His accidents, mishaps and mistakes have become legend.

The story went like this: there was an unfortunate incident involving a female cleaner. There was an investigation and he was found not guilty. Fire stations were built with an all male environment in mind. The cleaners never knock before entering a room. They would walk into a washroom and see a man drying himself after having a shower and not turn a hair. There was no such thing as locks on the washroom doors. It just opens and cleaners walk in with the sole purpose of emptying the bin or cleaning the sink, with total disregard to what you may be doing. It happened to me on a daily basis. I always had a shower after cycling to work. I would be in my washroom and a hand would go past my naked body to reach the rubbish bin!

The officer hearing the case told the man he would have to move him to another station. Instead of posting him, he asked him where he would like to go – I'll never forgive him! The bloke said that he had always wanted to go to Soho, and he got it. For him, it was like winning the lottery, and I was sentenced to a six-year headache.

It was an understatement to say that this man had a reputation for stupidity. It wasn't long before we heard a catalogue of his past blunders, and it wasn't long before he started a new chapter.

As a motor driver and a TL operator, you would have thought that he would be a benefit to the station. But no, just the opposite. He wandered into the office one day and asked if he could put the TL through its paces in the yard. That was OK; it was something that the TL operators liked to do to keep in practice. Ten minutes later he came back red-faced, and confessed to me that he had elevated the ladder from its housing without putting the outboard jacks down. A real no-no; it could have tipped over! This was a man with 15 years' service who should have been able to work unsupervised. In a way, I felt sorry for him and at least he had confessed, but I always ensured that he was supervised from then on. If only I had used my loaf, I could have been rid of him. It wasn't until a few days later

I noticed a great scrape in the brickwork on the first floor of the station. He had not just elevated the ladder, he had been waving it about and hit *my* station and as I had not seen him, I could not prove anything. Unfortunately I had to wait until he did some real damage, and even then the Brigade was still reluctant to shift him.

I tried to get someone who would take seriously my concerns about this man. I have no doubt that every officer in charge of a station has experience of negative reaction from above; it is as though they don't believe you; that you have some ulterior motive for your concerns. Instead, all you are interested in is the health, safety and well-being of everybody.

I had inherited the Sub. Officer from the old Whites, so he was as wise to the signs of harassment as I was cautious. We made a plan from the start to interview this man regularly to ask him if he had any problems, because we could see that he was his own worst enemy. Is it possible to harass a 6'2" grown-up man? This was not someone straight out of training school and I was really keen not to let anything go wrong. It didn't become that critical, but it very nearly did.

I could write a complete book on the mistakes and misfortunes of this man, but here are just a few examples:

He was sitting at the mess table eating supper; he sneezed, and his snot flew out across the table. Not only did he spray most of the watch, but a lump went straight into the toughest bloke's supper!

One day, after duty, he walked out of the station straight into a fight that was already in progress outside the station, and was bundled down Shaftesbury Avenue in a cloud of dust, blood and spit. He returned to the station bewildered and bleeding. He really didn't know what had gone on!

He was a very greedy man. That's not a problem; a lot of men eat more than their fair share. But after we had all finished a meal he would make sure that he was last to take his plate back to the serving area. He would stand with his back to us and pick over the leftovers from the others' finished plates!

One evening he was driving the ladders and it had gone out without the other fire engines. He had finished his supper. The washing up had been done and the 'hounds' had made up a complete meal from the scraps left on their plates. When Hazard came back they told him that the mess manager had made one too many suppers. He cleaned the plate.

In Piccadilly there is a contra-flow bus lane; it's 'no-fireman's-land'. It is separated from the main part of the road by a narrow section of pavement like a central reservation. If you go into it on a call you can become trapped behind a bus. It was a hazard that was well known to the drivers. It was also well known that it must be avoided. Hazard was driving me on a call and he went straight into it. There we are in the embarrassing position of having the lights on, the horns sounding, and going nowhere. To make matters worse, a friend of mine was standing at the back of the bus waving!

He became a target of ridicule. We officers tried to defend him but it was impossible; every shift there would be something new. He came into the office and told me that his shoes needed repairing. We get issued with two pairs of shoes; they used to have leather soles and had to be sent away for repair. The cobbler used to collect the repairs each week. I said, 'OK Hazard, get the Leading Fireman to put them in the book.' Then he told me that he had no other shoes. 'Where's your other pair then?'

'They're in the menders.'

It was one of those days and I ran out of patience and I swore at him. Then the prat tried to get the Leading Fireman to back him up in raising a complaint against me for swearing at him! If it wasn't for me, he would have been like the fox at the end of the hunt; the hounds would have torn him to pieces!

I told him that he would have to wear his only other Brigade issue shoes – gym shoes, really cheap black plimsolls, which we called 'Tenbys' after the maker's name. They squeaked on the plastic floors as you walked. It was a very funny sound and it creased us up every time he approached the office. Both pairs of shoes were condemned, so he had to wear them for a month!

One man each shift is appointed in strict rotation as the mess assistant. It is his job to help the mess manager prepare food, set the table and wash up. Some blokes are quite happy with these domestic chores but others will wriggle as long as possible and come up with the most absurd excuses to get out of the job. After supper, the washing up was a communal affair; the whole watch would get stuck in. This was a very noisy and often hilarious activity. I always washed my own plate but sometimes I had to go down one floor, back to my office work, while the bulk of the washing up was done – the screaming, singing, shouting and the clattering of pots and pans would always spark my laughter.

One time I wandered back up to the kitchen to see Hazard with a slice of buttered toast stuck to the side of his face. What with the blank expression on his face and the bread just hanging there, I had to hide in case he saw me laughing. As soon as I could, I got him and the Sub. Officer to my room to find out what had happened. At first he wouldn't say anything. I told him that I wouldn't take any action unless he wanted me to and if he didn't tell me if anything was wrong, how could I help him? I had already told everyone that I would not stand for any fun and games with food. In the end he told me that a fireman called Bob Sorrell had thrown the bread but not at him – the original target had ducked! He asked me not to say anything because 'Bob Sorrell hates me more than my wife!'

Bob was a great big man and an ex-Royal Marine. I stuck to my word and never made an issue of it; I just had to keep a constant eye on the situation. This eventually became known as the 'Ninja death-toast incident'.

There was another startling mess room incident. After a meal had just been finished, Woody said, 'I couldn't half do with a tooth pick.' Hazard produced a well-used one, which he somehow stored in his pocket knife, and with all sincerity said, 'You can borrow mine if you like.'

One evening he came into the office and asked if he could have a word with me. He would often do this and I always treated our private conversations seriously. I would shut the office door, which was normally wedged open or, if it was unoccupied, use the Station Commander's office.

'Sit down, Hazard, how can I help you?'

'Well, Guv, I've decided that I would like to have a serious go at promotion.'

I had to keep a straight face; he really was not a good prospect. How could I put this to him gently?

'It's not that I don't think you're capable, but I do think that you have left it too late.' He was in his early forties.

'Right then,' he said. 'I'm going to learn German.'

That was it. He left the room leaving me stunned and bemused. For some time after he carried a German phrase book with him at all times and would study during any spare time. However, one time, the Sub. Officer sneaked up on him and discovered that within the covers of the phrase book was concealed another form of gentlemen's literature!

Somewhere along the line I lost a couple of the old Whites. Tony Cooper and Tony 'Knocker' White had just had enough – they were twenty-year men and wanted a quieter life. They both swapped places with men from Sidcup Fire Station, and I got a couple of fresh faces but lost two experienced, highly qualified firemen. Also, it was at about this time that the first black man came onto the White Watch. 'Hayden Julian-Julian Hayden!' He was all right, no problem and had a couple of years' experience gained at another station. There were not that many black men in the Fire Brigade back then and there had been some racism, but there was no such thing at Soho. There were no problems of that kind.

We had picked-up a job in Cork Street, W1. Famous for its art galleries, it's a street full of life in the daylight hours but after the shops are closed, it is a wasteland. It was a summer Saturday evening. I think that it's just coincidence that most of my most interesting and spectacular jobs took place at the weekends. It was also Hayden Julian-Julian Hayden's first fire with us.

Cork Street is one of the furthest addresses on the ground, not as the crow flies but by having to stick to the one-ways. It was an office block of five floors, and the fourth floor, a solicitor's office, was blazing. Flames had burst through the windows and smoke was issuing from the roof. I sent an assistance message: 'Make pumps four'. I did not consider the possibility of persons being involved as it was not residential and the door was locked.

The crews were getting to work, starting up BA and gaining entry. I sent my first informative message: 'Offices of five floors 15 metres by 60 metres, 20% of 4th floor and 10% of roof alight. It's about five minutes into the job'.

Hayden came up to me. 'Guv, there's a dead body upstairs.'

'What do you mean – a dead body?'

'There's a woman on the fourth floor and she's dead!'

'From the fire?'

'No, her brains are beaten out.'

I had already 'made pumps four'; now I had to send a 'person reported message' to cover myself. I know that as well as two further fire engines and an ambulance, I am expecting a senior officer. As soon as a 'make-up' message is sent, a senior officer is always ordered. So I decided to go inside and take a quick look just to make certain of the circumstances.

The woman was not involved in the fire, so I told the crews to leave her undisturbed and get back outside to meet the senior officer.

It turned out that the woman was a cleaner. Her son's mates had copied her keys and were robbing the place when she arrived. I suppose they did not expect her to be working on a Saturday. The bastards had beaten her with a fire extinguisher and set light to the place. They were cool enough to lock the front door before scarpering.

Cork Street is just around the corner from West End Central police station. The police asked us to go to the station where we were all finger-printed to be eliminated from the enquiry. It was quite a sight seeing a row of smoke-stained firemen standing in line, getting their fingerprints taken.

I was not called to take any further part in the case but I did hear that the police apprehended the culprits. Poor Hayden must have wondered what he had let himself in for.

## Chapter 17

# OXFORD CIRCUS UNDERGROUND FIRE

The White Watch's next great adventure has often been described as the greatest London peacetime disaster in respect of casualties where nobody was hurt.

Oxford Street could once be described as a World renowned shopping street, but in recent years it has taken on the appearance of a Turkish Bazaar. It has a long and mottled history. It is on the route of a Roman Road and was once called the 'Tyburn Way'. This was the route where prisoners were taken from Newgate Prison to be hung on the Tyburn gallows. On this final journey they were allowed to stop off at a hostelry of their choice for a last drink, and the London Mob would hurl abuse along the whole route!

Victorian folk called it a lurking place for cut-throats, and it reverts to this description in the modern-day early hours – a conduit for the drunk and drugged making their way home from places where only the young and fearless stray. Waiting for the clubs to chuck out at 0300hrs, it is lined with unscrupulous looking illegal cab drivers waiting to snare stranded revellers. The London black cab drivers are, on the whole, hardworking and respectable. But, nobody in their sober mind should ever get into one of these death traps.

It was the main route for the fire engines to and from many parts of the ground. Regularly we would see marauding kids bashing the living daylights out of each other. And nobody wears any clothes anymore, even in midwinter!

Whether for work or pleasure, Oxford Circus Underground station is the hub of many Londoners' journey. Now it was to become the scene of the most serious fire to that date ever to occur on the London Underground.

For their actions, White Watch received a letter of congratulations from Assistant Chief Officer, Joe Kennedy. He was the officer who was finally in charge of the fire. He was also the OIC of the northern area of the London Fire Brigade. The northern area was far bigger and had more resources than most County Brigades.

I am proud to list the crews who were recognised for their 'Professionalism, enthusiasm and dedication in dealing with the fire'. Add to the above, bravery.

These were the men that rode with me that night:

### A24 Pump Ladder
Sub. Officer Steve Short
Fm. John Denny (JD)
Fm Ian Cheeseman (Cheesy)
Fm Eddie Martin
Fm Dave Field (Frank)

### A24 Pump
Fm Graham Underwood (Woody)
Fm Rick Swain
Lfm Brian Mills (Badger)
Fm Bob Sorrell

### A24 Turntable Ladder
Lfm Barry Shilstone (Baz)
Fm Roger Borg (Joe)

We were so lucky that night; I was sure that firemen would die in that inferno. I can thank a man called Harry Banks. He was the Station Officer at Euston, a great big man who looked like a superhero. All he said as the hose was being thrown-out was, 'Guide lines Ray!' Then everything started to fall into place. I don't mind confessing that this was the test. Was I up to it or not?

When we deal with fires in large installations of any kind, where there is any chance of BA men becoming lost, we lay out guide lines. A guide line is just a length of rope which is attached to an immovable object at the entrance, and the BA men take the line into the fire in order to find their way out. They have a short line attached to their BA set with a snap hook at one end that can be clipped over the main line, so that they are attached but can still move away a short distance to work. Attached to the main line are tags of different lengths, which tell the firemen which direction to follow. Short tags – way out, long tags – way in.

The call came in on 23 November 1984 at 2159hrs – fortunately, a time when many travellers had reached their destination. It was uncanny that there was this settled period on most night shifts. Like that time at home just after the kids have finally gone to sleep.

As the fire engines turned left into Oxford Street from Charing Cross Road, about half a mile away I saw a great pall of smoke rising up through the street lights. I had been a Station Officer for just over a year. I would have liked to have had a bit more experience. I really wasn't expecting fires as big as this. There were a thousand thoughts running through my mind. I just had to concentrate on what I was trained to do, make some sort of plan. I decided to treat it like any other fire. Go back to the basics and do them correctly. Start the BA, set up the control, and get water. Oh, and ask for help! With Harry Banks' help we got it moving.

Oxford Circus is a multi-line station with a warren of tunnels. There are five entrances to the station and at this stage smoke was pouring out of the one exit, but the others were clear. You had to wear BA just to stand out in the street; the smoke was hot and pulsated against your skin. As the men were pulling on their face masks, I knew how they felt and what they were thinking – hearts pounding, fingers fumbling with the familiar equipment; a sort of numb feeling in the brain, operating on auto-pilot; like me, reverting to the basics. None of them had used a guide line in anger. This was no ordinary fire. Nothing could have pre-pared us for this. Nothing like this could have been replicated in training. This was real danger; this was the ultimate. The one where the only sane humans to venture inside would be firemen.

There were no London Transport staff to give me information. It was so hot at the entrance that the fire could have just been confined to that exit and staircase a few feet below the surface. Perhaps it was just a pile of rubbish? No, it turned out to be a hundred feet down. There was no way that I could tell the extent of the fire or the whereabouts of the seat.

Some Soho firemen had entered part of the station that was clear of smoke to evacuate persons. The movement of air within the station caused by the passage of trains made the smoke throb. Suddenly, one entrance was clear and the others smoke-logged, then vice-versa. It was a bewildering situation. Far away from me, on a different plane, on the platform where the fire was located, a train arrived.

It's desperate at the start of a big fire; any big fire, and especially where you are in charge. You think that you are never going to get through the escalating responsibilities. There is so much to get your head round and it all has to be done at once. Before you get one thing sorted, another crisis is thrown at you. There are not enough men, every duty is important, nothing can be set aside, and you have to stay clear-headed enough to get them done. Men's lives depend on it – depend on you!

A fireman ran to me. 'Guv, there's people trapped in the control room!' This was where it got even more complicated. I had a major fire with people trapped. I didn't even know about the train, with an unknown number of people on board, that had stopped at the platform at the level of the fire. I had to find another BA crew from somewhere.

I knew that control were waiting for information but cannot find anyone to send messages. Everyone was busy; the drivers throwing out hose and getting water. Pedestrian barriers at the pavement's edge were adding to the complications; we had to climb over to get gear from the fire engines and hose had to be passed through them. I had to take my attention away from the fire to send my own messages: 'Make pumps eight. Persons reported, BA required'. In those days, if you asked for additional BA, an emergency tender was sent with the pumps.

The next thing I can remember is Lfm Barry Shilstone standing next to me with a bright red face. 'Where the fuck have you been?' For a few moments poor Barry just stared at me. Then he told me that he had been trapped in the ticket office, but had got out bringing the station staff with him. Heroically, he had gone into a smoke-free area without BA, found the control room and was about to lead the people out when the smoke descended. He had to usher the people back into the room, get them on the floor and pray. Suddenly the smoke lifted, and he dashed them out. I didn't have time to congratulate him or make sure he was all right – I just gave him something else to do. Barry later told me that he thought that he, and the station staff he led to safety, were on the brink of death.

Meanwhile the train on the fire platform, which was part full, had stopped. The driver and the guard saw smoke and closed the doors. The driver then attempted to get the train away from the station but a passenger had pulled the emergency cord and the train could not move. The doors were opened again and the passengers were encouraged to leave the station. This was at 2210hrs, four minutes after we had arrived. How they got out alive, God only knows. As they were escaping, the conditions were worsening and the driver said that he could hear cracking and popping as he left the platform.

The fire had been allowed to develop because after a passenger reported that they could smell smoke on the platform, a member of staff went to investigate, instead of calling us immediately. When firemen did reach the platform it was incredibly hot, and visibility was virtually zero. The dangers of working in smoke were never more apparent. Somehow they searched the train and extinguished the fire.

As the platform was being refurbished, the burning had started in a cross tunnel which had been sealed at both ends to form a builder's store full with all sorts of combustible materials. In the official report the cause of the fire was recorded as: 'Disposal of smoker's materials; motive unknown'. Either builders had been careless, or matches or cigarette butts had been pushed through gaps into the store.

The smoke was now appearing at adjacent stations: Tottenham Court Road, Piccadilly Circus and Green Park. In total, over 1000 people were assisted from trains and stations. (We became the sole members of the supremely exclusive 'one thousand club' after that!)

Most of the time I did not know where my men were; all I could see was the drivers trying to adjust the water pressure from their machines surrounded by miles of hose. (The water pressure increases as it travels downwards.) I had about 50 men under my control from all the local stations, and they kept coming back to me out of the smoke asking for more equipment. I have to say that our personal radios were, and still are, rubbish. They were bad enough above ground, but as soon as you entered the Underground you had a better chance of getting someone's attention by throwing the radio at them! If I'd had good communications with the men at the front, the fire would have been put out much more efficiently.

We got it out at 0153hrs the next day and then I was able to go down to the platform and inspect the damage. On the way down, the staircases were stained with smoke. You could see where the firemen had found their way down. There were trails left by their hands following the tiled walls. The trains had been moved by then and the whole platform was like a blackened cave. All the tiles had spalled off the tunnel surfaces; it was hard to believe that this was a railway station.

The best way to describe the extent of this fire is to repeat the 'stop' message. 'One train and a system of cross tunnels between the Victoria and Bakerloo lines 100% damaged by fire. 10% of Bakerloo line platform and train damaged by fire. Three miles of tunnel damaged by heat and smoke. Approx. 400 people rescued from five trains. Fifteen persons removed to hospital. Four jets and 100 BA sets'. It eventually took 30 pumps to provide all the manpower and equipment. It was by far the biggest operation in London in many years.

What was important was being re-united with my men and knowing that they were all right, just completely black and knackered. We went back to Soho, checked our equipment, got cleaned up and waited for the next shout. There is no capacity in the Brigade to allow time for recuperation and this is a factor when stress and trauma start to accumulate.

A few weeks later there was a mass debrief held at Paddington, the Area HQ. It was impossible to contribute to the proceedings, as there were too many people there. Consequently, I wrote a report telling of my concerns about the operation and made a couple of suggestions that I thought could have improved our performance. The Brigade had a good communications system called Diktron, which was cable connected but only carried on special appliances. I suggested that as Soho had nine Underground stations, it would be a good idea if we carried this equipment. I also suggested that we should change the standard quantity and size of hose carried on the fire engines. The men had experienced great difficulty in manhandling large diameter hose, as it got heavier the further they went down into the station. The bulk of the hose carried is 70mm diameter and I proposed that the percentage was reversed giving the inner London stations additional 45mm hose. Not only did I not get a reply, but when I insisted on a reply the senior officer that I was dealing with threatened me with discipline proceedings!

I gave up after that.

# Chapter 18

## BUSY WORLD

On the side of all fire engines there is a detachable station nameplate. When trucks go away from the station to workshops, these plates are taken off and replaced on any spare that is put on the run. Beneath Soho's nameplates was written 'Busy World' in fireman's chinagraph pencil scrawl. We were certainly living up to that! But that was nothing to what you would find written on a piece of paper if you happened, in a moment of boredom, to take off the cap in the centre of the steering wheel!

Firemen are great charity workers. Whether it is for some fallen fireman or sick children, you can rely on them to shake tins or complete some physical feat to raise money. The easiest way to raise money at Soho is to stand on the forecourt and shake tins. The White Watch raised £000s over the years for the Anthony Nolan Bone Marrow Trust, just by giving up their stand-down time and shaking tins at the theatre crowds. We once ran a half marathon for the Family Centre in Brewer Street, but our most inventive money-raising scheme was the infamous car wash. It seemed that nothing could be organised at Soho without a hitch!

We have always had a good relationship with the Palace Theatre. One of the ladies who worked there was Egyptian, and she knew of a sick child in Egypt who needed to come to London to have a heart operation. She asked us if we could help raise necessary funds.

One of the hounds came up with the idea of a charity car wash. It is a popular fundraiser nowadays, but back in 1985 it was ground breaking. We decided to do it on 16th March and it was advertised around the ground and on Capital Radio. There was even a banner outside the station written in Cantonese. We were between nights on a Red Watch day shift and the Reds helped us in between calls. Even the Station Commander got his hands wet.

We were touting for customers at the start, but by lunchtime Capital Radio were broadcasting it as a delay on the traffic news! Of course, that attracted even more cars. We had a conveyor system. In at the side entrance – washed and rinsed in the yard and leathered as they exited through one of the appliance bays. 50p a car – what a bargain! The

Brigade photographer put in an appearance and I have a lovely picture of the bald spot on top of Colin Townsley's head – he hated that!

We cleaned everything from cabs to Jags. The first highlight of the day was a young lady who very kindly showed us a beautiful pair of breasts. Every time her car stopped she lifted her top. The whole station leathered her car!

It was a great day; the money was not yet counted but it seemed like a lot. The next highlight was about to happen!

At about 1600hrs we'd had enough. Time to get something to eat and get ready for the night shift. The men were clearing up and I was in my room when I heard a clatter outside. There is a vision panel in the Station Officer's room, which overlooks the appliance room. I looked down to see a Porsche wedged against one of the doors. I thought: oh no, here we go again.

The singer, Paul Young, had heard on the radio about our venture and decided to give his support. Instead of entering the station by the side entrance, he came through the bay door under the banner advertising the event just as it was closing. If he had stayed still, the automatic door would have stopped and returned. But he reversed and pulled the front bumper off his car.

I was getting changed and wasn't on duty so, *unfortunately,* the officer in charge was Colin. He had to investigate and write a report on the incident.

Mr Young was brought up to the office. He was shaken and stirred. Colin was taking down the details and in walked one of the men and asked for his autograph, not for himself, you understand, but for his daughter!

To make matters even more surreal, Mr Young's bodyguard was an ex-marine and he knew our ex-marine, Bob Sorrell, and they were chatting in the yard while all this was going on.

We received a letter from DACO Jones thanking us for our efforts in raising £900 by washing over 700 cars, but then we received another one saying: 'Don't ever do it again!'

When I was first in charge I wouldn't let my watch go out to what was called 'on the doors' or a 'door jolly' – standing on the forecourt of the station watching the world go by in stand-down time. The White Watch Soho were not the flavour of the month with the Brigade, and knowing the complications that could have arisen, I thought it prudent to keep a low profile. But in the end I relented. It was one of the station's great attractions, as long as we were doing something productive i.e. collecting money for an authorised cause or giving out fire prevention leaflets. I also made sure that we were correctly dressed at all times. You never knew who was passing the station and could cause you grief.

It was great meeting people from all over the world. In the course of a day the whole world literally does pass by Soho Fire Station. Firemen from all over the world call in just to say hello, swap some uniform and look around. There was a lot of pressure applied when they didn't speak the language. Your individual way of explaining something to a foreigner would be capitalised on and repeated forever more. Like the time I was explaining to a group of blank-faced Germans that we had previously been visited by Germans who had left a framed photograph of their station. I pointed to the photograph and said: 'They came from here'. As if they would recognise the place – there was no inscription on the picture; it could have been anywhere!

Once we were visited by a fireman from Denmark. He was a youngster and he was short of money. Unofficially, I let him stay at the station for a few nights. He thanked us and went home. A few weeks later, he was back and stayed another few nights with another watch. We got him out to play volleyball with us. He was useless, and we began wondering if, in fact, he was a fireman. When questioned about the job, he knew nothing! What a bunch of dummies we were!

I think that it was because we had this continual contact with foreign firemen that we had so much empathy after 9/11. As I watched the disaster unfold on television, my heart went out to FDNY. If that had happen in London and 400 firemen had died, it would have been almost half of the shift on duty in London. The whole station was involved in collecting $50,000 towards their widows and orphans fund. The Station Commander at that time, Graham Ellis, was instrumental in making contact with the Soho Fire House in Lafayette Street. Some of the firemen went over with the cheque and formed a lasting connection.

1985 was a busy year for us. We were plagued by a series of fires in the old Bourne & Hollingsworth department store in Oxford Street, which was being demolished and is now the modern Plaza shopping centre. Two four-pump fires and a six in the months of July and August encouraged the police to investigate, and a security guard was found to be the arsonist.

A couple of months later on 3rd October, we were called to smoke issuing, King Charles Street, SW1. This is Westminster's ground so just the pump, with me in charge, and the TL were on the initial call. King Charles Street is adjacent to Downing Street and St. James Park. Dawn was approaching; it was just getting light and because the park, with its lake, is so nearby, I looked into the sky and said to my driver that I thought it was mist. Ed 'the bastard' Martin, one of the last of the old Whites, who stayed with me until the end, said, 'Sorry Guv, but that's smoke.' Indeed it was. The Foreign Office, another building enduring extensive works, was on fire – well on fire!

Westminster did not have a Station Officer on duty so I was in charge. They did have a very good and experienced Sub. Officer, Pat Millea, who was soon to transfer to Soho on the Red Watch. Pat led the firefighting and I organised from the outside. We're at the centre of the British Government – don't do it wrong Chilton, the whole world's going to be watching! I never underestimated my surroundings– I knew what was at stake.

I immediately made 'pumps 6, hydraulic platform (Simon Snorkel) required'.

As the Foreign Office is at the end of King Charles Street and adjacent to Horseguards, I stated that the additional appliances should rendezvous in Horseguards. I had been advised by my TL operator that an HP would be best at that location as there is a considerable flight of steps, which would restrict access for another TL. The fire involved the upper floors and was spreading; I needed to protect the buildings either side and fight it from both directions. The fire had started in faulty electrical equipment in a carpenter's workshop, and had spread unnoticed through an accumulation of sawdust and went on to cause considerable damage.

My unpredictable burden, Fireman Hazard, approached me and asked permission to 'save the west wing'.

He had a plan to scale the scaffolding, take a line of hose and get to work on the roof where the fire was beginning to show. He was a big strong bugger and quite capable of hauling hose in his teeth. I calmed him down and suggested that he got another man, took the line of hose up the TL, got off onto the roof and work from there. I sent one of the Leading Firemen with him to make sure that his actions did not cause any danger to the men working inside and, although less dramatic, it was the safer option. It also got him away from any potential mishaps that might involve me! As it happened, it was a good move and he did some sterling work.

What with Mrs Thatcher looking out of her windows and all the television cameras, it was a wonderland of publicity for the Brigade. As you can imagine, the fireground soon became swamped with senior officers and the politicians of the day.

It eventually went to 12 pumps and the Chief Officer attended. It was nearly over, just the damping down to be done when I was stopped in the street by our Divisional Commander, Mr Jones. He told me that the Chief Officer had said that 'This was the best example of firefighting he had ever seen'. Well he would say that wouldn't he! It was his Fire Brigade and the world's press were watching. Nevertheless, I latched onto this as a tribute to the firemen.

The year was still not over and on 8th November we were called at 0940hrs to Little Russell Street, WC1.

After the start of a shift and roll call, we check and test our equipment and complete some essential paperwork, then retire to the mess for tea. We were supposed to start work at 0930hrs but the men usually kept me talking to drag it out as long as possible, so we must have been in the mess when the call came in.

Appliances were ordered from Soho and Euston. As our TL was on another call, a Hydraulic Platform was on its way from Barbican. Smoke was issuing from a window on the second floor of a four-storey terraced building divided into flats. Members of the public told me that they had seen a hand sliding down the smoke-stained window.

As I did not consider this to be a fire that was going to spread, and did not require assistance, I sent a 'Persons reported' message. I ordered men to rig in BA and I entered the building in order to estimate the conditions. I didn't have a deputy on duty that day, so I had to have a quick look without getting too involved, just for peace of mind. While I was inside, the scene outside was taking on comic proportions.

An extension ladder had been pitched to the affected window. Hazard had climbed the ladder and had smashed the window – with his hand! He had sustained serious cuts and glass had fallen onto the man who was footing the ladder. He now had a shard of glass embedded in his hand and another shard was buried in his helmet. The situation then deteriorated even further; Hazard slumped over the ladder, as he was about to collapse due to loss of blood and had to be assisted down the ladder by another fireman. In the few minutes of my absence, World War Three had broken out, and I had to order a second ambulance to remove the injured firemen.

Meanwhile inside, the BA men came up against a completely different set of obstacles. There was so much rubbish in the flat, they had difficulty getting in the door. The bedroom where the fire had started was jam-packed with furniture, heaving with bookshelves, with a mattress on the floor. The remaining floor area was covered with household effects. There were overflowing ashtrays, lighters, spent matches and a candle in a medicine bottle. There was a saucepan filled with spent matches and a plastic waste bin containing the charred remains of cigarette packets and match boxes.

It would be safe to say that I didn't have to search far for the cause of the fire, and that the occupier was a heavy smoker!

When the BA men got into the bedroom, they found a man collapsed by the side of the bed. They dragged him out of the flat, and while on the staircase he was resuscitated by Temporary Leading Fireman, on loan from Euston, John Holtham. I recommended him for meritous conduct and he received a Royal Humane Society award for life saving.

The man was revived, brought to fresh air and was then removed by ambulance. He did not recover and later died in hospital. One of the firemen who rescued him (he was the first man into the bedroom), Clive Lewis, and myself had to give evidence at the Coroner's Court.

I found out later that the dead man was called Miklos Krasso, a revolutionary Hungarian émigré who was a cult figure of the new left. He had been a leader in the ill-fated 1956 Hungarian revolution. He escaped Hungary, studied at New College, Oxford and died all-alone in a shithole in London.

I interviewed Hazard after his hand had healed and he returned to work after six weeks' sick leave. As usual he was very apologetic and could not justify his stupidity – just that he was stupid! Why not use your axe? It is also basic good firemanship not to ventilate a fire until it is under control. It's the OIC who decides when that time is right. I was already writing regular reports to my superiors about his unpredictable behaviour, but as is usual they were reluctant to take any action.

In 1988 he finally broke the camel's back. He was operating the TL on another station's ground. Another fireman was working on his ladder and he trapped his feet! Even then the Brigade took no action before examining his actions. It was down to me to suspend him from operating TLs, then he requested that he be permanently relieved of this duty. Additionally, I had to remove him from driving completely as the after-effects of the accident caused his driving to deteriorate even further. When he was first questioned by a senior officer, he explained that he had no excuse, only that he was tired, as he had been working all day at his second job!

Then a fireman from Edmonton, Nigel Peck, contacted the station and asked if anyone was interested in a mutual exchange of workplace. I still look upon this man as my saviour, the man who did me the biggest favour ever. While he was with me, 'Greg' Peck could do no wrong! It was time for another mug to take their turn with Hazard – I'd done more than my fair share!

While all this fireground action was going on, there were still many station-based problems. When I talked to officers from other stations, they were amazed at the scrapes and confrontations we had while trying to manage the fire station – from stolen cars dumped in the basement car park, to cockroach and mouse infestations, to intruders on the station. Returning from one call we once caught a wino walking out of the station wearing Cheesy's clothes. I don't know what Cheesy was moaning about – at least he left his cast-offs in exchange!

The police were often appearing and asking to use the station for surveillance. There are several windows that overlook Chinatown and they wanted to observe drug-dealing activities. While wanting to co-operate with the police, at the same time I was conscious that the station could itself become a target. I always asked the police to be discreet, and mostly they were, until one day a plain-clothed detective ran past my office door with a gun in his hand! From there on, unless they had the Area Commander's permission, I would not let them onboard. However, I would often return from fire calls to find strange high-powered cars and motorbikes in the yard, and very tough looking men who were attached to some obscure police department waiting to raid some property in the West End. It was the only place they could find to park and maintain their secrecy.

The front door was a constant supply of surprises. Not only welcome visitors from foreign brigades but people in all forms of distress. People locked out, people stabbed, mugged and those who had been knocked down in the street. We often had to take the appliances off the run to deal with some emergency involving the public. The White Watch saved the life of a man who was suffering from a nut allergy and whose airways had become swollen.

Everything to test our ingenuity turned up at the front door, from young men, in what started out as a prank but was now something more serious, locked in handcuffs, to women with swollen fingers from rings that were too tight. One of these ladies was so scantily dressed that the whole watch crammed into the watchroom to help. I opened the door one day to a man that was really bloodied and beaten. I thought that he had been mugged. He had been walking along outside the station and got his legs tangled-up in a windblown bin bag and went down like a ton of bricks. He had had his arms full and fallen flat on his face. He was going to a job interview and his shirt was ruined. He got washed up and I gave him a clean white t-shirt and off he went.

At one stage we were at risk of becoming a refuge for all the stranded, moneyless children of firemen. Well, I always told my kids that if they were in difficulty, and I was not around, to go to the fire station.

Sometimes the doorbell rang and you got a pleasant surprise. I tried to get in a little nap at lunchtime, and the blokes were thoughtful enough to try not to disturb my slumbers. There was a knock at my door. It was one of the best men, Fireman Chris Andy, known to all as 'Candy' (C. Andy – get it?) He told me that there was a man who wanted to speak with me – and he was wearing a suit! I went down. I did not know this man who introduced himself as the owner of Rules restaurant, one of the oldest and best restaurants in the West End. He invited us to come and have Christmas dinner on him – the whole Watch and guests: food *and* drink! Bloody hell, obviously he didn't realise how much alcohol a fireman and his wife can consume in the space of a few hours! What a wonderful man, what a great night. We had an upstairs dining room all to ourselves with liveried staff attending to our every desire.

Undoubtedly the most unpopular visitor to the station was a certain kind of senior officer. Mostly they were polite and understood the rules, but occasionally one turned up with the intention of bullying and lambasting those who were less able to stick up for themselves. All of my men were polite and followed procedures, but some officers seemed either to forget or were so badly educated, that I would find them wandering around the place without my permission. They would be up on the first floor meandering past the office door without even acknowledging me, the OIC, let alone reporting and stating their business. This led to some quite heated exchanges and on a couple of occasions I refused to let them on the station. Any senior officer with any kind of responsibility to the station has every right to inspect any aspect of the station's activities, and as it was my responsibility to ensure that everything was in order, I was quite happy to accept a 'bollocking' if anything was wrong, but it had to be done correctly.

When any senior officer arrives, whatever his rank, it is laid down that he has to speak with the OIC of the station. That is the Station Officer even if the Station Commander is on board. The senior officer should go directly to the watchroom where he will ring 'one bell'. More naval stuff being piped aboard. There was a system of bell signals, which were used to indicate certain times of the day and to summon personnel. But now that all stations are fitted with a Tannoy system, the bell signals are virtually redundant. However, 'one bell' is still used to summon the OIC and the dutyman to the watchroom. The dutyman will report first and announce the status of the station to the senior officer. I would have to find my uniform jacket and cap so that I could report correctly dressed.

If it were an officer that you knew, it would just be a shake of hands and a welcome but if it were a stranger, I would be required to give a salute and introduce myself. The visitor would state his business and I would take him to the office or to see the Station Commander and offer refreshments. All very polite, but some of them were not worth the time of day. They didn't know how to report and sometimes they would completely disregard the procedure.

I had a policy whereby the dutyman would keep strangers downstairs and call me to attend. I believed that the upstairs part of the station was ours; it's as private as your own home and guests were by invitation only.

Two of my old school Station Officers would wind up the know-nothings. I did a bit of temporary at Euston on the Green Watch and the Guv was a man called Aggie Weston. He may just have been the toughest man in the world; he was as fit as you like and really looked the part. Furthermore he was an expert in unarmed combat! Not your namby-pamby martial arts, but unarmed combat.

When he was required to report he would wear a mixture of uniform. He would wait for the senior officer to say something. If they did, he would not get changed but he would, at least, mellow somewhat. If they did not challenge his strange appearance he would really give them the run around.

John Peen at Soho would always report properly dressed and wearing his cap. You should only salute an officer if he is wearing his cap and they would invariably have to scrabble around to find their cap. John would raise his hand as though to salute, then just as the other man did the same, John would remove his cap leaving the senior with his hand flapping around in mid-air. It was a matter of supreme timing and always worth finding a vantage point to view the show.

Why was there this belligerent attitude towards senior officers? They are the other side – the enemy. You have to understand that firemen are really only interested in doing their operational role correctly. They will tolerate all the bureaucratic dross that goes with that, but they just want to fight fires and anything that interferes with that tends to get short shrift. The senior management often came up with elaborate schemes that had operational efficiency right at the bottom of the list.

For example, at one time, Euston Fire Station was closed for a complete refurbishment. The fire engines and men were temporarily working out of Clerkenwell, still protecting the same area but from a different base. This interfered with their attendance times and there was part of their ground which was much nearer to my station than their temporary base. The problem was that the initial attendance to a fire in this area was completed with a pump from Manchester Square and our TL. The TL carries only a small amount of firefighting equipment and if it was the first to arrive at a fire, the crew were risking their own safety by having to get to work on their own. The TL only rides with two men and, although it carries two BA sets, they cannot use them unless another fire engine is with them to provide BA control. You must have a minimum BA crew of two and you must have a BA control officer.

All the Station Officers complained about this and wrote memos to back-up their concerns. Eventually a Divisional Officer from Area came to see me. After I had explained the whole rigmarole yet again, I am still astounded by what he said; 'Can't you hold the TL back for a few minutes?' Just imagine if somebody died and the press got hold of that! I managed to convince this man of his idiocy, and got the predetermined attendance changed just in time for Euston to move back into their smartened-up station. It only took 12 months of complaining!

Meanwhile, deep in the bowels of Lambeth HQ, a strategy – a whatergy? – was being hatched. It was decided that when a large fire occurred or a long drawn-out incident was foreseen, instead of ordering reinforcements from stations located near to the incident, as was usual, a number of fire engines would be sent to a station near to the incident and this would be used as a 'Forward Control'. This procedure was formulated shortly after the Brigade had its fingers burnt after the Poll Tax riots. That day they had only one senior officer on duty to cover the central area. Our poor old Blue Watch took the brunt of the whole affair in Trafalgar Square with several cars alight, a range of builders' portacabins ablaze and a violent, screaming mob.

Now this plan might have made good sense in the case of a fire which would stay in one place. But not in the case of a civil disturbance that could change its location at any time. The Brigade were anxious to try out their theory, and as the police had received information that further riots were expected, the Brigade decided to create a 'Forward Control' at Soho. At the start of a night duty, four additional fire engines were ordered into the station to standby, just in case. Rioting did break out about 2300hrs on the other side of the River in Kennington Park near the Oval. But instead of sending appliances near to that location, we had to suffer the ignominy of setting off in convoy with our pump at the head, on the bell, like some travelling circus.

What's more, nowhere included in the strategy was any provision for the supply of catering for the thirty persons who were away from their stations around a mealtime. We could provide tea, but not food. The senior officer in charge of the exercise gave the mess manager £5 out of his own pocket, and sent him out for biscuits. Then he whined like a stuck pig when he received no change! In an act of petty revenge, he took a whole packet for himself!

Can you wonder at our despair, and why we treated some officers with suspicion and contempt? It is certainly the case that senior officers should try to remember what it was like to be a fireman, but the further they get up the management chain, the easier it is to forget or even care. Oh, I know that they have to consider a far bigger picture and I understand the constraints of appeasing Governments, but why can't they at least give the impression that they are on the same side? In my eyes, their credibility was further depleted by the fact that they could not possibly understand how a Soho TL driver felt after two 25-shout night shifts. Is it any wonder that some of them are the enemy?

*Chapter 19*

# LIFTS, LOCK-INS AND FLOODS

The personnel on the watch were always changing. I was happy to see men move on through promotion, but I had problems handling my disappointment when men transferred just to go to another station. I could not understand why they would want to leave Soho. Moreover I could not understand how they could want to leave me! In nearly every case I felt that my contribution to their progression was being stolen, especially when they were young or had joined me straight from training school.

Sometimes your spirits are lifted when, out of the blue, you get a really good addition to the watch. At the start of 1986 my old friend, Steve Colman, was posted to the watch as a Leading Fireman. I now had Steve and my old stalwart, Barry, as Leading Fireman. Brian Mills had moved on through promotion.

I had been on duty at Westminster on Steve's first day. He was only 18. He arrived late, got a bollocking from the Guvnor for being incorrectly dressed and went off to a massive wharf fire all on the first day – an unfortunate baptism. He went non-stop uphill from there and our careers have followed a very similar path, both culminating in around 20 years at Soho. In 1982 he was awarded The Queen's Commendation for Bravery when he rescued a young boy from the blazing fourth floor of a hotel. He had reached the fourth floor by climbing the dreaded hook ladder and received burns to his hands and legs into the bargain.

It was good for my morale to have junior officers who worked relentlessly and contributed to the office fun. The camaraderie and banter is not just restricted to the mess room.

Having blokes who would get the work done without encouragement made my job that bit easier. I liked to be on top of the office work, but that didn't mean that we couldn't have a laugh at the same time. There is a lot of routine administration and all the officers, including me, had to pull their weight. This work is routine and sometimes tedious, but it still has to be done correctly. Preparing the laundry, getting shoes and boots repaired, ordering stores and maintaining the petty cash was all part of the job.

Even the emergency calls are not all excitement. Mostly all the calls that come in are emergencies to somebody, but to us they were routine. Most stations, due to the peculiarities of their grounds, have a cross to bear. It may be rubbish chutes alight in blocks of flats or grass fires in the summer. Our burden was automatic fire alarms (AFA). In a highly built-up area with lots of shops, offices, hotels etc., you are always going to get a vast amount of accidental actuations. In some buildings, the false alarms were so regular that it was difficult to treat each call as serious, but it is essential that you are operationally prepared when you arrive at every address. Start treating these calls casually and you will soon end up in trouble.

Calls to anything other than fires fall under the broad umbrella of 'special services'. There are two types of special service. They are either provided free of charge and classed as humanitarian or, if asked to do something that was not essentially an emergency, the Brigade would issue a standard charge. For example, filling water tanks or dealing with chemical spillages.

Another feature of any built-up area is that every building has a lift. Most of them are liable to break down, get stuck between floors or the doors just won't open. Lift incidents can take a considerable amount of time and sweat to set right and make safe. Some of the equipment is so old that it needs all your skills to safely release the occupants.

Stored in each lift motor room there should be a set of equipment that can be used to hand-wind the lift carriage to the correct level. Sometimes this is missing. Moreover, with old obscure lifts, it is hard to figure out how it works. The station would attend some lifts so regularly that the firemen would leave messages in the dust for the other watches who they knew would attend at some time or other.

A regular added complication to 'persons shut in lift' was the calls that came out-of-office hours to a locked building with the security guard shut in the lift. You have to either gain entry or hang about waiting for a key holder to arrive before you can release the red-faced guards. Other out-of-hours calls were in the early morning to release office cleaners. Very late at night it was invariably jolly drunken people who, for a short span of time, thought it would fun to get into the lift together. Once the lift stops because it is overloaded and it starts to get claustrophobic, the fun quickly changes to panic.

This wonderful old photo, taken in 1929 was left at the station by a veteran gentleman fireman. Notice the children at the window!

'The Pride of the Avenue.' The West End is still asleep but the fire engines are out on the forecourt ready to be washed for the day shift. (2006)

Her Majesty's Lord-Lieutenant presents The Queen's Commendation for Brave Conduct.
(London Fire Brigade, 1976)

14 years later, Ray Chilton, now with 'whole roof off', receiving the Long Service and Good Conduct Medal.
(London Fire Brigade, 1993)

The depths of the burnt-out Oxford Circus underground station. Leading Fireman Brian Mills and Ray Chilton, smoke-stained members of the 1000 club.
(Martin Lloyd-Elliott, 1984)

The White Watch at its best. Ray showing the wear and tear of too many sleepless nights. (Robert Walker, 1999)

The Royal Opera House. A mobile crane hangs precariously above Covent Garden Piazza.
(London Fire Brigade, 1998)

The conclusion of a grim task. The removal of the corpse of a burglar fallen from a roof top in Leicester Square. (London Fire Brigade, 1996)

Coptic Street close to the British Museum. A hydraulic platform at work removing injured building workers. (London Fire Brigade, 1998)

Farewell 'Little Chris'. At least 500 firemen show their respect. (London Fire Brigade, 2002)

Lifts broadly fall into two categories: cable operated and hydraulic. A lot of the newer lifts in smaller buildings are hydraulic, and because the motor rooms do not have to be directly under or over the shaft, they can be positioned anywhere. In the more extreme cases you would find them in adjacent buildings.

Get three or four 'shut in lifts' in a day and you earned your money. During warm weather, just climbing the stairs to reach the top of a high building wearing fire gear left you sweat-soaked. That was even before you gained entry to the lift motor room and began to hand wind the lift.

The worst lift incident I ever attended was when I was a fireman at Westminster. It was in a block of mansion flats called The Winter Gardens in Marsham Street, SW1. Lift engineers had been working on the top of the lift carriage and it started moving upwards out of control. One of the engineers had managed to jump off the carriage at an open doorway and was trapped half in and half out. The other man was crushed when the carriage reached the top of the shaft. All the time we were working to release them, blood was dripping from above. Talk about nightmares – is it any wonder I have difficulty sleeping?

Another routine call was to persons locked in or locked out. Nowadays the Brigade charges for lock-outs, but previously we were 'cheap as chips' locksmiths. Even since the changes, the punters have learnt that if you say that you think that you have left a fire or a cooker switched on, the Fire Brigade will attend, free of charge, and open the door. We would try to get in without causing too much damage but just in case, you had to get the 'customer' to sign an indemnity waiving the Brigade's responsibility for any damage.

Friday was the night for lock-ins. I cannot count the number of times we were called to release the last person left inside a locked office block. Of course, as soon as the ladder comes off, the crowds arrive. It was free entertainment – especially if the victim was a young woman in a skirt. The firemen would climb down the ladder keeping as close as possible to the already embarrassed female.

On several occasions, I was called to cinemas when they were closed after the performance, to release customers locked inside. Before the advent of mobile phones, the stranded folk would have to attract the attention of passers-by to call the Brigade. This was a particularly complicated operation, as the main doors of cinemas have locked chains passed through the internal handles of the main doors. We worked out a method where we could wedge the chain against the door and then cut it through the gap between the doors with an angle grinder.

Not just pretty faces then!

Anyone who knows the ground will realise that road traffic accidents are not high on the list of calls attended. Apart from a few thoroughfares, which criss-cross and surround the ground, the traffic is at a crawl. It did speed up in the early hours, and we did attend collisions down on the Embankment and in the Hyde Park Underpass, but most of our incidents involving motor traffic were restricted to the slow moving and unusual.

When I was a Leading Fireman we were called to the Swiss Centre, Coventry Street. This building had a car park whereby the cars were taken to the upper floors by an internal lift. I never quite discovered how it happened, but one driver managed to drive into the lift shaft without the lift car being there. The car had fallen engine first to the bottom of the well and caught fire. The driver tried to escape the car but perished when he became trapped between the car door and the wall of the shaft. Every RTA after that was a little less dramatic, but nevertheless extraordinary.

Motorcycle and cycle messengers seem to have little regard for their life and limbs, and we had to extract several trapped under buses and cars. Most of the actual car crashes either involved some kind of street furniture or the vehicles had left the road and smashed into buildings. My final RTA involved a Black Cab, which had bounced off another car and then headed perilously towards a set of railings. As the cab hit the bottom of the railings, they upturned and shot through the windscreen towards the driver's head, missing him by inches!

But the most bizarre happened in Lyle Street in the centre of Chinatown. My fire engine was returning from a call on Westminster's ground when the call came over the radio, via the police control. My first thoughts were how could there be an RTA in Lyle Street? There is no possibility that cars move at anything more than 10mph. Anyway, on went the sirens, up Charing Cross Road. Coppers were at the Lyle Street turning, waving us in. As you turn left, you cannot see very far up the road as it bends away to the left. When we turned the corner we were met with a sight that defied comprehension. There before us, at the side of the road, were two cars, one completely on top of the other! A gentleman from Canada, who was used to driving a car with a foot-operated parking brake, had pressed the accelerator to the floor while his hire car was in reverse and it had ridden, straight up, on the bonnet of the car behind, and was now perched with its rear wheels against the windscreen. Nobody was hurt, but all and sundry were scratching their heads in puzzlement.

Another type of incident that is consistent with concentrated areas of old properties, is flooding. Burst pipes, neglect, and heavy rainfall would all contribute to the horrible amount of damage from leaking water. There is an underground stream that flows under the Duchess Theatre in Catherine Street, Covent Garden. When there was heavy rainfall, we were always called to help with the pumping-out.

Domestic premises were the worst. In most cases you could stop the flow of water, but the damage was quite another thing – just as destructive as any fire. When you find basement flats with the furniture floating around, it is impossible to console the occupiers when their treasured possessions are floating out of the door.

However, when a commercial property is involved, there can be a lighter side to the calamity. We received a host of automatic fire alarm calls to a hotel in Mayfair. To some hotels, the fire alarm sounding and the consequent arrival of the Fire Brigade is an unwanted aggravation, and at this place we were an irritation. The staff were oblivious to the seriousness of our attendance. That was how it was when we received yet another call to their alarm on a warm summer's evening.

If water enters the AFA system, it responds in the same way as if it were smoke. Most of the attendance was standing out on the pavement chatting while a junior officer had gone to inspect the affected area. It got a radio message back that water was percolating through a ceiling on the first floor. So I went upstairs to the first floor with a few firemen, and as we entered the corridor where the original crew were waiting – crash! Down came the ceiling! The water was not just percolating, it was cascading. All hotels have a system of pipe-work that supplies the internal firefighting hosereels, and as soon as water is released, a flow-pump kicks in to increase the pressure. This pipe had fractured, causing high pressure water to flood into the corridor and it was filling up like a scene from Titanic. With the help of the hotel maintenance men, we were desperately trying to find a shut-off valve. In the meantime – crash! Down came the ground floor ceiling. At that moment a coach-load of Americans had arrived from Heathrow. The dining room had been laid out with a welcoming buffet; now it was covered with sodden ceiling tiles.

At first we could not stop the water; we were sheeting-up and moving furniture out into the street. The Americans were evacuated, and they sat out in the street around the tables and chairs surrounded by their luggage.

It never ceases to amaze me that people can so readily accept their quickly deteriorating surroundings. These tourists' first sight of their hotel was to see it floating down Curzon Street. Seemingly unconcerned, they were more interested in talking to the firemen.

On the subject of floods, when I was at Soho as a Leading Fireman, the West End was hit by a tremendous downpour. It lasted for about half an hour but the station received over 60 calls in that hour. I know because I had to fill in the register of calls. There were so many fire engines on the ground that firemen from Beckenham (ten miles away) were called to fight a fire in Wheelers, the fish restaurant in St. James's Street!

Old Compton Street is the heart of the gay community – always busy, always lively. On 31st January in the early hours, we were called to a fire at No. 32. On the ground floor there was an illegal drinking club, with prostitutes working in the two upper floors and a peep show in the basement. Just a run-of-the-mill place of work in Soho!

Old Compton Street is so near to the station that you hardly get time to get rigged before you are in attendance. As soon as we arrived, I could see smoke issuing from above the front door and the windows of the first floor. It was a freezing cold night and the street was unusually deserted. There was no one with information about the premises. There were no signs of life, but I had to presume that there could still be residents. The smoke was not punching out, but drifting, which is a signal that it's a smouldering fire, waiting to accelerate once fed with oxygen.

I got the boys rigged and told them to get the door open carefully and then stand back. At the same time the water was got ready. A few seconds after the door was opened, sure enough – whoosh – the flames burst out into the street.

Martin Lloyd Elliot was riding with us that night. In the beginning he was with us just to take photographs, but the station got to him and in the end he wrote his book 'City Ablaze'.

The firemen fought their way into the basement and up the stairs. There were no persons involved. The only thing that prevented the whole building being involved was a closed door leading to the second floor staircase.

When I got inside and the fire was extinguished, I found that the fire had originated in the basement and I didn't have to search for the cause. I just had to follow the scent of petrol.

A good job with good action photographs. You don't get many of them (see front cover).

A regular call to Old Compton Street came in on Sunday mornings. Roxy Beaujolais, the landlady of the Three Greyhounds, searing her Sunday roasts – again! This pub was eventually the last non-gay drinking establishment in the street and was the White Watch's regular watering hole. We loved Roxy and I think she loved us!

Any fireman will tell you that a call to a smell of burning can test your abilities more than an inferno. Somewhere in a property, something is overheating or smouldering and you have to find it. We were called to a smell of burning in Compton's on a busy night. Compton's is a large gay pub. We had just received delivery of a large, handsome man of Italian descent who had transferred to us from 'boring' Paddington in search of some excitement! Alfie Comparini has perfect manners and a tongue of silk. None of the above is true except the large and Italian.

It is very difficult to clear a big pub with throbbing music shortly before closing time. It is even harder to locate a smell!

It is a common occurrence in pubs with bare floorboards that fag ends drop through the gaps and cause the accumulated dust and fluff to smoulder. Even if you can get water down though the boards, you still have to saw and lift the boards to make sure it's out. Sometimes a less drastic method is to work by removing part of the ceiling below. This was what the landlord wanted.

Alfie was working while standing on a step-ladder. In walked a member of staff. Alf said, 'Watch your backs boys!' He got a reply quicker than that. 'Don't worry yourself ducky; you've got nothing I want!'

Again, in Old Compton Street, I was called to a person collapsed in a flat with a reported smell of gas. We got in the door, no problem. I couldn't smell gas, but as a precaution I didn't turn on the lights. I was in a bedroom in total darkness with someone in bed. I thought: 'Oh fuck! Here we go – a decomposed body'. So, in torchlight I gingerly pulled back the covers. The poor old lady asleep screamed only slightly louder than me!

I didn't know that there were any old ladies even living in Old Compton Street!

Adjacent to Old Compton Street is Moor Street. Cafes, sex shops and most buildings with prostitutes (sorry, models) working in the rooms above. We were called to smoke issuing from the rear of one of these properties. Nothing obvious was showing, but I'd had several fires in this street so it had to be investigated thoroughly.

The firemen entered several of the upstairs bordellos. Entering a prostitute's workplace has to be handled delicately. It's simply 'not cricket' just to burst in. In one property, Mick, the Sub. Officer, stopped a man on the stairs and, quite matter of factly, was asking him if we could get to look out the back windows. The man appeared quite agitated, gripping his waistband and reluctant to speak, reluctant to hang about. We realised then that he was an escaping punter. No wonder he wasn't interested in speaking to the firemen. Perhaps he thought it was a raid.

Part of my job was to inspect the fire precautions in different types of properties. Most of these visits would be arranged in advance. But when we received a complaint from a member of the public, we had to investigate immediately. It was usually a case of blocked fire exits or overcrowding. The callers were usually people with more than just civic responsibility at heart. You would find that you were in the middle, and became the mediator, of a long running feud, or that you were the 'revenge' aimed at a club where entry had been refused. People would phone the police and complain that some club was dangerously overcrowded. The police would then pass the complaint on to the Brigade. Firstly you had to speak to the doormen (usually off-duty firemen) and ask to see the person in charge. The manager, or whoever, would then be obliged to show you into the club. I could then inspect his fire certificate which would tell me the club's capacity. Now, whatever the nature of the establishment, a crew of firemen will cause a stir. The firemen can make the most of this but I have to talk seriously to the responsible person, and when that person is male and wearing a leather cap, make-up, thigh-length boots and hot pants, it is hard to take the relevant section of the Fire Precautions Act seriously.

Under the Fire Precautions Act we were also required to carry out inspections in any premises where there was entertainment. This included all the theatres, and that was an experience all to itself. Part of the inspection had to be carried out during the performance. Not only did we get to see bits of all the shows, but we also got to see backstage, under the stage – in fact, everywhere. We also got to meet the performers and see what goes on backstage while the show is in full swing. It gave you the opportunity to learn something of the layout and it was a relief from the day-to-day.

The London Fire Brigade once had a house magazine called 'The London Fireman'. In 1982 it became 'The London Firefighter' but it still retained its chumminess, giving us details of who had joined the Brigade and who had left, developments in equipment and pictures of any interesting jobs. It's gone now, but not before it deteriorated into a vehicle of corporate propaganda. Previously, once a year they published a league table of stations with the greatest number of serious fires. As the Brigade tried to change its image, this list disappeared – lots of fires were not politically correct. Nevertheless, Soho was always in the top five, but in 1987 we were at the top of the table. In '86 I was in charge of just 3 four-pump fires, but by November '87 the White Watch had already handled five fours and two sixes. We completely missed another four-pump fire in Beak Street. The TL picked it up on its own while we were on a separate call. Fire engines from Manchester Square and Euston assisted Steve Coleman and the TL driver.

One of the more interesting of those fires started at 2256hrs on 4th July. The Lindsay House restaurant in Romily Street was unusual, in that the diners reserve a room and then they and their guests have a slap-up private dinner party.

On this night, all the diners were dressed up in their finery when smoke started to rise from beneath their feet. Romily Street is less than a stone's throw from the station, but even before we arrived, there was fairly thick smoke throughout the ground floor.

Before we can start to investigate, we have to get the restaurant evacuated, but the staff and diners were reluctant to leave. They were quite prepared to stay at the table with their eyes watering and smoke rising all around. The staff were thinking about the pennies they were about to lose. In this type of restaurant it wasn't as though something else could be chosen from the menu and they could start again. As diplomatically as possible, I persuaded the manager that there was no alternative.

The density of smoke was now increasing, but there was no sign of fire. As a matter of course, the kitchen is the usual suspect, but in this incident it wasn't; so now the fire had to be in the fume ducting. What with all the eateries in Soho, we were the fume-ducting experts. Years previously, Ron Morris had advised me to 'make-up' on fume ducting to be on the safe side, especially if the fire was not obvious.

Always follow the 'old grey fox's' advice. Ducting can run anywhere, and all along its course there is a danger that the fire will penetrate the metal and then spread unseen into wall and floor cavities. Then you have a hidden fire which has to be exposed by cutting away timber and removing sections of wall and, no matter what, you are going to be in attendance for a long time and will need a lot of men.

We had to wear BA as the smoke was so thick, and as we had to cut and take up about 6m² of floorboards, cylinders didn't last very long. The fire had indeed burst out of the ducting and had severely damaged the floor joists. It took about two hours of hard work before we could make the place safe, much to the displeasure of the restaurant and the diners.

They should have gotten their rotten ducting degreased more often. We were always being called to smoke issuing from ducting, especially from those restaurants with charcoal grills. Kitchens would be working at full belt, unaware that black smoke was belching out into the night sky.

Duct fires are the city fireman's chimney fire and are usually started by flames leaping from pans into grease-lined ducts, but sometimes they are caused by burnt-out extraction fans. They are fought much the same as chimneys, in that you can attack from the bottom, the top or at an intermediate level by cutting into the ducting. No matter how you do it, you have to access the whole construction to ensure complete extinction.

Little did we know that the busiest part of the year was still to come.

*Chapter 20*

# THE GREAT STORM

I reported for duty on the night of 16th October 1987, expecting just a normal duty. Early in the evening, the teleprinter started to spill-out messages predicting dangerous weather conditions. The Great Storm was heading our way and out of control!

By about 2200hrs we were chasing around the ground to various items of street furniture etc. that were in, what the Fire Brigade terms, 'precarious positions'. These calls climaxed with a collapse of scaffolding in Covent Garden. Then just before midnight we were called to an address at the Oxford Street end of Dean Street. As we entered Oxford Street, the lights went out. They didn't go out all together; it was like a relay going down the street. The whole of the West End was plunged into darkness. Next I was ordered with the pump to standby at Hornsey – where the fuck's Hornsey?

Each station has an emergency generator that has to be brought into action if there is a power cut. Hornsey's didn't work. As it was a one-appliance station and its fire engine was out dealing with storm damage, a pump had to be in the station to deal with any emergencies that may be reported directly to the station.

It took ages to get there because roads were blocked with fallen trees. We only stayed in the warm, dry station for a short while, and were then out to trees falling down around Alexandra Palace. Then, as dawn approached, we were sent home, clearing damage on the way. Everywhere was a wasteland. The usually busy streets were deserted. Public transport was up the spout and people were staying indoors.

When we got back to Soho, the telephone was red hot with calls from the oncoming day shift. Most of the Red Watch were going to be delayed in getting to work. Some, who had suffered storm damage to their own properties, would never make it at all. The Station Commander's wife was ringing the station from home in Hastings to get her husband back because the chimney had gone through the roof!

My relief that day was Colin Townsley, but his house had suffered structural damage and he was not going to get in. If there was no officer of an authorised rank to take over from me, I had to stay on duty until

**148**

area staff could get an officer from the next shift to relieve me. Only trouble was, there weren't any. Some of the Whites and I had to stay on, keeping the station afloat, working with the more intrepid members of the Red Watch. The pump did not stand still.

At times like this, when Control was swamped with calls, it starts 'batch mobilisation'. This means that each appliance would be given a list of calls to attend. The usual messages were not sent, unless assistance was needed. You went from incident to incident until the list was exhausted. Then you would get another list over the radio and so on.

I was up on roofs all over the place. In Regent Street we had to retrieve scaffold boards which had blown from the back of Austin Reeds, over the roof and were now in a dangerous position, threatening to drop onto passers-by six floors below in the street. At least we were given breakfast in the staff restaurant.

Every time I got back to the station, I was expecting to find a happy face that would let me, if not go home, at least give me a break. I finally got off the run at 1530hrs and laid on my bed until we started again at 1800hrs.

Another night of torment followed. Out with more lists of damage. No rest, barely time to get some food inside you.

At 0802hrs the next morning, I was just looking down at the blurred image of my breakfast and down they go again – Fire, K Shoes, Quadrant House, Regent Street, W1.

We arrived to find a shoe shop heavily smoke-logged. The premises consisted of ground, first floor and basement with five floors of offices above. I was met by a member of staff who had arrived, opened up, saw smoke and made the call. Lights were showing up on the first floor, I asked her if there could possibly be anyone inside. She told me that the cleaners might still be there as they locked the door while they worked. So I sent the first BA crew up to the first floor to search. The ground floor was smoke-laden; it was almost certain that the fire was in the basement, but rescue comes first.

I was standing with the shop assistant out on the wide pavement of Regent Street and out came the fire. Bosh! A great rush of heat and smoke blew us backwards, almost off our feet! Another BA crew was preparing to go down to the basement to fight the fire. Instead they had to take immediate action to assist the firemen on the first floor. They could no longer get back down the stairs and had to smash the windows to escape. A ladder was pitched and they were able to get out with smoke rising from their clothing. I had three firemen cut by glass and we still had not got round to getting some water on the job.

More trucks were arriving and I got another BA crew inside. They were trying to get down the stairs, protecting themselves with water spray. They had great difficulty as the fire kept flaring up and it was incredibly hot. As they edged forward, it seemed as though the fire was in a separate room. Eventually they located a store-room, which was full of burning boxes and collapsed shelves.

When buildings have basements that protrude out under the pavement, they are required to have pavement lights. These are thick glass blocks in a metal frame that can be smashed to allow the basement to ventilate.

Eventually this fire went to eight pumps and we had to smash out the whole pavement light and introduce a mobile smoke extractor because the smoke was so thick and was not dissipating. The fire investigators came to the conclusion that a cigarette end had dropped through a broken glass and had started smouldering away since the early hours.

When we got back to the station there was already a cartoon on the banter-board showing firemen in dresses jumping from an upstairs window shouting 'Women and children first!'

The banter-board was something exclusive to Soho. At the old station it was a blackboard where every occurrence was illustrated and captioned – an ongoing comic illustration of station life. Now it was a notice-board in the mess where cuttings from newspapers and magazines, which could be associated with the watches or watch members, were pinned. It had to be monitored, and anything that could cause real offence had to be removed.

The next time I saw Colin Townsley, he told me that I was a lucky bugger because I was always picking up the big fires and now I could add the night of The Hurricane to my CV. A month later he was dead. A selfless hero who died while attempting to rescue a victim of the Kings Cross Underground fire.

*Chapter 21*

# THE KINGS CROSS UNDERGROUND FIRE

All the firemen who attended that awful fire, which took 31 lives, carried out their dangerous and, in the later stages, grim tasks with determination, thoroughness and courage. They should be held deep in the hearts of all Londoners for ever more. The removal of burnt bodies is a harrowing task, even to the most experienced.

I feel uneasy writing about this. It wasn't my fire. I didn't go, and I don't want anyone to think that I'm taking away any form of glory or imposing on their private memories. I know the story has been told many times – possibly too many. But for reasons of posterity, the circumstances should be made apparent.

The call came in at 1930hrs on 18th November 1987. Kings Cross belongs to Euston Fire Station and was in full swing getting the folk of London home from work. At the time of the call, Euston's trucks were out on another call and the next nearest machines were ordered from Soho, Manchester Square and Clerkenwell. When they arrived they saw no smoke and entered the station.

Calls to underground stations are a very regular occurrence. On this occasion, the call was to an escalator alight. Overheating escalators came in like clockwork. I know what the firemen were thinking as they entered the station, getting ready to search the machine room and inspect under the now stationary staircase. Everything seemed normal.

Major underground stations present a particular problem to the OIC of the first attendance. It is a basic rule of control that the OIC stays outside to oversee operations. However, it is much more efficient to organise from the station control room. They have CTC and you can communicate with the whole station. Also, it is from there that you can get trains stopped and give the all-clear. Additionally, you can borrow the expertise of the station staff.

When the Fire Brigade are called, whatever is happening has usually happened. They get there and deal with, almost, the aftermath; the catalyst has long passed. This incident differed in that it hadn't actually happened and when it did, the firemen, instead of being the saviour, became part of the tragedy. If smoke was coming out of that station, Colin would not have been able to go inside and the firemen would have not entered the station without wearing BA. Nothing would have prevented the disaster, but the tragic outcome might have changed.

After that fire, the men of Soho Red Watch had a certain look about them. Some have never recovered. Others could no longer do the job and some went away to other stations. But they are still the Watch that is the most together.

The repercussions of Kings Cross fire hit the whole station. Everybody was affected in some way. It affected me in such a way that it still makes me feel guilty and sad. I had known Colin for about seven years. We had a lot in common. He was a cyclist and he rode in most days. Like me, he was partial to a bit of jazz and a good book, so we always had something to talk about. We were both blessed with two daughters of a similar age, little girl and big girl, and were going through the same parental tribulations.

He was a big, strong, fit man with an ego to match. When he entered the room, you certainly knew he was there. That's how he got the nickname 'Tonka' – the indestructible toy. We got on, and I still hold on to things that concern our acquaintance. Firemen don't send postcards to each other but I have one from him. After he died, I always regretted that we had never socialised away from the station. Relationships like that can easily be neglected when you are on different shifts and everyone is so busy – there will always be some other time.

I was at home when I heard the news that there had been a horrendous fire at Kings Cross and that a fireman had died. It was national news. Friends and relations started to phone. They had heard on the news that the man who had died was a Station Officer from Soho station, married with two daughters. From that description they feared the worst.

I got everything in order at home and went to the station as soon as I could, and spent the next week or so helping good man Ray Firth, the Station Commander, with anything he needed me to do. Although a separate department of the Brigade organised the funeral, there was still a multitude of things to do.

At one stage there was a blind panic when we couldn't find Colin's wedding ring. He never took it off and his wife was desperate. It could have gone missing anywhere after he was removed from the fire. It was found, thank God, and rushed to Mrs Townsley.

I wrote a letter to 'The Independent'. I just wanted everybody to know what kind of a man he was. 'On the surface, Colin was larger than life – a hard man who did not find it easy to tolerate those who did not reach his high expectations or the high standards he set in all the respects of his life. But scratch that surface and you would find a gentle, sensitive, creative man, who adored his wife and his daughters and had a great affection for his men, Soho fire station, cycling, music and literature.'

He had 25 years' service and he had waited for 19 of those years to get his job at Soho and he loved it.

The station became the centre for Londoner's gifts, messages and flowers. I was out in the yard one day and a motorbike courier rode into the yard with a stack of money. 'Here yar mate. We've 'ad a collection.' The money – £000s – was stuffed into my hand and off he went. It went on like that for weeks; strangers were just walking off the street with donations. After each performance, the cast of Les Miserables appealed to the audience for donations to one of their firemen. Then they were waiting in the foyer with buckets. Every night they brought the money over to the Station. Our safe was bulging until a special account was set up.

One night the Blue Watch Station Officer, Shiner Wright, got a phone call from a nightclub in Kingly Street. Could he come and collect some money, but not until the club was closed? Shiner got permission to leave the station at 0300hrs. When they arrived they were asked to take a seat and a completely naked exotic dancer handed him an envelope containing £1,700. That pleased old 'Shiner'! Well it was Soho and the show had to go on! I had to stand guard over the safe that weekend until we could pay it in on the Monday.

It was a very emotional time. The Brigade's Senior Welfare officer, Anne Wilmott, was at the station on a daily basis. Some of the Red Watch talked to her, but others kept their feelings to themselves. One day she could see that I was in need of some counselling and she took me to a quiet room and helped me to come to terms with some of it. Until then I never really appreciated what Welfare and Counselling were about. Since that day, right up until I retired, I had regular contact with Anne, a wonderful woman with the fireman's interests at heart. She helped me, not only with my personal problems, but advised me on any welfare problems I had with my men.

Saturday 28th November, the day of the funeral, approached. The busier it became, it was impossible to keep the place running as a simple fire station. Colin's coffin, covered with a Union Jack, was mounted on our TL and driven up Tottenham Court Road, past Kings Cross Station to St. Paul's Church, Covent Garden. Six of the Red Watch rode the TL acting as pallbearers. The streets stood still with respectful Londoners lining the pavements. The firemen based at Soho lined the pavements outside the station and firemen from all over London and the nation formed guards of honour at Kings Cross, St. Paul's Church and at the crematorium in Lewisham.

I was asked to take care of Mrs Townsley. She didn't really want a Brigade funeral, but believed that it would have been Colin's wishes. She did not travel with the coffin but was to be taken, unnoticed, to the church by car.

It had already been agreed that I should escort her through a side entrance in Henrietta Street. I will never forget sitting in that car and being driven out of the station. I find it hard to describe my feelings in going from the quietness and the shadows of the deserted station into the bright daylight of the avenue lined with our firemen and the public. How many times had he turned-out through those doors? This was like no other time.

Some wonderful words were said at the service, but it was a hard time. Afterwards, when the TL left for the crematorium, I went to the pub. A man, not a fireman, with whom Colin occasionally cycled the route to work, followed the entourage to the crematorium on his bike just as a sign of his respect.

Later, it fell to me to open Colin's locker and sort out his personal possessions. It was one of those things that has no connection with reality. I found a bag of fruit that was probably part of his supper. I did not know what to save. In the end, I saved his best undress uniform and everything he had ever written and took it all to his home.

In the proceeding weeks, months and years, I got to know Colin's family, especially his daughter, Sally, who is the same age as my Lizzie. Later on, this lovely young woman would phone me at the station and ask if she could park her car. Time flies by that quickly.

Mrs Townsley knew that the whole station were there if she needed anything. But she was an independent lady, a real fireman's wife. One of the Red Watch firemen lived nearby and he helped her out with any household repairs etc.

What hurt me the most was that because we had the same family make-up, all through my life I would be doing all the wonderful family things that he would be missing. Something changes in a man when he becomes the father of daughters. The protective instinct is overpowering – a challenge to your masculinity. You have to come up to their expectations. It's peculiar. In your eyes they never actually grow up and become independent – they only get bigger.

Each following year there was some sort of remembrance ceremony at Kings Cross Station, and later at a church nearby. I tried to get a fire engine to the church service right up to the tenth anniversary when I think it was a mutual decision to let it rest in peace.

The tenth anniversary service was held at St. Pancras Church, Upper Woburn Place. The church was bursting with dignitaries and senior officers. Colin's family were in their rightful position at the front of the church. When the service was over we all stayed standing as they headed out. As they came up the aisle with all eyes on them, Sally was searching for a friendly face and she found mine. She put her arms around me and for a few seconds she was my daughter and she had lost me. I'm not ashamed to cry. I hope everything has gone well for those girls and they remember their dad. My chest still gets a bit tight when I think of him.

I did make sure that there was some lasting memory of Colin's existence at Soho Fire Station. When we wear the BA, attached to the set is a yellow plastic tally. On this tally you enter your name and air pressure. I got BA workshops to make us a tally with Colin's name permanently embossed. I got one of his men to unscrew the hook where Colin hung his fire gear when he was off duty and replaced it with the tally. My gear hung next to that space until the end.

A plaque is mounted on the wall of the appliance room from the official Kings Cross enquiry team. There is also a plaque presented by some French firemen from Clermont Ferrant who came over for the funeral. Colin had established a link with these men and often visited them during his holidays in France.

It may seem a tad melodramatic, but I decided that the best thing I could do for him was to stay at Soho until I retired and look after his station. That gave me a good excuse to give up any thoughts of leaving.

After Kings Cross, the station became even busier. It seemed as though every traveller was smelling smoke on the Underground. With nine stations to deal with, we were called several times each shift. It was not just a case of inspecting the stations and making sure they were safe. If the smoke was reported in a tunnel, we would have to empty a train and ride on it through the tunnel at walking pace inspecting the route. Prior to the fire, if there was a small smouldering in the tunnels, London Underground staff would deal with it but now it had to be done properly; they had to call the Brigade. The calls took so long to deal with that there was no time to do the everyday work. It didn't get better; it got worse. Every station had to be fitted with automatic fire detection and they started to go off. LUL also installed hand-operated alarms on the platforms and how many times did the hooligans bash them? It drove us mad and it frustrated the travelling public. Both the station staff and the firemen came in for abuse. It was quite understandable knowing the hardships of travelling on the London Underground, but it really was for their own safety. Some people thought it was some kind of exercise but we never close a station or empty a train for any other reason than a reported emergency.

Still, none of that helps if all you are trying to do is get home.

*Chapter 22*

# SHINER AND THE NIGHTMARES

Now is probably as good a time as ever to tell you about Station Officer John 'Shiner' Wright. He was in charge of the Blue Watch for several years until he retired. I don't think that I would offend anyone by saying that he was a scallywag. His antics are those of a legend.

He was always late on his first day duty. I would be in the mess having breakfast at the end of my second night duty, waiting for Shiner to phone and report that he would be late. He always had some lame excuse but it didn't matter what he said because he spoke in such a hurried way that you knew that he was just behind schedule. He sometimes rode a bike from his home in Finchley; no Lycra for Shiner, just some old tracksuit and his Fire Brigade issue officer's gloves. He had a voluminous red moustache and a shaved head. Only problem was that when he shaved his head, he always missed a bit!

I first met him when I was a Sub. Officer. In those days the 'A' Division commander was a Mr Colenut – a dapper, no-nonsense gentleman who would stand for no form of malarkey. All the officers who were in charge of stations attended regular Station Officers' Meetings, where we could discuss our problems and get given a few more. At the first one I attended, I was quite taken aback by this group of world-worn, gnarled, senior men grumbling about the job. It didn't take me long to join the gang!

Everybody took notes and most of us took notebooks, but not Shiner. At one meeting Shiner grabbed the notebook of the man sitting next to him and threw it onto the Commander's desk. Without looking up, Mr Colenut said, 'When you're finished, Wright, we'll get on.'

He used to attack me with spring-loaded contraptions that would explode when weight was taken off them. He would put them under cups and books, anywhere. After another busy night, I was getting changed to go home, all on my own, away with the fairies in the locker room. He had rigged my cycling shoes. As I picked them up, bang! I jumped out of my skin. I grabbed a waste bin, filled it with water and chased him screaming, like a girl, around the station. I cornered him in the appliance bay and gave him the contents of the bucket. His Blue Watch were cheering-on the usually controlled Chilton. That was the day that the Blues elevated me to the status of folk hero.

There are loads of stories about his antics, but my favourite is when he had the audacity to get 'Tonka'. He mixed Ajax with his talcum powder and when he dowsed himself after a shower, he turned blue!

It was not well known that Shiner was once the youngest Station Officer in the London Fire Brigade. He was destined for much higher things, but he liked station life too much and stayed as the Guvnor at Euston on the Red Watch for many years. He told me that he had always wanted to give Soho a go, and transferred when he must have had at least 25 years' service.

He was always broke and wasn't too shy to ask for a sub, but he was a little shy when it came to paying it back. So when I had a £5 bet with him, I didn't expect to be paid. I know this sounds fantastic but he had some chums in the French Foreign Legion and he would go off on beanos with them in Marseilles. He was heading off for one of these expeditions and I bet him that he would not be back in time to start his next shift. Sure enough, the phone call came. He was still in Marseilles and wanted me to get him some more leave. He paid up! I pinned the £5 to the inside of my locker where it stayed until he retired.

Nothing in his life seemed to go without a hitch, even his retirement do. He arrived, the worse for wear, sporting a black eye! The new Red Watch Station Officer, Bruce Hoad, and I burnt his £5 and put it into a tasteless chalice as a parting gift. After I had gone home a fight broke out; this spilled out from the pub into Macclesfield Street and the police were called. Who was at the centre of it? White Watch – you already guessed. I suppose it was a fitting farewell to a man who had always been on the limit.

The next time I saw him was less than a year after he retired and it was at his funeral. The drink had always been his downfall, and I believe he drank away his pension and it killed him.

My next big and exciting fire was, as usual, created from fantastic circumstances. We were called at 2020hrs on 24th September 1998 to a fire next to the Franco Restaurant, Jermyn Street, W1. Named after Henry Jermyn, the Earl of St. Albans, the street was now world famous for its shirt makers and boot makers. The Franco had once been a luxury establishment called A L'Ecu de France. Jermyn Street is full of history; it was once home, not only to Gladstone, but Isaac Newton.

In more recent times it was more important to the White Watch because, while on a call, we were approached by a German fireman with the most magnificent set of whiskers. He had very little English and we had even less German, but being a fireman he did share the joke. 'Funf – ein' – '5 – 1,' I shouted (the score by which the England football team had just beaten Germany!).

When the call came in, the pump ladder and pump were ordered from the station, but the TL was ordered via the radio as it was returning from a call on Kensington's ground. The PL & P were delayed by heavy traffic, and the TL arrived before us and got stuck trying to turn into Jermyn Street due to parked cars. There was already smoke drifting high above, but high buildings were hiding the location of the smoke. The TL had to be manoeuvred through a narrow gap and then all the trucks were able to pass. About half way down the street there was a group of people. As we approached, the TL stopped after being hailed by a security guard. This was at the rear of the old Simpson's departmental store. The guard told us that he thought that the smoke was coming from their roof. I told the firemen to start getting water ready and got the TL to work to inspect the rooftops. Once the TL was extended, the crew could see that we were in the wrong place. The TL had to be made up and the hose dragged further down the street. This delay saved a fireman's life. As we neared the building which was actually on fire, there was a great explosion and a sudden increase in fire. An acetylene cylinder had exploded on the roof. It went off like a bomb; instinctively everybody ducked.

I had a building of six floors; the ground floor was a bank. The rest of the building was multi-occupancy, but belonged to the bank and it was being refurbished. Moreover, I had cylinders involved. That meant that I could not risk allowing the firemen to get too near.

There was scaffolding around the building and in the stairwell, which served the upper floors; workmen had been removing an old lift shaft. The fuse board had been bastardised by the contractors, in order to supply temporary power to the whole of the area being refurbished. The cause of the fire was recorded as electrical overheating and I can imagine that all the cables in the lift shaft had been glowing just before the fire.

The roof, top floor and the staircase from ground to roof were alight. Entry to the ground floor was impossible due to the intensity of the fire and the instability of the stone staircase. Stone stairs are likely to collapse when subjected to extreme changes in temperature. The intermediate floors could only be reached by climbing the scaffolding. The fire, which had started on the first floor, was being allowed free passage to the roof because, with the lift carriage removed, the shaft was now a chimney. The fire had also penetrated a door on the second floor and was spreading into that area.

My first action was to get the TL to work as a water tower. I could not allow men to go anywhere near the roof because there may have been more cylinders. In the vast majority of fires, firemen will always get inside to fight the fire. Standing outside and squirting water is for wimps! Next, I had a report from the police that a man was trapped by the smoke in an adjacent building. A crew was sent to find this man and he was brought to safety.

As Jermyn Street is reasonably narrow, I got another jet to work from the building opposite. That just about had it under control. I had got water onto the fire and a BA crew into the second floor and nobody was hurt. As the senior officers arrived, they all had a go at increasing the appliances in attendance and it finally went to ten.

Back then the management thought it was a good idea to hold a debrief after every make-up, and the crews that attended were called up to Paddington. Usually someone gets criticised over some part of the incident, and the officer who was acting as chairman had decided it was going to be me. He was a nasty piece of work and he seemed to have a real down on Soho. Maybe he was jealous. He started to have a go at me, which he would have been better to do in private. The firemen leapt to my defence and verbally pinned him against the wall. This man also tried to stitch up a good officer who was in charge of our Red Watch. At night, he would conceal himself in a darkened doorway opposite the station just to catch us out. Can you believe it? Nothing better to do! He caught this man standing out on the forecourt incorrectly dressed. The Brigade didn't proceed with the case but eventually got us. He was the instigator of the blackest period of Soho's history.

He sent us a Station Commander who was to challenge my sanity and that's enough said.

Although the Station Commander had an office next to the main office, he did not have any other facilities on the station. He had to use the Station Officer's washroom and had to provide his own messing arrangements. This was not instigated by the station, but by the Brigade. There was habitual word play at Soho and any Station Commander had become the 'Station Banana'. If the 'banana' in position was a decent chap, the men would break the rules and ask him if he wanted messing. Any food provided would have to be paid for but it was cheaper and better than going out into the West End. As was my want, I did not like the 'banana' being in the mess. It was the place where the men could vent their feelings and it was restrictive having them around.

In October 1990 I was told that a female was being posted to the watch from training school. Having lived through the previous episode, I was scared. Two of the old watch were still with me and they were also scared. I put my concerns in writing to the Station Commander but got nowhere. So, as none of the other watch members had any experience of working with women, I asked if a personnel officer who was experienced in equal opportunities could come and speak to us. This was refused. They told me that they would not have to come and speak to us if the recruit were male. Everything had to be equal!

Although I had been on a very basic equalities training course, I was quite unprepared in the intricacies of 'woman management'. I had joined a men-only institution. I had not worked with any women during my service, but I had learnt something from the previous discipline case, and with that under my belt, I set down the ground rules to the watch and just hoped that I would get it right.

Two women came to the station at the same time, which was policy; the other went to the Red Watch. After some early teething problems, everything went smoothly. The young lady in question was quite amenable and ready to join in the humour and I tried to treat her as any other new arrival. I thought, sod the equality – she was a girl! I would not protect her from any of the hardships of the job, but at the same time I would not allow her to be, in any sense, bullied or degraded. She will still laugh at this. I banned her from eating bananas in the mess, especially on the second night, unless she ate it by breaking pieces off! Not funny? Well, shame on you!

I can't say it was easy for me, but as I was a married man with two daughters, one particularly forthright, I thought that my natural ability would prevent any repeats of 1981.

As I have already said, I have only worked with three women and they have all survived and continue working at stations, which takes some guts. I hope that any female reading this will understand that I was cautious in my management. Although I have no problem with women in the

Fire Brigade, I did have a problem with the problems it caused – the problems that arise from having one female working and sleeping in the same room with 10 men.

The most obvious of which did happen. A serious relationship developed between one of my best men and the new girl. This proved to be a very difficult situation, not helped at all by the Station Commander's interference. At a time when I need support and guidance, he was like a wet fish.

The problem was that the rest of the watch, including me, did not know how to handle the matter. After all, there are a lot of commercial businesses that do not allow this sort of thing. Although they would not admit to it, I eventually found out that the Brigade had a written policy, which advised against partners and staff who are related to one another working together on the same Watch. This document came my way from a helpful source, but it did not solve the problem.

The man involved is a stubborn git and has the ability to dig his heels in to a great depth and will not give in.

I gave them both my advice as a twenty-year man, both in marriage and the Fire Brigade, that it would be better for their relationship if they worked apart. It takes a very strong bind to be able to spend time continuously with the same person, no matter how much love is involved.

I was in despair. Harassment was beginning to raise its ugly head. I came home after a night shift and I sat in my kitchen. I was so concerned about this that, like a madman, I was writing another memo sitting at the kitchen table. Suddenly I thought, 'What the hell are you doing?'

But what was I going to do? Nobody was taking any notice of me, let alone helping me. I decided that I would try and speak to the man who was in charge of the area. This was an Assistant Chief Officer, and Station Officers do not talk to ACOs directly. Protocol says that I must go through my line manager (I would have liked to run through my line manager!). An old chum of mine was working as the ACO's assistant, so I rang him.

'Do you think the ACO would talk to me?'

'Of course, let me speak to him and then I'll put you through.'

'Yes, Mr Chilton.'

I told him all about it. He had no prior knowledge of the problem. The ACO told me that he wanted to think about the situation and asked me to call him back at the same time the next day. When I rang, these were his very words:

'Well, I went home. I thought about it, tossed a coin and it came down on your side.'

He waited for my reaction. There was none. I thought, surely he's joking.

Then he said, 'No seriously, I discussed it with my wife, and I have decided that I am going to move them both.'

When I got back to work, there was already an instruction for me to take an appliance off the run and go to Paddington HQ with the couple. The man who handled the meeting was our Divisional Officer and he confessed to me that he had no prior knowledge either. They were both transferred to separate stations but on the same watch. Later I managed to get the man back because his skills were being wasted where he was; he had all the qualifications and he's a great bloke.

I have to tell you that they are now married with a wonderful daughter and they are both still my friends. I think that I take some credit for that and, even if I don't, I'm very happy with the way it worked out.

How did I do it? How did I manage such a fiercely independent group of people? Firemen are all expected to use their initiative and make instant judgements in emergency situations without referring to their superiors, and then again in separate, unconnected and less urgent conditions they are expected to follow the rules and abide by the decisions of their leaders. Where do you draw the line? I'm afraid it's impossible; you can't have one reaction without the other. They apply the same self-determination to every set of circumstances. All I could do was try to make sure that they understood the consequences.

I never really tried to analyse it until recently when I heard Mike Brearley, the once-England cricket captain, describe it perfectly. He called it 'tough love'. Firstly, you have to genuinely be on their side; you can't pretend because they will find you out. Then you have to make them understand that you will stand no nonsense; that your love is in no way namby-pamby. You can never let them down and by that you stick to all the rules yourself. If someone needs straightening out, they get it face to face; if someone needs a bit of help, they get it with no conditions. Until I heard Mike Brearley, I didn't know how I did it, but now I do.

Later on that year, I had either gone off duty early or taken a night off. The Sub. Officer, Steve Short was in charge and he was called to a man on a tower-crane threatening to jump. He was 170 feet above ground on a building site in Northumberland Avenue, W1. Steve was a very experienced man; he was the original Sub. Officer.

This man had climbed the crane with the intention of ending it all. Steve and Fireman Rick Swain climbed the tower. The man was out on the jib, which was about 80 feet away from the main tower. Armed with a safety belt and a line, which was attached to the jib at intervals, Steve made his way out to try and get the man down. As he approached, the man stopped him when he was about 20 feet away. Little did this man know that Steve was probably the best man in the London Fire Brigade to be talking to, as he was a Lay Preacher with a great respect for humanity. The man hadn't eaten for two days, and Steve managed to get some food and drink to him, and then persuaded him to come down.

Afterwards, the man said: 'I thought about jumping but that fireman changed my mind.'

Steve was made an honorary member of the Samaritan's Supporters Club and was presented with this honour by the actress Liz Frazer. One visitor to the station who was more than welcome – a beautiful lady.

Steve Short went on to become a Station Officer in charge of the White Watch at Clerkenwell, and we were to meet on a regular basis and handled a lot of incidents together.

I ran the White Watch my way. There was no point in putting up with no rest and the travelling if you did not enjoy the station while you were there. I could not accept some of the changes which the Brigade made to work routines. Back in the old days, we stood down after lunch on a Saturday and the whole of Sunday. After the Brigade stopped this, unless we had something specific to do, I tried to maintain the tradition, although on Sundays we did work in the morning. Well, the Area Commander did once make the mistake of saying to me that the men at this station need some time for rest and recuperation!

## Chapter 23

## PARADISE

My name for my fire station – Paradise. After any incident, I would say: 'Come on boys. Let's get back to Paradise'. Saturday morning is a fine time to be in Soho. It's quiet; not many natives – just the regulars and a few wandering tourists. We kept up the traditional Saturday scrubout. It was a good time to get outside on the forecourt and socialise with the passers-by. I got to speak to the most interesting of people from all around the world.

At 0930hrs I would stir them up, into boots and leggings (me included), out into the yard for a bit of drill. Nothing fancy, just pitching ladders and getting jets to work. In between each drill, I would give them some Q&A. This invariably degenerated into much falling about with laughter. I had the same old questions about equipment, procedures and topography, but they never remembered all of them and only the real stalwarts could remember where Ernshaw Street is located. There is always one road on the ground that even the best has trouble memorising. For me, it was Garrick Street. Named after the famous actor, I knew where it was; I could just never put a name to it!

Training was something about which I had the best intentions, and if there was a quiet time, I would try to get the men out in the yard. But it was always interrupted by fire calls, or we were short of men for one reason or another. When we had a youngster on the watch, it was essential. We had to find time. Even if it was the boy on his own, we would always train. We used our equipment in anger so often that there was not much of a training need. If there was, we would get it done when time allowed.

Not every fire was headline news. Not every special service was worth remembering, but some of the crazy things that happened could only have happened in Soho. Late one night we were called to the Dominion Theatre, Tottenham Court Road, to assist the police.

London's homeless are very crafty when it comes to finding a comfortable place to sleep. The 'Phantom of the Dominion' made his nest high up in the flies. The flies are a space above the stage from where the scenery is raised or lowered. As the theatre was emptying at the end of a performance, The Phantom would sneak into the building and sleep in the comparative comfort and warmth above the stage.

On this particular night, he had been spotted by theatre staff and the police had been called. 'Time' was the current show, and above the stage there were high wires stretching from one side to the other. The police were trying to catch him, but as soon as they got near he moved away – balancing on the wires, with no safety net!

Theatre staff, five firemen, the police officer in charge and an Inspector, who told me that he was a trained negotiator, were gazing upwards open-mouthed with necks craned, amazed at the agility and balance of The Phantom.

The Inspector asked me if I could do something. I'd had some experience with people in precarious positions high above the ground. They fall into two categories: those who are in such a distressed state that they deserve a fireman or a policeman to risk their safety by trying to prevent them from jumping; the others are attention-seekers who, quite frankly, are best left alone. I had been involved in the rescue of a burglar who was swinging around on scaffolding trying to evade the police. Then, she, yes a lady burglar, decided that she would rather jump than be caught. That's when I decided that I would remain an onlooker; unless the firemen got into difficulties I wasn't going anywhere. I was 100ft up in the air waving around at the head of the TL with my life in the balance, remembering the promise I made to El. I felt safe on the ladder. I would have felt safe on the building; it's the getting from one to the other that's the scary bit.

The Fire Brigade has orders that limit the amount of assistance that we can give to the police. I am not allowed to risk the safety of the firemen unless it is a life-risk situation. I can provide equipment; I can show the police how to use it, but I cannot get involved with the apprehension of a suspect.

I told the inspector that, in my opinion, the Phantom would be best left alone. I suggested that we all go outside, leave him alone, and maybe he would disappear. He wasn't really committing a crime. The problem would go away and we would be able to go back to bed. At least that was what I was going to do. We went outside and after a while the police joined us. Fifteen minutes later we went back inside and the Phantom had returned to his underworld.

Another similar incident took place in Gresse Street, which is tucked away behind Tottenham Court Road and named after an artist who was nicknamed 'Greasy' because he was so fat. Passers-by had called the Brigade because two youths were calling for help from a seventh floor balcony.

I got the TL to work and I sent a crew up the internal staircase. The door to the flat was locked. The OIC of the TL, who was at the head of the ladder, told me that there was no emergency, but that the youths were just locked in. He told me that he could bring them down the ladder to save breaking in. As they were fit and well, I agreed and he walked them down one by one.

At about that time the police arrived and discovered the youths had been picked up by an older man and lured back to his flat. He had locked them in and had gone out for food and drink. When they saw the state of the flat, they realised that they were in trouble. There was evidence of drug abuse and a blood-stained mattress on the floor, and they were frightened. They had broken a window to get out onto the balcony. The police asked us to get away; then they lay in wait for the man to return.

A case of attention-seeking took place one busy Saturday night in Piccadilly Circus. A young man was performing on top of Tower Records, about four floors up. He was dancing up and down the parapet, evading the strong arm of the law. A crowd was gathering to such proportions that police had to take control. The crowd were whooping and cheering the acrobatic display. Like everyone, I was looking up, but I became aware of a strange presence. I looked round to see a C-P30 look-alike. Yes, the whole bit – a golden robot. Suddenly he shouted, 'Jump you boring bastard!' The police stepped in and arrested him. Even Luke Skywalker could not save him.

Sometimes you look down at the call-slip that is shoved into your hand with disbelief. 'Child hanging from a tenth floor window, Dufours Place, W1'. Most of Dufours Place is taken up by a single tower block. It is located very near to Carnaby Street and all the narrow passageways of east Soho. In the middle of the afternoon it is thronging with humanity and the crowds were gathering, transfixed by the spectacle that was unfolding.

As we were racing to the scene, I told Eddie, who was driving, that this must be a 'mickey' (fireman-speak for a malicious false alarm). We turned into Broadwick Street and, just where it widens at the junction with Berwick Street, I could clearly see the tower block, which really stands out as the tallest building around. There was a human form hanging from a window. I was still sceptical. I thought: a student prank, a blow up doll – and then it started wriggling.

It was a mentally disturbed old lady. She had climbed through a pivot-type window and was only suspended by her clothing, which had caught on the window handle.

There were police on the scene and I sent a crew chasing up 10 flights of stairs. This was not the time for a casual stroll; this was life and death. Outside, up went the ladders, but even at full extension (100ft), the man at the head could not reach the flailing woman. We had a Camiva TL, which has a limit stop that can be bypassed to get a further extension. This must only be done in extreme circumstances as the ladder can become unstable.

During all my time I had never seen this switch flipped in anger. One of my best men, Ian Cheeseman, was operating and Stephen Day 'Arnie' was up top already on tiptoes with arms outstretched. Would it reach? Would the extra weight of the woman on the ladder be enough to topple it over? As strong as he was, would Arnie be able to hold her, especially if she started to struggle?

The switch was flipped and the extra extension was being added just as the crew, who had gone upstairs, dragged the woman back inside. To the cheers of the crowd, we made-up the ladders bringing Arnie back to ground. Phew, back to the station and a quick change of pants!

The poor old dear was being looked after by Westminster's Mental Health unit. I told them that I thought it would be better if she kept on the ground floor.

All of these incidents have elements of danger, surprise and sadness. The desperate states that people get themselves into are not something that can go by without some effect on you.

People threatening to jump were regular calls for the TL. They would be called to all the popular suicide locations: Tower Bridge, Highgate Hill (aka Suicide Hill), and all the high places from which people jump. The two-man crew would set out unaccompanied on these missions, and they would join up with the local crews at the scene.

One of these calls turned out to be most distressing. That night my most reliable and experienced Leading Fireman, Mick Stanley, was in charge and Cheesy was the operator. They were called to The Holiday Inn, Coram Street, WC1; a hotel on Euston's ground. A young woman, who was full of drugs, was six floors up on the roof, and threatening to jump. She had already made an attempt at suicide. The ladders went up with Mick at the head, but as he neared she jumped. Mick managed to grab her clothing just as she launched herself but was unable to hang on. She slid out of his hands and she hit the ground right next to Cheesy.

I did my best to do a bit of counselling. I told them that I would get them over to Welfare but neither was interested. That did not mean that they got over it quickly, if they ever have.

There are two types of false alarm: those made with good intent and the malicious 'mickeys'. We started to get a series of imaginative mickeys. The more usual form is a call to a fire at some anonymous address such as, say, Oxford Street – no number given and made from a phone box or nowadays by a mobile phone. The calls we were receiving were much more complicated – crashed underground trains, cinemas on fire with people involved, and one was to a school bus overturned in Trafalgar Square with children trapped. As you go to these calls, half your brain is telling you that it is a false alarm, and the other half is going into disaster mode. We were pissed off, not only with the stupid calls, but that we might miss genuine emergencies.

Just as criminals return to the scene of their crime and arsonists like to see the results of their handiwork, false alarmers like to see the fire engines with their blue lights and sirens flashing by. These calls were so regular that we started to look out for the same face in the crowd. The boys spotted him first; well he was obvious – a short, round man with a beard walking on crutches.

He was a vagrant who used to hang around outside Leicester Square Underground station. This station is the nearest to the fire station. Some of the boys had heard this man speaking with a Welsh accent.

Every time we received a mickey, I asked Control if the caller spoke with a Welsh accent. As often as not they identified him. All I had to do now was nab him at the scene.

Late at night we received a call to James Street, Covent Garden, to another elaborate fire and I spotted him in Long Acre. Once we checked that there was no fire, and the call had been made by a Welsh man, I sent the boys to chase. We left the fire engines and were all running after a man going as fast as he could on crutches, back down Long Acre towards St. Martins Lane. We cornered him outside the Sussex public house, where he was so exhausted that he had to sit down on a bench. What do I do now? I quickly decided that I would have to make a citizen's arrest!

I didn't know what to say so I said, 'I arrest you in the name of The London Fire Brigade.' Fucking hell!

One of the firemen, Graham Underwood, 'Woody', who boxed for the Brigade had to be restrained. 'Can I give him a dig Guv?'

The Welsh man kept saying that it was not him; it was his brother. He didn't attempt to leave; well there was no point, surrounded by 10 ugly firemen! Once the trucks had negotiated the one-ways, I was able to call for the police over the radio. They took him away, and the next day I first had to attend Bow Street police station to give a statement, and then go straight into court.

I was told that he was pleading guilty and that he had previous. He had already been convicted for making false calls in his home town of Merthyr Tydfil. As I sat in the court, he was asked to plead and he said, 'Not guilty, it was not me – it was my brother!'

A prosecution lawyer had to be found before the trial could proceed. Finally, the judge remanded him for psychiatric reports. I did not have to re-attend court but I heard from the police that he was put away for six months. When he returned to his old haunts, there were no more calls. He must have been cured of his obsession – the blue lights!

Of course 'It was not me – it was my brother' entered the White Watch vocabulary.

I must tell you a little of Graham Underwood. He transferred into Soho from somewhere in the South East; Erith, I think. When I first met him I realised things would never be the same again. He looked like a muscular Del Boy/XXL Bob Hoskins' love child. Apart from the obvious 'Woody', during his time at the station other pertinent nicknames were created – 'Mad Dog' and 'Dangerous Derek'. He was a driver with a style all of his own. Once his mitts were locked on the steering wheel, that was where they stayed. It was not driving in the normal sense – more like wrestling. Most of the men who have driven me have been safe and sensible; there have only been one or two who made me nervous. Not because they were dangerous, but that they only had one speed – fast! Until I got used to Woody's unique style, I was, er…apprehensive.

The first time we sat around the mess table with him, the Sub. Officer looked at me with that knowing look saying, 'Hold on to the seat of your pants!' He was like a living, breathing, express train in everything he did. And funny – we were all in stitches.

Everything was a laugh including the infamous 'Showdown at Wendy's'. Woody's theory was that everyone should get the joke, but not everybody can understand the fireman's sense of humour. After a few pints in the West End, it is time to get something to eat. Everybody was supposed to laugh when the clown went straight to the front of the queue but some bloke took it seriously and off it went. Wendy's and Cambridge Circus turned into The Last Chance Saloon! The next day the Station Commander and I had to do some serious pleading round at Bow Street to make it go away.

The trouble was that you could not help but like him but it was touch and go at one time. I was on the brink of getting rid of him when we received a complaint from a local pub. I really had to read the riot act to some of them. It was time to shape up or ship out for all of them. This was the 'wide awake club' and he was the founding member. They were part of the watch who decided that sleep was for wimps and stayed up all night. They got into bed just before I came round to get them up, dead to the world.

Nothing pleased me more than when an officer at another station spoke to me complimenting my men. Westminster had a stinker one night and Peter Simpson needed a TL in a hurry to rescue some people from the upper floor. Mad Dog was spot on, first hit. There are some who can talk a good fire and there are others who just did the business. I was very lucky; I had a dozen of them.

*Chapter 24*

## ANGELS

The next conflagration was a horror. My increasingly wrinkled brow gained a few more lines that day.

The 30th April 1989 saw a 10-pump fire at Angels, theatre costumiers in Shaftesbury Avenue. They are Europe's largest suppliers to the film and television industry, and some of the costumes are priceless.

It was always a sure sign that we had a job nearby when the running call box outside the station was opened just before the bells went down. The tour was almost over and we were sitting at breakfast. The 'wide awakes' were off to Cornwall surfing for four days. They were in the mood already, wearing surf wear, Hawaiian shirts and Bermuda shorts. Sometimes I was just too tired to enforce the rules and it was funny.

I went downstairs; we nearly always ran down the stairs. When they built the new station, the pole they installed was too fat. It was too big to get your hands round and the only bloke who could do it was Alf – hands like Parma hams! The dutyman was already talking to a young man who, it turned out, worked for Angels.

Angels is just past Cambridge Circus and as we turned out, smoke was issuing, clouding the avenue. My first problem was the central reservation in the road outside. It made parking awkward, and proved to be a restriction throughout the whole operation. My Waikiki firemen, now in fire gear, were getting on with the usual BA and water.

The premises took up four terraced properties – a row of four shops with the same name above the door, with offices and store rooms on the four upper floors. Smoke was now showing at the upstairs windows.

I spoke to the man from Angels who, by now, had run back from the station. I discovered that the fire was in the basement and that there were no people inside.

I took a couple of the blokes with me to have a quick look inside. Where we entered, the smoke was not too thick, but as we moved further on through the interconnecting shops, it was getting thicker. We shut the doors and went back outside, and I sent the first assistance message. As the fire was reported to be in the basement, I already had four pumps in attendance. I just had to confirm with control that this was now a four-pump fire.

In the initial stages of a serious fire, there is so much to do you just have to rely on the men and the other officers. You try to do your part but it is impossible to control every move. You make sure that the BA control procedure is adhered to. Don't let the firemen enter the building without water, tell them which way to go, but what goes on inside is down to them. The actions of the men can be predicted but the spread of fire cannot. It is a wicked devil once stirred by the addition of oxygen; it leaps to its own defence.

The first BA crew inside included my Leading Fireman, Steve Coleman, and a senior Sub. Officer from Euston, a man who had seen more service than me. Anyone who has been in charge of a serious fire will tell you that you rely heavily on the information that you receive from inside the building. You are dependent on a quick and accurate assessment of the conditions. It takes a good man at the front that knows what to tell you.

The BA crew made their way to the back of the property to a staircase that led down to the basement, and they found a fire at the top of the stairs, which they extinguished. As it was so smoky, their vision was down to zero. The Sub. Officer told me over his personal radio that the fire was out and that I could start to ventilate. We only ventilate a building when the fire is out. This should be done by opening windows from the top of the building and working downwards. I found a couple of my blokes and told them to ventilate. As there was more than one staircase, I said to use one away from the fire-affected area.

As they were making their way upstairs, fire burst through the ground floor. The initial crew had not found the bulk of the fire, just part of it. At that stage I had no suspicion that it was arson and several fires had been lit. The whole of the basement area, full of clothes on racks, was now alight. Here we go again. Two firemen gasping for air on the first floor in part of the building, which had been relatively smoke free, and a fire that, instead of being out, is going like a train. Was nothing to go smoothly?

A ladder was pitched to the window and the men climbed down. I tried to recontact the BA men at the fire-face – were they in the basement? No reply – fuckin' radios! I kept calling; they could only have been about thirty foot away, but no reply. The fire was intensifying; the smoke was now pushing out into the street. Everyone was working flat out; I'm the only one with a pair of free hands. But as OIC, I am expected to remain outside in a position where I can control the incident. That was where I was, but I had to locate this crew. I am also expected to stay calm and collected – whatever happens.

I grabbed the man from Angels and asked him if there was a rear entrance. He led me to a single door, which I tried to put-in on my own, but it wouldn't budge. I was getting frantic, concerned for the safety of Steve Coleman, one of my oldest friends. Not just another fireman, although that would have been bad enough, this was a man I had known since 1974; my little girls had been his bridesmaids. I returned to the front of the building and there they were, streaming with sweat, smoke still rising from their clothes and low on air – fuckin' radios; they had not received my frantic messages.

At 0811hrs, another full attendance was ordered as a further call was received to a block of mansion flats around the corner in Charing Cross Road, which were being affected by heat and smoke from Angels. Only ten minutes had passed since our arrival, but it was like starting again. I had to call for more assistance: 'make pumps six', and get more BA men inside and down into the basement. In that 10 minutes I had used up so much nervous energy, I was exhausted.

At that point, a senior officer arrived, and as I had made pumps six, he had to take over control. He then made pumps ten. A multitude of senior officers of various ranks were soon arriving and the 'stop' was finally sent at 0935hrs. At one stage two firemen from Euston were taken to hospital with cuts caused by broken glass.

The stop message read, 'Shop and Offices, five floors, and basement 20 × 20 metres. 50% of basement, 25% ground, first and second floors; staircase from basement to second floor damaged by fire. Five jets. BA'. Same as all calls. (Seven calls had been received to the same incident.)

The only good thing to come out of it was that the nasty senior officer who rebuked my suggestions over Oxford Circus was reported to the Fire Brigade Union for not complying with BA regulations. He had been wandering around inside the fire, when he should have been wearing BA and booked in with control. Oh, and the only way we could have established any kind of contact was with the Diktron communications equipment!

Once the fire was out, I was able to get a look inside; the amount of damage in the basement was amazing. I made my way up to the roof. On the top floor I noticed that the heat had been so intense that the plastic fire alarm call-points had melted. The photographs of that fire taken from outside and above the building do not do it justice.

Arson was confirmed. There were several seats of fire, but who set it? The man who came running to the station, the man who stood beside me and saw my desperation at the prospect of losing firemen! I don't know what he was up to, probably trying to gain some sense of importance. That must be some kind of syndrome. 'I was the one who found the fire – aren't I clever?'

I have to say that when I got back to the station, I had had it. I was so tired, wondering why on earth I was doing this job. No amount of pay or job satisfaction could compensate for the physical and mental bashing I had taken. Nobody else knew what I was going through – except Shiner. Silly old fool, he found me and gave me some of his special medicine, offered a few words of understanding, and made things all right. The temperate Chilton, no alcohol on stations, no drinking on duty, was never more grateful for a large whiskey.

Nobody tells you when you go for promotion of the stresses and strains of the job. There were times when I just had to put the responsibility out of my mind. The bells go down in the middle of the night and you are called to an important building, let's say the Institute of Contemporary Art, housed in a magnificent Nash building in The Mall. There is an entrance to this building in Carlton House Terrace where some of the most cherished buildings in London stand. We would get regular calls to their AFA, usually late at night, after some function. I always did what I was supposed to do: search the building and make sure that the fire alarm would reset, then wait a while just in case it reactivated before returning to the station. Then I go back to my room and my bed. It is then that my mind would go into overdrive. What if I had missed something?

AFA calls were a pain. There were times when we would have to stay in attendance at an AFA waiting for the key holder to arrive. I would always try to gain entry if I could do it without causing damage, but there was no point in smashing into a building when you were 99% sure that it was a false alarm. The local residents would complain about the constant ringing alarm but we would just have to wait for a key holder, who was making their way from somewhere in deepest Essex, and you could not leave the place without inspecting the interior. So there you are at 2am, sitting outside in a cold fire engine waiting for a couple of hours in the confined space, which is not a pleasant place, especially after a curry supper. No matter where you are or whatever you are doing, a fireman farts! You look round disdainfully and all they innocently say is, 'What, what?'

Another real annoyance was the rogue alarm, which would repeatedly self-actuate all through the night. This was even more frustrating on a Sunday night when nobody was about. After three calls to the same alarm, I would take the fuses out; it was obvious that they were defective and would not work correctly even if there was a real fire. Also four fire engines were tied-up for a considerable time on a futile exercise and possibly missing a bona fide emergency.

The thing that I held the most precious at Soho was the firemen and officers. Not just my watch, but also everyone working at the station and the adjacent stations. In my 18 years I have only ever had harsh words with one man from another watch and that was soon forgotten. Everyone obeyed the rules, even my version of the rules. They only needed telling once. It was also very rare that I had any problem with stand-bys as I always pointed out my idiosyncrasies when they reported to me. I used to tell them that this is my station and everything in it belongs to me, so look after it. Keep your boots on the fire engine and your feet off the chairs and do as you're told. All in a light-hearted manner. The youngsters looked at me with fear, but the more senior men realised that it was just a case of 'you scratch my back, and I'll scratch yours'. More naval rhetoric; the scars left from the cat o' nine tails itched to distraction.

It is just simple politeness, but also a Brigade Order that all Brigade personnel must report to the OIC if they want to enter the station outside their normal working times, except for the hour before they are due to come on duty. Due to its position, the station personnel would always want to park their cars to go shopping or to go out with their families. That was an added bonus; I got to meet their families as well.

The constant coming and goings of the firemen from other watches helped generate the great atmosphere that I believe was unique. I could walk into the mess – the social centre of the station – and enter the best room any fireman could wish to walk into. I never experienced this bonhomie at any other station. How I miss it now that I am retired. The humour was spontaneous and would not easily transfer to paper. That is, unless you can find some amusement in the following. A moustache was regularly drawn on the TV screen with a chinagraph pencil. Then there were screams of laughter when the moustache lined up with a face! When they were short of decorations for the Christmas tree, mashed potato took the place of snow! Dipping your biscuit in another, unsuspecting, person's cup of tea. Such laughs, such fun!

It has to be understood that this is a rough, tough job and the men have to be equal to that. A consequence of this is the way they talk to each other. The language is strong and so are the insults. Not many subjects are taboo. Only wives and children are excluded. Even grandmothers are not safe!

I can still remember the first time that I sat in Soho's mess room (it was on the ground floor at the old station – Bow to the east). It was located at the front of the building, with windows which looked out onto Shaftesbury Avenue. There was a separate section where the officers ate, known as the 'piggery'. When I stood-by as a driver on the Red Watch, I found it hard to understand what the Reds were talking about. The conversations were punctuated with their own slang, which I only began to understand once I was stationed there. Then there were all the nicknames. You could go for years not knowing their real names. Some of the blokes had several names and you just had to guess who was being spoken about. Nowadays, in these modern times, nicknames are frowned upon. To me it was just another indication of acceptance. The more popular you were, the more names you had. I never had a nickname – at least not one I've heard!

In the old days, before mobile phones were the size of a battery, the only means of contacting a fireman on duty was the exchange telephone. This was a pay phone hidden away somewhere on the station. At the old station, it was in a booth on a staircase landing. The phone would be answered and a shout would go out, 'So and so wanted on the A and B!' This referred to the A and B buttons on an old-fashioned pay phone. You would make your way to the phone booth where the light would be out; the bulb was always broken. As you were about to enter the darkness, one of the blokes would leap out and frighten the life out of you. At the new station, we got so fed up with messages being written on the wall behind the phone that we put up a white board. This was then called the 'wailing wall!'

The prank of hiding in the dark was transferred to the basement gear room where we hung our fire gear when off duty. Put your hand in, along the wall, to find the light switch and another hand would cover it! Stand by for a heart attack! You would never enter the gear room when the lights were out; the experienced learnt to switch on their torches. As they say, 'If you don't possess a wicked, twisted sense of humour and the skin of a rhino, don't join the Fire Brigade!'

The equal opportunity regime had reached such ridiculous proportions that when a new recruit was posted to a station, the instructions state that nicknames are not allowed. In one case, when a young man was posted to Euston, the whole watch was being lectured by a woman from headquarters about the rights and wrongs of nicknames and the treatment of recruits. She asked the new boy if he would find being given a nickname offensive and, if so, what would he find offensive? This young man was just about to enter Fire Brigade folklore, big-time. He said, 'I wouldn't mind as long as it wasn't something horrible like 'fuckface'.' What! The whole room went into a stunned silence. When the story filtered down to Soho, we were just impressed.

As soon as we got our next call with Euston, I wanted to know who this man was. Innocent and polite as you like! He was never called by this name, but he was given special privileges whenever he stood-by with us. I would even offer him my seat in the mess – a demigod!

What nonsense, nicknames not being allowed. It's all part of it, part of the job. I think it is primarily a male thing but in any group, any team, any service, nicknames are created. It has something to do with bonding, acceptance and, dare I say it, affection in the er … most manly of ways. Some of them are ingenious, others more basic and simply a 'Y' on the end of a name. I have known them to originate from Dickens or some other obscure character hidden away in history – anything that characterises the individual. It is amazing how creative they can be. There was a man on our Red Watch simply called 'singer'. Now where did that come from? There was a singer with the same name. Hardly anyone would have heard of him, but Paul Hale was Casey Jones and he sang 'The Runaway Train'. It took me years to fall in.

When I was a Leading Fireman, the Soho mess room was a madhouse. At any time, day or night, it was incredibly noisy but nothing could be compared with the times they decided to get out the Escalado. Escalado is a table-top game and it is based on horse racing. The Whites would pick their horse and bets were placed. I was the new boy and every new boy was encouraged to bet on the white horse. The different coloured horses were arranged on the starting line, a handle was wound and the horses raced up the table. The bloke doing the winding was urged-on by the screaming mob! The white horse always shot off into the lead, but fell back just before the finish. I thought it was a one-off but it did it every time! The betting was only nominal, but the poor old Leading Fireman was fleeced. The screams encouraging the horses were unbeliev-able; alarmed passers-by would stand outside the window trying to make out the havoc which was resounding out into the avenue.

There was no better time than meal times, especially supper, which we took at 2030hrs irrespective of the Brigade's attempts to change our meal times. If the calls allowed, we would all try to sit down together.

A good mess is essential for good morale. If there were any problems doing the cooking or getting shopping, I wouldn't think twice – I would do it.

There was no getting away from it. The mess manager was the most important bloke on the watch. 'The Food Baron' was far more important than the OIC. We had three great mess managers. Roger Borg, who is Maltese and has never been able to shed his nickname (even his family call him 'Joe'), had fingers in many pies (no pun intended). He could get you tickets for any show in the West End. He and Steve Short once sold every seat for one performance of the 'Phantom of the Opera' to raise funds for the Welfare Fund. The whole theatre was full of firemen and their families. Besides his wheeling and dealing, Joe was a fantastic cook and a man with a great sense of humour. Eventually he suffered a bit of bad health and he had to leave the station for a less strenuous job in the Brigade. Joe and the Phantom of the Opera were to feature in another Soho sensation.

A call came in during supper. Fire at Her Majesty's Theatre, Haymarket. The performance was in full swing and an electrical fire had developed in the basement. By the time we arrived, the theatre had been evacuated. There was Joe and his wife standing with the audience on their wedding anniversary! The damage to cables was so extensive that the per-formance had to be cancelled. An American lady asked me how she was going to get her money back. She had paid a vast amount of money to a ticket tout and would only receive face value from the theatre. Once the job was over, we were invited in for a drink. There cannot have been many more bizarre scenes. A gang of smutted firemen and Christine, The Phantom, and the cast all in costume, happy because they were finishing early sharing a drink. Coke only for the firemen!

Nothing could be further from my mind that, in years to come, my association with 'The Phantom' would become much more personal and special; in fact, a special relationship.

After Joe, it was Eddie Martin's turn to take over the mess keys (each watch has a separate, secure, pantry and fridge). Eddie, like Joe was a survivor of the harassment case, and he stayed with me until he retired.

He had the sharpest tongue in the mess and anyone, no matter who, would get a lashing. Contractors, who were carrying out repairs or maintenance in the kitchen and its surrounds, were reduced to a quivering mass if anything was not quite correct. He was my enforcer upstairs. The same went for anyone who did not observe the correct messroom etiquette. Wash up your own cup and never make a cup of tea without asking if anyone else wanted one; this included me. No one was left out, especially visiting senior officers. It was great. Stand-bys from other stations were another ready target for correction. They were already at a disadvantage being in unfamiliar surroundings. It was best when they had some spunk and gave it back to him – then we would all cheer! The poor old standby, if he left something on his plate he would get, 'What's wrong with that mate?' That's how he got the nickname – Ed the Bastard.

One evening I walked into the mess and found a standby from some station out in the sticks who had not reported to me on his arrival. A red rag to the old Station Officer. He stood up to apologise and towered about 12 inches above me! I let him have my seat, and would have given him my supper if he'd wanted it!

Eddie was great, a constant source of humour. He would pronounce certain words wrongly and these words became instant 'watch-speak'. 'Windowscreen, binoclearars, peter bread'; fuckin' peter bread! I gave up trying to make him say croissants correctly.

He appeared to be tireless. Not only was he the mess manager, he drove the ladders, did the shopping and generally worked his nuts off. On the fireground, if anything needed doing, Eddie had done it; I'd never have to ask. This leads on to a short tale of mismanagement. In the early days, the second Station Commander at Soho was a nice man. I thought he was a good chap; he just made an elementary mistake when we picked up our first job with him.

It became a six-pump fire at the St. Martins College of Art in Charing Cross Road. To the unfamiliar, Charing Cross Road in the early evening is gridlocked, a seething mass of humanity and stationary traffic. Smoke was belching out of the second floor windows with persons reported. Fortunately the hundreds of students had long gone, and there were just a few cleaners and maintenance staff left in the building. As usual, every-one is working inside, mostly in BA. So that only left the drivers, Eddie and me outside sending messages and getting water, coping with the traf-fic and the theatre crowds. In London nobody goes around you, not even for fires! Nothing is more important than getting to the theatre on time.

Until the take pumps arrived, we were flat out, especially Eddie who was running out twin lines of hose. The first hydrant was broken, so he had to find another and then run out a jet to go into the building. By the time the Commander arrived, Eddie was having a well-deserved breather but the fool couldn't resist having a go at him, daring to know why he wasn't inside helping his mates! That was it, off the Richter scale. The poor man spent the next six months apologising.

By the way, that was the job where Cheesy rescued the shop dummy, the same that I had sent 'persons reported' for! 'Cheesboy' was a new boy then but destined to become a 'Soho Lifer'.

When Eddie retired, Steve Day took the helm. Another control freak who for years had been called 'Arnie' because of his fitness regime, but we soon realised that another nickname was much more appropriate – 'Napoleon'. He was raised in a Fire Brigade family. His father started in London but retired as a senior officer in Kent. Both his father and I took every opportunity to push him towards promotion, but with no success. Napoleon admitted that he had no intention of leaving Soho and that his only ambition was to become mess manager. I thought he was joking! Who could blame him and who was I to argue?

It was a habit of mine that after the evening office work was done, and the rest of the watch were either at work or out on calls, I would inspect the station and catch the same people every time for leaving their lockers unlocked. I would then make my way to the mess and chat to whoever was cooking. They didn't realise that, at times, these conversations were my saviour; they were all great suppliers of common sense and a conduit to the feelings of the watch. During these interludes I would help with the cooking. Having run the mess on two occasions, I did realise the thanklessness of the task.

Prior to Soho, mess food had been pretty basic fare and the suppers were usually pretty unhealthy fry-ups. Naturally, at Soho even food was branded with substitute titles. 'Clutch plates' – beef burgers. 'Babies' heads' – steak and kidney puddings. 'Tortoises' – meat pies. 'Cow juice' – milk, and, for some reason, tea was a 'mug o' spit!'

Apart from the damage to our arteries, these meals needed constant attention and successful cooking was a gamble. This was because the station was so busy and the mess manager was on the run. Any cooking had to be removed from the gas and re-started after each call out. As the mess manager's cooking abilities and our tastes became more adventurous, it was realised that one-pot concoctions were the solution to all the interruptions. Therefore, chillies, curries and pasta dishes became the new tradition.

The messroom was not just the room where we ate, but also the TV room. The television was switched on all the time. I would often find it talking to an empty room after returning from a shout when everyone else returned to bed. The telly could not even be switched off at meal times because the pressure of the banter became too much. We would try, but it always had to be switched back on. It was the lion's den; if you could hold your own in there, your survival as a fireman was guaranteed.

All the great occasions of 18 years were observed in that room. All the great sporting achievements and failures, I can think of no better place to watch England play football. We were on duty on the night England were knocked out of Euro '96. No sooner had the final whistle gone than we were out to the riots that spread outwards from Trafalgar Square.

When there was a total eclipse of the sun, there was a row of firemen out on the flat roof looking through little holes in bits of paper and special glasses.

I always said that the hardest part of my job took place in the mess each year, when I had to draw the names out of the hat to see who was going to get some leave at Christmas. There was nothing I could do about it. There were only a certain amount of men who could be on leave at the same time. We had decided that this was the fairest method; it was just miserable to have to do it and tell family men that they had to work Christmas Day.

From the mess room, a door leads outside to the flat roof and, up until 1999, it was an uninviting paved area that had a couple of bench and table combinations and a self-built barbecue.

In the spring of that year, the Brigade was contacted by the producers of the BBC programme 'Home Front in the Garden'. They wanted to do a make-over at a fire station with a terrace. They were offered a choice of two: Clerkenwell and us. Of course, Soho was chosen. Not only did we have this big rectangular, bare canvass, they could also make an additional feature by touring the ground. I had to follow a car towing another car mounted on a trailer in a fire engine around the ground while being filmed. We did that trip four times before it was a wrap!

The men who did the actual construction admitted that they were amazed at the place – the constant in and out of the fire engines and the humour of the men. They were so struck that they made their own video separately from the film crew and it was based on 'Dad's Army'. It had us in fits. They would arrive very early in the morning, like all of us, to avoid the traffic, and were greatly amused to find some of the Whites sleeping under the Soho moon in the middle of their handiwork. Whenever there was any hot weather, some of the men would sleep outside, as once temperature inside the station had raised, it would not cool down.

The transformation of the terrace was great – not just a make-over, but quite a substantial creation. It pleased everyone in some way and the Whites were filmed at the end of the project to get their opinion. We were all sitting on the new raised circular bench and spontaneously they wound-up the rest of the Brigade by saying that now, not only did we have the best station in the Brigade and the best ground, we also had the best garden. It was just a wind-up, but some fell for it, especially a fireman from Battersea who sent us a great long e-mail giving us the operational statistics from his station! Get a life mate!

A story about the terrace pre-'Home Front'. One of the old hands on the Red Watch, John Wilkinson, a 'lifer' who has now passed away, made an effort to brighten up the place. He bought some growbags and tried to cultivate tomatoes. They never came to much – small, green marbles and they were never going to be edible. Magically, overnight they all became magnificently ripe. Somebody, patiently, hand-painted John's tomatoes bright red! We all laughed, but 'Wilks' didn't, but then he never did! God bless him.

As Christmas nears, each Watch sets a day aside to have their Christmas dinner. Even if you were on leave, you would try to get in for the meal. We would all put in a bit extra for the meal and have a whip-round for the cooks' Christmas box, which we handed over that day because of the extra work. If there was ever going to be a meal that was interrupted, this was it. If not during the meal, then during the dishing-up, the bells would sound. In accordance with Brigade Orders, these were dry occasions for the Whites. As the years went by and I mellowed, I started to contribute a few bottles of wine. We still had to be sensible – professional firemen after all. One year my fire engine went out and was out for some time at a flood. When I arrived back and returned to the mess, I found them drinking the wine straight out of the bottles! Woody was pouring wine into his mouth until it overflowed and spilled down his shirt. I was just about to explode – they'd filled the bottles with water – bastards!

Once the Christmas dinner shift was over, we would invade the West End for a White Watch piss-up, but that's a whole separate chapter.

## Chapter 25

# COOKS, CRABS AND FEARS
# (THE BEST AND WORST OF TIMES)

Occasionally the whole station became involved in a jape. The most memorable was born out of a seemingly weird fascination with crustaceans. The Whites had a job in a Chinese supermarket. The call came in after supper, but before we had washed up. We got back past midnight and the dirty plates were left in the sink. When this happens the dutyman would usually wash up while he made the tea at 0700hrs. Unbeknown to the dutyman and me, a dead spider crab had made its way from the supermarket in a galvanised bucket and had been concealed in the depths of the kitchen sink. I heard the dutyman's screams from my room. When we went off duty, we donated the crab to the Blue Watch. 'We are the Blue Watch; everybody hates us, but we don't care!' A poor, sad bunch, deprived of friendship, they adopted the crab as a pet until it began to stink!

As a consequence of this, the fable of 'Colin the Crab' was created. The spider crab was replaced with a large, vibrantly coloured plastic crab, which the Blue Watch allowed to become the station mascot. He took up residence in the mess room false ceiling. He travelled the world in firemen's luggage and was photographed in the most exotic of settings, perched on some lovely ladies who were only too pleased to oblige when they learnt of Colin's high status. He sent postcards from Australia, New Zealand and Thailand; he even came with my family to the South of France.

Poor Colin became the victim of a kidnapping. The Greens held him captive and a ransom note was sent to the Blues. When this was not taken seriously, an amputated claw was sent. The Blues mounted a rescue mission and found him in a Green Watch locker, cellotaped, blindfolded and mutilated. The kidnapper had to be tortured!

On the subject of the Green Watch, Manchester Square were pulling a fire engine around the West End collecting money for some good cause. As they went up the avenue and past Soho, the Greens, very considerately, decided to cool the pullers with buckets of water. Well, it was December. The Guvnor of the Square swore vengeance. He has retired now so there should be no problem in my telling this tale. Early one morning the Square's trucks arrived at Soho heavily armed. They climbed into the station and mounted a dawn commando-style raid. The attack involved copious supplies of water and smoke bombs. That'll teach them!

Adjacent to the mess is the kitchen and from there a whole catalogue of stories were shaped around the station cook. Most station cooks are women of a certain age, and for a long time they were the only females working in fire stations. They were usually local ladies, who lived near enough to get in for 0730hrs to cook the breakfast. They could be relied on to produce homely, basic food, keep the kitchen clean and tidy and just about save you from food poisoning.

It is naturally accepted that a good cook is a protected species; they are treated politely and with respect. If anyone was rude to the cook, they felt the wrath of the whole watch. It's just that the Brigade would occasionally employ oddballs, and then seemed incapable of getting rid of them.

When I was at Westminster there was a large German lady who used to soften the marg by massaging it in her warm hands. (The mess could never run to butter.) If she happened to get any under her fingernails, she would simply scrape it out with another nail! Not a lady to cross. I was frightened to go into the kitchen. When she left, the station had no cook to do the Christmas dinner. Nobody wanted her back but the Blue Watch were working on Christmas day and managed to persuade her to return, just for that day. She cooked the turkey and the Blue Watch told her she could take some home for herself. They got a few slices of breast each, and Doris lugged the remainder of a 20lb turkey home in her shopping bag!

The next cook at Westminster was called Marjorie and she was crazy. She would run out of the kitchen screaming that she had seen a ghost. She wore a plastic shower cap while she was cooking.

Back in those days we used to have station fire drills. If there is a fire inside a fire station, there is a procedure we have to follow. The dutyman has to inform control, a firefighting crew has to be organised and the fire engines are driven out of the station to safety. The call bells had to be operated manually, as none of the old fire stations had such a thing as a fire alarm. As the most likely place for a fire to start was the kitchen, the cook had to be given training to summon us to the kitchen. At

Westminster, the kitchen was on the first floor. Marjorie, wearing her shower cap, was trained to run out onto the balcony at the rear of the building, banging a saucepan with a metal spoon and shout, 'Fire!'.

One day we were at breakfast and Marjorie had left the kitchen. After a time we noticed that she was missing and we heard a man shouting. We went to investigate. Marjorie had heard a strange moaning and had gone right down to the far end of the station, where the window cleaner had trapped his fingers in a sash window. She promptly fainted, probably thinking it was the station ghost and the window cleaner had to shout for help!

Back in the '70s and '80s, Soho had a fine old lady called Frances. Most of the time you would not have known she was there; she got on with her work and went home. She was reaching the end of her service when I went there and a replacement had to be found.

This was the time when the Brigade was just getting into equal opportunity mode and cooks could only be employed from the Job Centre. It didn't pay that well, so you can imagine the type of people who applied from our local Job Centre.

The first man they took on was a 'gentleman of the road'. His address was the local men's hostel. He would cook our dinners. We would get normal-sized meals and he sat out in the kitchen with a plate piled to overflowing. There was a side door that led from the kitchen out into Gerrard Place, and we discovered that he was passing out food to his mates. They were standing in line at the latest free soup kitchen. This was also the door where the butcher and the milkman would deliver their goods and later call back for their money. That was when the mess manager could not be found for love, and especially money.

Next we had a very nice lady who appeared to do nothing all day but read. This was in the days when the Station Officer had the authority to sack the cook. This particular Station Officer was a graduate of the Soho school of charm. He told the cook that she had to leave. When she asked why, she was told: 'Because you can't fuckin cook!' Another one to enter the annuals of station history.

Next came Greta; she lived in Paddington and was straight out of the typical fire station cook mould. Basic food, and a bit like your mum. She knitted cuddly toys, which we bought for the kids and she gave the money to charity. If she had travel problems, the TL would go round to her flat and bring her to work. (Don't tell the Brigade!) You could wind her up rotten and then she would start to curse us in language quite unbefitting a lady. We looked after Greta when she retired. A nice present, flowers, and a proper do in a pub.

It was then that we were invaded by a harridan; a woman who was as unpredictable as the weather. I'm sorry but she was unstable. As she was African, we had to be particularly careful that she was treated correctly, but she tried us to the limits. Some of her peculiar exploits were just indescribable. All the watches were reporting her crazy behaviour to the Station Commander. By the time he took us seriously, it was too late; she had gone past her probation time and therefore could not be dismissed for simply not being up to standard. Because of his neglect, we had to suffer two years of madness.

She was a lousy cook and spoilt more food than she prepared. The mess managers would give her instructions, which she did not carry out, but there was nothing we could do about it. She complained about non-existent racial comments, which I had to investigate and report. Nobody was stupid enough to make any such comments. A West Indian cook had been our weekend cook for years, and he was a smashing chap. Marius worked at Soho for at least 15 years with no complaints from either side of the serving hatch – another cook who had his own retirement do and went back home to St. Lucia, the proud owner of his own fire helmet!

Eventually the Brigade listened to sense, but not until after this woman stood on the draining board and shouted out the kitchen window that she was being raped! What did they do with her? She was moved to Knightsbridge where she made them suffer until she was moved again. The Brigade still did not have the ability to sack her.

By the way, at one time Knightsbridge had a gay cook who became so involved in the men's 'wellbeing' that he used to come into work early and brought round the early morning tea. As a stand-by it was very scary to find this man standing by your bed asking, 'And how many sugars would you like?'

As another little aside, a friend of mine, another Station Officer, was being stalked by the cook at his station. She waited for him after work and would phone his home. The Brigade investigated my mate's complaints, but the woman was only moved. If the roles had been reversed, any fireman behaving like that would have been sacked.

After the mad woman, we were sent a lovely young lady who was a good cook but with a distinct disadvantage – she was a vegetarian who would not touch meat! On her first day, Eddie handed her four pounds of lambs' liver!

Our next long-term cook was a man who told us that he lived with his brother. But when we saw his brother, there was absolutely no similarity in their looks. He was a just about all right as a cook. He caused us no problems. He was reliable, and as we were so grateful to be rid of the mad woman, he stayed with us for several years. The cause of his demise was neglect by the Brigade.

I started to get complaints from the men that they were suffering from skin rashes. Not just my watch, but all the watches were complaining. I did the usual and raised the flag. Samples of the water were analysed and were found to be below standard. The water storage tanks were inspected and it was found that they were dirty and needed relining. Instead of getting a reputable company to carry out the work, 'Arizona Builders' turned up. The substance they were using to repair the tanks was dangerous to breathe, but they were working without protection in a confined area and this stuff was drifting all through the station. Also, this product should have been left for a week to cure before refilling the tanks – as soon as it was touch-dry they filled-up. The cook was the first to use the water and it burnt his hands. He finally had to resign due to the damage caused to his hands. Just imagine if anyone had taken a drink of that water.

We had to take the station off the run. A separate water supply had to be installed and a mobile washhouse was installed in the yard. We later found out that the tanks did not even comply with the Water By-Laws and new tanks had to be installed. This went on for months. Eventually we were given the all clear to use the water supply, but the men were still coming out in rashes. Then they blamed the air supply equipment, so that all had to be cleaned and upgraded. Still there was no cure. Now it was the atmosphere in the West End that was the problem, and as they could do nothing about that, it was a case of like it or lump it. Is it any wonder that station personnel are so disgruntled with the management?

Oh, and they also came to test our ears. Somebody somewhere was bothered that the constant sounding of the sirens in the confined space of the fire engine cab was damaging our ears. I never 'heard' the outcome of that survey!

Being a fireman you will often be asked about the extremes of your job. What is the worst thing you have ever seen? The funniest? And the best? Not much is actually funny; it may be strange, it may be fantastic but every fire or special service is somebody else's disaster. We were often in fits of laughter at things in the street, like the day we were driving up Tottenham Court Road and saw a completely naked woman lying on the pavement sunbathing. The shoppers were simply walking around her! We stopped to see if she was all right but she was far, far away with the fairies. We were close to a psychiatric unit attached to University College Hospital. The police had to be called. The rest of the Brigade who were listening to the radio were then able to share in the amusement when I had to state the reason why I needed the police to attend.

The funniest? Well, if I have to. We were called to smoke issuing from a ground floor mansion flat in quite a posh block in Bloomsbury. There was indeed smoke issuing – quite a lot of it. I banged on the door and it was eventually answered by a rather bedraggled, middle-aged woman. Oh, all right, just a bit older than me. Her hair was all over the place; she was wearing a dressing gown and stank of drink.

She said in broad Scottish accent, 'What do you want?'

She was oblivious to the fact that her flat was on fire. The smoke was eye-stingingly thick. When we got inside, the place was a real dead-dog shithole, with filth and rubbish everywhere. We followed the smoke into the kitchen. The woman was still with us proclaiming that she did not want us in her flat. In the semi-derelict greasy, grimy, kitchen a pound of pork sausages was being incinerated under the grill. The woman looked around in disbelief.

'Look at ma fookin' kitchen!'

Once we recovered from split sides, we started to open windows to let the smoke out.

Woody, who had been searching the rest of the flat called me. 'Come and look at this Guvnor.'

I went into what could be loosely called a bedroom, which was also smoke-filled, and found her old man still asleep in bed!

Also in the running for funniest was a call to a fire in a ladies hairdressers in George Street, W1. This was late at night. The whole of the ground floor was smoke-logged but I could not see any fire. Instead of smashing the glass front door, I told the men to have a look for an entrance where a forced entry would cause less damage, and would not entail us having to wait for a key holder to attend. They managed to slip the lock of a door, which led into the basement, which was connected to the shop. The smoke was thick but it was not hot. As we are searching in the darkness for the source, the shop stereo goes full blast into the original James Bond theme! We all fell about; Fireman Robbie Ervin '2-Bob', the current watch loose-wire and genuinely funny man, was at it again.

I discovered that the cause of the smoke was a cigarette, which had been partially stubbed out in a plant pot that was now full of smouldering compost.

The worst. Coping with persons under trains on the Underground is the worst. I don't care what anyone says, but you never get used to it; it just gets a bit easier to handle because you know what to expect. It's not like a burnt body or people run over or trapped in crashed cars. Firstly, you have to cope with the oppressive atmosphere of the Underground. Then the smell in a confined area. Then the danger of crawling along underneath a train to reach the casualty.

The whole thing starts back at the station when the call comes in and the dutyman shouts, 'One Under. Piccadilly Circus.'

The call slip is thrust into your hand. You read it for yourself just hoping that it could possibly be wrong. You then start to drag on your fire gear, turn to the blokes in the back and remind them what equipment you want them to take into the station. The regular fire engines don't carry all the gear needed for lifting or moving trains; this comes in on the Heavy Rescue Unit, usually from Euston.

The trucks arrive at the Underground, which has usually been closed or at least is in the process of being evacuated. The station is unusually quiet. Everybody is coming out as you are going in. All you can hear is the firemen's boots and the clanking of equipment being carried. You make the long journey down to the platform. It's long because you don't really want to go down. Your body is going through the motions and it is sheer willpower that's making you go on. You know what you are going to see and do. I know this bears no comparison to the work of rescue squads at major earthquakes, and it's small fry to anyone who has had to recover war-torn bodies. I know that it's our job and we have to get on with it, but it's still grim.

When you reach the platform there is a gaggle of people, station staff and transport police, standing where the casualty is trapped. We have to ensure that the track power has been switched off. I cannot allow men onto the track until this is confirmed. British transport police will go on the track with the power on, but we have strict orders to the contrary.

Then there is the ripped and mangled body. Oh, why can't they just take a handful of pills and stay in bed? I know it's stupid, but it's neither the blood nor the smell; it's the whole thing – the clogging atmosphere on the platform, the dirt and the dust.

If they are still alive, we have to try and free them, but if they are obviously dead the train is rolled off the body. There is always 'that moment' when the body comes into sight. Then it has to be lifted onto the platform and taken away. Horror strikes again and another image is branded into the memory.

The trapped, live casualties are the worst. The wounds are big and dirty from the train dust. The carriage may have to be jacked; it may have to be levered away from the tunnel wall. Any actions where the train has to be moved are particularly dangerous. It is essential that the firemen under the train can hear each other. I have had to shout at the top of my voice to get the ever-increasing crowd of officials gathering on the platform to be quiet.

Whatever the firemen have to do, one under is always a shit job.

The peculiarities of each incident stay in my mind. One Christmas Eve we got one at Oxford Circus. It was a smartly dressed man and he had gone under with his shopping, which was spread along the track with his body. After the body had been removed, I was walking away when I saw something on the track. It was long strip of skin that was fused to the live rail. A London Transport man was still down on the track. I pointed it out to him and he just pulled it off with his fingers and dropped it in a rubbish bin.

The police were concerned that one at Piccadilly Circus had been pushed. Apparently there was a gang of men who were suspected of a series of pushes. This poor man was decapitated. We went under the train just to be certain, only because that is what we have to do, but I was glad when the police decided that it was a crime scene and the body had to be left in position.

They weren't all that horrible. We did get some out alive. On one occasion I had to get the Air Ambulance down to a man who was badly injured in Embankment Station. The helicopter landed in Embankment Gardens next to the station.

On another occasion the blokes were crawling under the train, only to be met by the person crawling out who wanted to know what all the fuss was about. Another man jumped so far and so fast that he was completely missed by the train, and only injured himself when he hit the opposite wall!

But the worst, the very worst for me did not involve a body. We were called to Tottenham Court Road in the early hours, long after the tube had stopped running. A drunken young man had tried riding the train in the gap between carriages and had been crushed. The body had fallen onto the platform and had been removed by the ambulance, but we had been called to wash down the platform. There was so much congealed blood, thick-like, soup. Even now, writing this, I'm going a bit funny. Sometimes, when I was awoken by the bells, I went into a bit of shock. Especially if I was really tired and had only just gone to sleep, I used to feel dazed and nauseous. I had seen much worse sights; it must have just have struck all the wrong notes.

When people demean my job, when some soppy politician tells me that I have the skills equivalent to that of a motor mechanic, that's when I would like them to see the firemen struggling to free the ripped and torn body of some poor screaming, moaning wretch who really only wants to die. To see them do it tenderly and humanely, all the time under a train. Just try and imagine the last bit – under a train.

What of the men's reactions, what about the effect on the new boy who gets his first, what about the old hand who won't tell you that he never wants to go to another? None of us is impervious to these horrors; it's just that you are a man amongst men and you're not supposed to show any weakness.

Every successful fire was the best. When you got back to the station, the empty BA sets were being serviced, the blokes were dirty and the morale was up around ceiling height. Those were fires that allowed me no self-recrimination – I had done everything right. Boy what a great feeling that was!

One of those happened in June 1990. Premier House is a big office block in Oxford Street. It had six floors and the fire was on the third. We were called at 2038hrs; the first call stated that the fire was at the rear of the building in Soho Square.

Soho Square, to the unfamiliar, is another twenty-four hour sea of humanity. In isolation it could be a well-kept square in the middle of any respectable village. At its centre is a black and white, part-timbered gardener's tool shed that has stood since 1870. There are two churches in the Square: The French Protestant and St Patrick's Roman Catholic.

It's a good job they are a good distance apart. One day, lumps of masonry started to fall into the street from St. Patrick's. We were called to an unsafe structure. We had a hydraulic platform on the run at the time; the ladders were off the run, which was fortunate as the vicar wanted to look at the damage. I went up with him. He showed no signs of fear, unlike me. I knew the operator! He had great fun, an intrepid man of the cloth who even laughed at my paltry jokes about being closer to God. I had to call for scaffolders, and stayed in place until they could make the place safe.

When we entered the square in the north west corner, the flames were bursting out of the third floor windows. At that time our only access was through a narrow archway. I asked the TL driver if he could get in there. The TL was manoeuvred through the arch facing the affected building. It was extended and a jet was taken up the ladder and opened straight into the fire.

Fires in modern office blocks can be hard to fight by using the regular point of entry. Reaching the fire by finding your way in smoke-filled staircases and corridors is dangerous. Also, any delay allows the fire to increase, causing more damage. I left the Sub. Officer in charge at the rear and took another crew around the corner to the main entrance. I made that my entry point for the sake of BA control. By the time this crew had reached the fire, it was virtually out. We just needed the BA to do the damping down.

This was when smoking in offices was still common, and a cigarette left smouldering in a waste bin full of paper was a regular cause of fire. Now that smoking is not so popular and insurance companies have created little huddles of smoking lepers out in the street, this type of fire is not so common.

A good job well done means slaps on the back for everyone!

## Chapter 26

# THE CARLTON CLUB

The White Watch's next adventure certainly made front-page news – worldwide! The Carlton Club is the premier Conservative Party club and they were in Government at the time. An explosive device containing 10–15lbs of explosive had been detonated in the hallway of the club, seriously injuring two people and extensively damaging the front of the building. A further 20 people were injured, and the Fire Brigade rescued and assisted a total of 23 people from the building.

It was said that this explosion marked a dramatic escalation in the IRA's terrorist campaign in mainland Britain, and was designed to cause maximum damage and injury at the heart of the British Government. Had it not been for the fact that voting was going on in the Houses of Parliament, there would have been at least 20 MPs dining at the club.

Located at 69 St James Street, SW1, the club had previously suffered bomb damage during the war and had been moved from Pall Mall to St. James's after the Second World War. It was located 100 yards from St. James's Palace and Clarence House, the home of The Queen Mother. This part of London is home to the noble and rich. Exclusive gentlemen's clubs are hidden away behind the fine facades. Two 18th century shops still exist and one of them, Rudds Wine Merchant, sends a case of scotch to the station every Christmas.

No warning was received and the bomb exploded at 2038hrs on 25th June 1990. Sir Michael Grade, who was eating at the famous 'Overtons' fish restaurant opposite, witnessed the scene and said, 'There was the most enormous bang followed by the sound of breaking glass. Smoke was billowing out of the windows. Within a short space of time the emergency services were on the spot. There was an extension ladder up to the third floor and they seemed to get the trapped people out very quickly. The speed of the emergency services was tremendous. They pitched a ladder and got some people out at the front.'

Soho's three appliances were ordered, backed up by Westminster's pump ladder. It was fortunate that Station Officer Peter Simpson was riding in charge of Westminster's machine. Westminster could often get to that part of our ground before us. This was especially the case that night, as the traffic was already backed up on our route down Pall Mall from Trafalgar Square. Peter had no hesitation in making pumps four, followed very quickly by 'make pumps six'.

As we approached, an enormous pall of black smoke was rising into the air, and rubble and glass had been thrown into the street. The portico of the front of the building had fallen onto the front steps. Even though the fire engines were arriving, there was an eerie silence. At that time of night the traffic would be creeping along towards Piccadilly. St. James's Street was filled with a smoky cordite haze. Peter's men had assisted a number of people down from the first floor, who were trapped because the staircase had collapsed. Some passers-by had been injured by the blast and had already been taken to safety. A number of police officers were suffering from smoke inhalation.

The pump ladder and pump drove past the incident to be away from the face of the building. The TL stopped short, waiting just in case it was needed. After a quickly shouted hand-over from Peter, my first action was to order five ambulances. The ambulance service made this a major incident. The Westminster firemen were up to their eyes in it working close to the blast site.

The building was on three floors and basement; fire and the explosion damaged 16 × 19 metres and 50% of the ground floor, 25% of the first floor and 15% of the basement. The area around the front door and the entrance lobby was where the most damage had occurred. The floor had collapsed into the basement. This was where the most seriously injured man, the doorman, was located. The floor had to be bridged with a ladder to gain entry and to reach the casualty.

It was a very fortunate coincidence that a man called Barry Davis had been nearby when the explosion occurred. He was not only a paramedic, but also an instructor with the London Ambulance Service. He went straight to the scene and played a major part in stabilising casualties and assisted with their removal. (Afterwards I made sure that his actions were recognised by the Brigade.)

Due to the unstable nature of the front entrance, I couldn't get any more of the trapped out by the front entrance. I sent the OIC of my pump around to the rear of the building. I did not have a Sub. Officer that night, so Leading Fireman Cummings was the man. He was the biggest bloke you have ever seen and had seen military service in Northern Ireland, so he was aware of the possible consequences of an

IRA bomb. Ladders were pitched and 23 people were either led to safety from the ground floor, or assisted down ladders from the first floor. This was a particularly difficult rescue operation, as a lot of these people were elderly and not used to descending ladders.

Fortunately, we had got all the people out when the police told us that we had to leave, as a secondary device was suspected. Everybody moved away from the building. I ended up at the top of St. James's with some of my men. Others made for the safety of Green Park. The TL crew were still waiting in Pall Mall.

The Salvation Army canteen van had arrived by then, but because they were separated from the bulk of the firemen, only the TL's crew could take advantage of their refreshments. The TL's crew, Barry Shilstone and 'Joe' Borg, were both bears and partial to a bit of grub. It was said that they were preparing for winter hibernation!

Meanwhile, I was protecting myself from any further blasts when the BBC's Kate Adie squeezed my arm and asked me if I was all right. See, even a poor old fireman is worth a bit of comfort from a famous correspondent. The police bomb squad had to declare a suspect vehicle safe before any further action could take place.

The Deputy Chief Officer was on the scene by that time. He said that he wanted to meet the officers in charge of the first attendance to congratulate them. Peter, Geoff and I made ourselves presentable and stood by. We stood by for ages; perhaps something more pressing had come to his attention. Anyway, we gave up on that and returned to the station three hours later.

This was another incident where you did not have time to consider the present danger. A further collapse, another explosion, anything could have happened, but the firemen just got on with it. No questions, no hesitation, they just got on with it. There were people to save and a fire to put out and whatever the circumstances, that is their job.

This was not the first terrorist incident that we had dealt with. We were often called to suspect packages and cars. It was usually just a matter of standing-by in a safe place waiting just in case of an explosion. We are not allowed to get involved with searching for explosives.

On one occasion we were called to a car alight in Norris Street, just off Haymarket. Standing in Haymarket at the junction, there was a policeman waving us in; in fact there were lots of policemen. Norris is a narrow street and once cars are parked down one side, it is difficult for fire engines to pass. As we turned left at the end of the street, there was a Mercedes that was a ball of flames. Something wasn't quite right. Why so many police? We were just about to get water onto the car when I asked a copper what had happened. The car had been hijacked by suspected terrorists and they had forced the driver to take them to the West End to set the car alight. There could have been a bomb inside! I quickly withdrew the firemen and we directed water onto the car from behind the protection of a building.

Another time we were called to The Bloomsbury Hotel to their fire alarm. I was met by some rather large men with tell-tale bulges in their jackets. Apparently, the security forces had been observing the hotel where suspected terrorists were staying. The terrorists had become suspicious, actuated the fire alarm and escaped. Just in case we happened upon a bomb factory, I asked the surveillance squad to search the part of the hotel where the alarm had been sounded.

The year 1990 finished with another bang – another four-pump fire. A gang of painters was working at night in a suite of offices in Bolton Street, W1 at the junction with Piccadilly. They had been washing down paintwork with white spirit. At 2143hrs one of the painters lit a fag! Bang! The whole suite was alight and smoke-blackened painters were jumping out of the first floor windows, much to the astonishment of the passing crowds!

## Chapter 27

# BIRDS AND PRANKS

I couldn't turn my back; the White Watch were always up to some sort of prank. One day after breakfast I had to go down to the watchroom for something, and they were all gathered around the window trying to get a look at the Curzon Cinema on the opposite side of the avenue.

The cinema manager was standing outside, looking up and scratching his head. The film showing was 'Prick up Your Ears'. During the night somebody had transposed the magnetic letters advertising the film from ears to arse! Now, I wonder who could have reached up to the cinema canopy unnoticed; perhaps a TL returning to the station in the early hours?

Once the remainder of the station heard of this, to the bewilderment and dismay of the manager, he had to rearrange his sign on many more occasions, but never discovered the culprits. But I knew who it was – 'Woody...where are you!'

Soho is not the kind of area where you would expect the Fire Brigade to be called to animals in distress, but we got our fair share. Mostly birds. They would get their legs tangled with string or wire then fly into trees and get snared in the branches. At one such call in Store Street, WC1, a pigeon with its feet bound together was flapping away caught on the front of a building with wrought ironwork around the windowsills. A ladder was pitched and the crowds gathered. All the windows of the surrounding offices were loaded with spectators. I decided that it was my turn to do a bit of work and climbed up to the second floor. Birds do not seem to appreciate that you have come to their rescue and they peck at your hands! Anyway I managed to cut it free – then it died; it just went limp in my hands. So instead of being released to freedom, it was taken away in a bucket and unceremoniously dumped in the station's paladin, much to the dismay of the audience, but to the amusement of the rest of the Brigade who heard my stop message – 'Pigeon trapped at second floor level. Released. Deceased!'

The Ministry of Agriculture called us to a bird trapped on their roof. Most of these big buildings have light wells in the centre, which allow daylight to enter the offices that do not face the street. To prevent birds from nesting and fouling, these areas are protected by netting, which is fixed over the light wells at roof level. This bird was not your usual London 'flying rat', but a beautiful bird of prey; it was some sort of falcon.

It was not in a very accessible position and a ladder had to be placed from corner to corner over the light well, eight floors up. A fireman then crawled out to reach the bird. This was a precarious, dangerous, exercise; it was so tangled that the fireman had to cut the netting to release it. Again, it did not realise that we were the good guys, pecking at everything in reach.

Once it was freed I was not sure what to do with it. The RSPCA would take too long to be of any assistance, so I decided to do a mercy dash across Central London to Regents Park Zoo, where I knew there were vets who could take care of the bird. Out came the old favourite – the galvanised bucket. One of the blokes had a budgie so he was promoted to expert bird handler, and on his advice we covered the bucket, which is supposed to keep the bird calm. I told control what I was doing and asked them to contact the vets. Control got back to us saying that the Zoo did not want it if it was a pigeon! Off we went, no sirens but blue lights – not taking any risks with the traffic, but at the same time trying to get to the Zoo as quickly as possible.

When we arrived, a vet was waiting for us. I don't know whether the bird survived but I sincerely hope that it did. The only falcon ever to be dashed across London in a fire engine!

One summer's day the fire engines were returning from a call and while going around Trafalgar Square, Ed the Bastard spotted an unusual bird using a pedestrian crossing. A shout came from the back of the truck, 'Look. There's a fuckin' penguin!' I told you that The Bastard got things mixed up and he was certainly no ornithologist. The bird turned out to be a guillemot that had flown off its migration route, landed in the Square and was exhausted. There was nothing else for it; it had to be saved and taken back to the station.

I knew nothing of this until I got back to the station and was shown the bird, who was now in a makeshift cage with the remains of a tuna fish sandwich for sustenance. The RSPCA had been informed and when the chain-smoking RSPCA officer arrived, not only had he to contend with our 'penguin' pecking viciously at his hands, but also the smoke from his fag, which was permanently attached to his lip and stinging his eyes. Whatever next! He didn't even put gloves on.

This is the last bird story – I promise. This involved another precarious rescue. You may ask, why risk the safety of a fireman just to save a bird? You just had to; otherwise you would have to face the consternation of the onlookers. People would step over a person collapsed in the street, but go into compassion mode big-time over any type of animal.

Just who noticed a duckling trapped in a storm drain I'll never know. But there it was, swimming around and twittering, about 15 feet below street level. This was a drain that let into the Thames. I can only think that the duckling swam in when the river was at a slightly lower level and when the level rose, with the tide, its exit became submerged. There was a Jacobs ladder going down but it did not reach the surface of the water so we had to tie an extension ladder together. It was lowered down and the head was secured, so that it would not drop any further into the drain. Then a fireman climbed down. He couldn't catch the duckling but was able to guide it into, yes, the galvanised bucket, this time tied to a line with a brick inside. The bucket was part submerged, the duckling was urged into the bucket and raised to street level. Then it was lowered back into the Thames to its waiting mother and family. Ahhh!

Cats were another source of alarm. We had them trapped on roofs, under floors and trapped between cavity walls. I even had one poor old moggy that had fallen from a roof and had impaled itself on some railings. It had also had an eye hanging out on a thread. I think its name was Lucky! Fortunately this happened in the early hours when there was no one about. We were all looking at the cat wondering what to do. Call the RSPCA? No, not worth it. Even us town boys could see that it was on its last legs. Fortunately, a fire engine from Knightsbridge that had been attending a separate call on our ground was passing and stopped. The old Sub. Officer who was in charge lifted the cat off the railings with the intention of wringing its neck, but as he lifted, it died. Not much else could have been done; at least it was out of its misery.

There are no more animal stories, unless you count mice and cockroach infestations in the station kitchen and a wind-up involving the local newspaper. The paper would ring up once a week for information on any interesting jobs. We were supposed to enter the details of anything interesting in a news book, but nobody ever did. They always managed to call at the busiest times. Believe me, I don't know who it came from or where they found the inspiration, but somebody told the reporter that we had been involved in the capture of an escaped baboon from London Zoo!

They went for it and contacted our press office for more details. That called for another serious case of bluffing from the old Station Officer.

The years are rushing by and in 1992 I was awarded the Long Service and Good Conduct Medal. This is awarded after 20 years' service. I don't know about the good conduct part because it didn't seem to matter how you behaved, as I don't know of anyone who didn't get the medal. I have known men who refused to accept it on those grounds, and others simply because they did not wish to shake the Chief Officer's hand.

When I received mine, the ceremony was held at the Commonwealth Institute in Kensington. I always encouraged my men to go to the ceremony, as I had learnt from past experience that these things are great for the family. It's one of the rare occasions that they get to see their dad, husband or son get some kind of formal recognition. Plus you get a drink and a bite to eat on the Brigade.

When the date for the ceremony is announced, all the old hands start scratching around to find a decent undress uniform that still fits. You do get a bit of notice, so I usually had time to order them a new one made to measure.

Even this occasion manages to produce a bit of amusement. To avoid the Chief having to fumble around trying to pin the medal to your uniform, you are given a hook on which the medal can be hung. The only trouble was that once the Chief had hung the medal, shaken your hand and a photograph had been taken, a lot of recipients couldn't wait to get away, and as they bounce back down the stairs, the medal jumps off. It falls from the first floor through the open staircase into the basement and, after the ceremony, half a dozen men could be seen scrabbling about searching for their medals. I had been warned about this and held mine close to my chest.

The Brigade's press office send out details of the awards to the local press and, as a consequence of this, the West End Extra wrote a little article and published my photo with the Chief Officer. You should see his blank, uninterested stare. As a further consequence of this, I started to receive letters at the station from some poor, short-sighted, infatuated woman. Perhaps, in fact, she fancied the Chief Officer! Then she started to phone, which was all very amusing for the men. I ignored the whole thing and, fortunately, it went away.

We went through a quiet time in the first three years of the '90s. Still as busy as usual, but no really big incidents. Jokingly, the men blamed Firewoman Lara Roberts, who started her service just as the excitement stopped.

The worst places on the ground were the hostels for homeless men and women. Alcoholics, drug addicts and the mentally unstable all living together is a recipe for disaster. Fortunately, more by luck than providence, that recipe has not become a reality.

When I first went to Soho, the ultimate horror was Bruce House, Kemble Street, WC1. The fire alarms were always actuating, sometimes several times a shift. Dealing with calls on a cold winter's night was particularly difficult, as the inhabitants did not want to leave the building. There was no point in provoking the residents, as not only were they unstable, but physical violence was always a possibility.

Once I did get an evacuation, I had to send a crew to inspect the area where the alarm was actuating. All of these hostels have the same smell; a mixture of stale tobacco, sweat, stale piss and disinfectant. As this was not the most desirable of jobs, I tried to rotate the crews who were doing the searching.

The alarms were mostly set off by people smoking in restricted areas. Lots of small fires were caused by people smoking in bed and the occasional serious fire was usually down to arson by one or other of the cranky residents.

In later years, Bruce House was converted into individual housing units for the homeless and became less of a problem. Just before it closed I was called, strangely, in the middle of the night to a man with his foot trapped. The bedrooms in this place were small cubicles, and somehow this man had fallen out of bed and trapped his foot in the gap at the base of the cubicle partition. I find it very hard to be patient when dealing with people who will not help themselves. This man was moaning and groaning. He stank, so did the cubicle, and at three in the morning my well of human kindness quickly ran dry. To make it worse, the firemen didn't want to get involved. This was really a rarity, but for some reason they just didn't want to co-operate. Perhaps they were still half asleep or had, maybe, picked up on my increasingly aggressive attitude. I ended up shouting at the trapped man, who only had to twist his foot to escape and then I forced his foot out of the gap. You should have heard him scream, but I couldn't wait to get out of that place.

Unfortunately, the problems at Bruce House just moved to other hostels: 90 Dean Street and St. Mungos, in Endell Street. The number of times the Fire Brigade are called to these places is incalculable.

The most startling incident in a hostel occurred in St. Mungos, Endell Street and it was a Red Watch job. They were called to assist the police with a man who had entered the loft space and was threatening to blow-up the place. Eventually he set fire to the loft. After holding-off, hoping the man would come to his senses, the firemen had to then get into the loft. As they forced open the hatch, the man, who was now also on fire, came falling through onto the fire crew and the police.

There were two women's hostels on the ground, both in Greek Street. One was very respectable, located in the House of St. Barnabas overlooking Soho Square. This is about the only 18th-century Soho townhouse retaining its original interior. While on calls to this address the ladies, who were responsible for the building, would always want to accompany the firemen when they searched it. They were very concerned about the welfare of their residents and the place was immaculate.

At the other hostel, a little further down the street, the residents were more down at heel. Some real crazy women – it was more like an asylum than a hostel. I was once told that they were the remains of women who had been wrecked by the ravages of Soho street life. Evacuation was very unpopular. The women would congregate in the sitting room on the ground floor. Some of them looked as though they had hadn't seen the light of day for years. As most of the calls were false alarms, I did not insist on the poor, lost creatures leaving the building. Even when the laundry was on fire, I let them stay inside.

In 1993 a very important milestone was reached. One of the firemen on the Blue Watch retired after completing all of his thirty years' service stationed at Soho. Bertie Wilson, apart from being a TL driver, had been the mess manager for as long as I can remember. What an achievement. How many shouts had Bertie attended? It's impossible to calculate.

When Ron Morris retired, his retirement function was held at the station, but that was the last that the Brigade ever allowed. Not for any particular reason other than the station would have had to be taken off the run and it wasn't really professional. This wasn't actually Bertie's retirement do but, all the same, we were quite surprised when it was allowed. Perhaps it was recognised that his achievements were exceptional and we were allowed to organise this little presentation at the station. Or perhaps it was because we called it a reception!

The Blue Watch did not have a Station Officer at the time so I suggested to the Station Commander that this occasion should not go unmarked. To his credit he pulled out all the stops. Apart from Bert's close colleagues and friends, the local MP, the Mayor of Westminster and the Chairman of the Soho Society also attended. Bertie and his wife looked suitably chuffed. There was no way he could have been 55. All those years at Soho driving the ladders had not damaged his looks – handsome devil, not a grey hair in his head.

## Chapter 28

# HOLY SMOKE AND BEANOS

On Christmas day 1993 the White Watch was due to go off duty at
0900hrs. Okay, we had worked Christmas Eve but at least we were
going home for the rest of Christmas. The bells went down just before
breakfast. 'Fire. St. Anselms Church, Kingsway, WC2'. All the standard
cries went up, 'Holy smoke' etc. This part of Kingsway is not on Soho's
ground and belongs to Clerkenwell, but as their Station Officer was off-
duty I was in charge.

St Anselms is not that old. It was built in about 1909 and was built to
replace the Sardinian Chapel that had been demolished for the creation
of The Kingsway. This was part of the last great Victorian metropolitan
improvements. A massive slum clearance was replaced by modern buildings and a direct north–south route through a particularly congested part
of London, which links up with The Aldwych and the Strand Underpass.

Smoke was pouring out of the main doors and from under the roof
slates. I immediately made pumps-ten! My driver said, 'Are you sure?' I
could tell, immediately, the sort of job we were going to have.

We had a hydraulic platform on the run and I got it into position right
at the front of the church and, even though it was restricted by trees, it
made all the difference as the fire progressed. Once we had made sure
that nobody was left inside, BA crews from Clerkenwell and Soho got to
work inside the church. I had so much to do outside that I didn't get
inside at any time throughout the whole job. Not only did I have to oversee the work at the front of the church, I had ladders pitched at the side
and the rear.

Everybody worked really hard and we managed to limit the internal
damage and save the roof. That's quite an achievement – nobody saves a
church roof! Once the fire gets into it, it is very hard to contain, as they
are so high and difficult to access. If fire gets a real hold in a church, it is
normally burnt to the ground.

Although I would never doubt the firemen's dedication in getting the
fire under control, I do think that there was an ulterior motive – like me,
they wanted to get home as quickly as possible.

At that time the 'A' Division control unit was a Range Rover, one of the early ones that were in the habit of turning over. My old Leading Fireman, Barry Shilstone, was driving to our fire and had to take evasive action at a set of traffic lights. He was only about 200 yards from the church and over it went onto its roof. This then turned into another incident as he was trapped in the vehicle. Fortunately, he was unhurt but he was suspended upside-down, wedged in by all the equipment and had to be cut free from his seat belt. I would have liked to see that!

As soon as my relief arrived, my fire engine was away. The fire was not on our ground and I did not even have to complete the fire report. I could leave that to the officers from Clerkenwell, who were very grumpy, as the call was recorded as being on Soho's ground.

I have to say that I couldn't have cared less; once the fire was out, I had Christmas Day waiting at home with my family.

Something that always got my goat was the uniform. My views might be considered to be as old fashioned as brass helmets, but I really think that some of what has been done in the name of modernisation has been detrimental, not only to the traditional look of a fireman, but also to his safety and wellbeing.

Firemen have three types of uniform: the operational gear that you see when they are on calls, an undress uniform which is worn when they are required to look smart, and work wear. However, officers are not issued with work wear.

When I started, the operational uniform was a double-breasted wool tunic with chrome buttons. At the waist, it had clips on either side where your belt and axe were hung. They looked smart but were not waterproof; they just absorbed water and became really heavy, like carrying a whole sheep around on your back. As they were used for ceremonial occasions, you tried to keep one of your three in good condition. Although now obsolete, they are still the only suitable uniform that can be worn for funerals and the like. So when the need arises, a Brigade-wide search has to be set in motion to find some in good condition. This fire gear was replaced by the dark blue firecoats and leggings and, as a consequence, away went the belt and axe. Although there was nothing personable about it, at least this style of uniform was comfortable, waterproof to an extent, and we still looked like firemen.

I can speak for all the firemen when I say that the withdrawal of the personal axe was the beginning of a decline in pride for the uniform, and began an unfortunate downwards dive towards demilitarisation.

We took great pride in our axes. The heads would be polished and the wooden handles varnished. They were so prized that some blokes found it hard to get them out of their pouches and get them dirty. They were more than just a tool; they were an emblem of your profession. Now they have nothing other than a torch, if you're lucky, and a whistle on a piece of string.

Next, London went over to the maroon coloured fire gear, which was a disaster. It is uncomfortable and oppressively hot in the summer. The jacket is too short and tight fitting, allowing no ventilation. It would have been better if it were longer and looser like the U.S. fire coats. The new helmet is totally impractical. Fire helmets may have changed in their construction over the years but had always remained basically the same shape. The 'space' type helmet covers the ears and has two distinct disadvantages. Firstly, exposed ears were a good measure of temperature; if it was too hot, your ears felt it and it was time to get out. Secondly, they restrict your hearing. The Brigade order, which dealt with the wearing of uniform, stated that fire helmets must be worn going to and returning from emergencies, but stupidly, you cannot use the appliance radio telephone handset without removing the helmet. And worst of all, the ambulance crews started to call us 'smurfs'!

The senior officer who oversaw the introduction of the uniform was interested in getting some practical feedback from the wearers. As we were wearing it a lot, he thought that we would be able to give him an accurate opinion. I sat the boys down and they raised all the points that I have already stressed, with the addition that if you are over 6ft, you cannot wear the helmets in the back of a fire engine as your head bangs on the roof (not something that would have entered my mind!).

Once his reply to my report worked its way back down the management chain, he said that we had not given enough time to assess the uniform, even though he had requested our input in the first place! However, he did say that he would come to the station and discuss our problems. He never turned up. This compounded our opinion that it doesn't really matter if the firemen are uncomfortable – a deal has been done with the uniform suppliers and you're stuck with it.

The real disservice was when they meddled with the undress uniform. Copied from a naval officer's uniform, the old double-breasted jacket was wonderful. U.S. firemen still wear it and it sets the job apart from other services. First they changed it to a single-breasted jacket and then to a tunic-type affair, and in doing so, all the tradition went down the drain. New isn't always good!

Another anomaly is the officer's uniform. On promotion to Station Officer, you get made-to-measure uniforms, but they don't provide officers with any form of work wear. These suits used to cost about £250 a time, and the trousers are all you have to wear to fight fires – a white shirt, black tie and black trousers, I ask you. El cursed the pile of white shirts brought home after a tour of duty! On several occasions I wrote reports asking for suitable work wear for Station Officers. I don't think that I even got a single reply. It would have saved them money! When I was first promoted, I used to write a lot of reports making suggestions that might improve the Brigade. After a while you realise that you are banging your head against a brick wall and give up.

The Brigade sends you a list of approved tailors where you can get your first uniform made. I went to a strange little shop in Clerkenwell Green where I expected to see 'Mr. Ben'! The man who took my measurements asked of my 5'8" frame if it had ever been in the Guards! Suits you, sir!

Previously, all the Station Officers at Soho had used a very old fashioned tropical outfitter called Alkits on Cambridge Circus. It closed down in the early '80s and then, for convenience sake, we used a mobile tailor. This man would take your measurements then get the uniform made back at his workshop. The only trouble was that when you tried on the finished article, it never fitted! He always had to go away and make some adjustments. He was also very willing to suggest that, instead of making you a uniform, he was open to making you 'something for the weekend' – a dodgy suit, or his speciality, a smart blazer.

Colin Townsley told me about this and advised me never to take advantage. Not that I would. If you saw what he made you would understand what I mean. But Colin had another reason. Apart from it being fraudulent, he said that he would always have something over a senior officer who was wearing a dodgy blazer. That was good enough for me.

The mobile tailor especially liked his visits to our station as he liked to visit Soho at the same time. After he had taken care of our tailoring requirements, he would wander off into Soho, where he would scour the second-hand record shops. This was all right, and something after my own heart, but I was never completely sure about a man taking your inside leg measurement who also made his own clothes!

At first I did not socialise with the White Watch and didn't go out for drinks with them. I thought that it was essential that I maintain some sort of separation from the men. It wasn't that I didn't like a drink, or that I didn't want to share their company, it was just that I was in charge. I didn't want to compromise my position. Once I had cemented my place in the pecking order, I started to go for a drink, but would only stay for a couple and then leave. After three or four years, I finally succumbed to the delights of occasionally drinking so much beer that it was hard to stand up. I convinced myself that this was good for morale! I persuaded myself that it was a good way of relieving the stress and it was bloody good fun.

It did not affect my authority. The men were able to separate socialising from station life. We tried to go out once a month; it wasn't possible all the time but we did have some great times. There is nowhere better than Soho for a good drink, as the watering holes are endless. Mostly our local was the Three Greyhounds in Old Compton Street. We would stand outside on a warm summer's night having a pint and watch the whole world pass by.

On the opposite corner from the pub is the Soho House. This is an exclusive members-only club. It seemed that all the current entertainment trendies were the only ones allowed entry. Watching the comings and goings of the rich and temporarily famous became an added attraction. One night, the dare went out that, surely a lowly fireman could get in there? Steve King, 'Victorian Strongman', took up the challenge. Not only did he get in there, but he waved to us from a room where a private party was in full swing – free drinks, the lot!

The best nights out were those that were unplanned.

One afternoon we were called to a smell of burning in a building in Regent Street. Like a lot of these buildings, it was multi-occupancy. As soon as we arrived, several of the occupiers told me that they had noticed the smell on and off all day. Now I have to initiate a full-scale search of a whole six-storey block of shops and offices; in all, about 10 separate properties. We looked everywhere and finally found part of the building being refurbished. The builders had removed part of a dividing wall and

in the process had set light to the expansion joint in the wall cavity, and
this was now burning unseen up through the building. I saw smoke at
roof level and in the basement, but was unable to get any access in
between.

From experience, I knew it was going to be a long drawn out job and
I would need more manpower, even reliefs. It was hot, sweaty, hard work
and we were there for hours. Once we had gained a couple of hours over-
time, we all looked at each other and unanimously decided that it was too
late to go home. Out came the mobiles: 'Sorry love...blah, blah, blah'.
Apart from the fact that by the time some of us would get home it would
just be a case of going to bed and coming back, surely we deserved a
drink and with London's blessing.

Some of us had no going out clothes with us, especially the cyclists, so
we had to mix and match uniform with borrowed civvies. It was a great
night; everyone was on top form. At some stage it was time to eat. Even
in Soho, it is hard to find a place that will allow entry to a group of 12
well-oiled firemen. We had hit on an Indian in Earlham Street, which
wasn't very full. We explained that, although we may be a bit noisy, we
were no trouble and they let us have the whole of their upper floor to ourselves. Even so, the noise was a bit much and we were asked to quieten
down. That was the night that when the naan bread arrived, it was so big
that Cheesy had to wear it as a sombrero, even though it was still hot and
burnt his poor old bald head!

The Christmas beanos started out as a simple drink in the West End,
but this was soon not enough and developed into two or three day binges
in foreign countries. The first one that I attended was on the overnight
ferry from Portsmouth to Cherbourg, chosen because there was no such
thing as closing time. The next was a little nearer to home. Some of the
boys had met a pub landlord at an England football match and he said
that we could go and stay at his pub anytime. Only trouble was his pub
was in Doncaster. Still, we said that anyone could enjoy themselves in the
West End on a Saturday night, but the White Watch could enjoy themselves on a Monday night anywhere. So off we set to a two-day lock-in.
The landlord, to his credit, treated us like kings and even laid on a
karaoke night, where I managed to make a fool of myself by annoying the
DJ when I insisted in swinging the mike, à la Roger Daltry, while singing
'I'm Henry the Eighth I Am!'

Our next 'mission' was to Dublin, which was all right, but the accommodation was very basic and we were not allowed entry to many places. They said that we were too drunk – how could they tell? The following year we went to Amsterdam and gained the dubious accolade of being asked to leave the worst hotel in town. In normal circumstances, and if we had had our firemen's heads on, we would have got the place closed as it was a death trap. It was the sort of place where we would normally be dragging people out, not sleeping in ourselves.

My trouble was that I could not stand the pace of these ventures. I was all right for the first 24 hours, but then I just wanted to go home. I'd had enough. And it took me about a week to recover. I don't know how the rest of them kept going, all that drink and hardly any sleep. After all, it wasn't as though we were getting a lot of sleep at the best of times. It must have been some sort of reaction to all the stress.

In 1994 a couple of writers and a photographer came to the station with the aim of producing a book about the Fire Brigade. This was one of a series of educational books on teamwork. It gave a basic description of the work of the Fire Brigade, plus a day in the life of Soho Fire Station and the White Watch. Not much of a book, but we all got copies, and for me it is another thing that I can look back on and see my station and the people who worked there at that time. As the Brigade insisted that the book portrayed a multi-racial, multi-sex establishment, we had to borrow Carmen from the Red Watch. She got one day overtime; we only got a copy of the book! I had forgotten all about this until years later when a fireman friend of mine who had emigrated to New Zealand, contacted me. He wrote saying that he had seen the book after his grandchildren had gotten it from the library. He questioned the fact that it was educational and not a horror story – all the ugly mugs had frightened the kids!

Of all the hundreds of calls to fire alarms, hardly any developed into serious fires. That is what a fire alarm is for – to warn the occupants that there *may* be a fire and to leave the building. The trouble is that we were so used to responding to the alarms and searching buildings, that when you did actually get a job it was a bit of a shock. Especially when it was one of the regular calls.

Before they modernised their fire alarm system, calls to the Mayfair Hotel, Stratton Street, W1 came in like clockwork. Steam from the showers, cooking, smoking, and water leaking into the alarm system, in fact, almost anything set off their alarms.

So when a call to their fire alarm came in at 0830hrs, nearing the end of a night shift and when the hotel was in full swing, I expected the usual. When we arrived there was still no reason to be concerned. The pump from Knightsbridge usually beat us to this address and they had already gone into the hotel. Some of the guests had mustered in the foyer. Not everyone reacts to the fire alarm though. Being right in the centre of town, this is a very popular hotel with overseas visitors. Reception was thronging. There was a row of taxis on the rank outside and coaches arriving to take tourists on sightseeing trips

The Leading Fireman from Knightsbridge had gone to inspect the area from where the alarm was activating. He had gone with a member of staff and another fireman. Unfortunately, the hotel had already sent someone to the affected area, and instead of reporting back that there was a fire, he had stayed at the scene and tried to put the fire out. That was how the fire managed to develop and now he was trapped.

We were all outside socialising, waiting for the Leading Fireman to give the all clear, but he can't raise me on his radio – fucking useless radios – so he has to run to tell me that I've got a serious fire in progress with persons reported.

The problem with this building, and many like it in built up areas, is that they are so big and tall that unless you are a fair distance away you cannot see smoke rising. This building had the added complication that the fire was on a side of the hotel that was hidden from view and fire engines could not access that part of the building. I had no way of measuring the extent of the fire. I could not even see where it was. I just had to rely on my junior officers and organise accordingly.

A suite of rooms was alight on the third floor, I did not know how many people were involved. I had already 'Made pumps six – persons reported', now I had to send an informative message guessing the extent of the fire and stating, 'Unknown number of persons involved'. Until the hotel staff had taken a roll call of guests and staff, there was no way I could be sure of any casualties. The firemen had just got to get in there and search.

It was one of those jobs where it would have been far better if I could have gotten inside. I was desperate for a senior officer to arrive so that I could relinquish control and see for myself what was going on inside. Fortunately, at that time of day, they are on their way to their bases and one arrived pretty quickly.

With a hotel as large as this, we would set up a control point on the floor below the fire in a smoke-free area. The BA men would book-in at this point and then proceed up to the fire. The smoke was thick, black and down to the floor. It had started in a television, caught the curtains and spread to the room furnishings. The BA men had already pulled out the member of staff who was overcome and now ready to be removed to a waiting ambulance. The whole wing was smoke-logged and they were still searching for further casualties. Suddenly the fire doors, which were preventing the smoke from entering the remainder of the hotel, burst open. The two semi-clothed, smoke-blackened, occupants of the room were being led and dragged by a BA crew. They were suffering from smoke inhalation and were quickly removed. They had come all the way from Canada. Welcome to London!

Fortunately we were able to restrict the fire to its floor of origin, but the smoke damage was extensive. It's not until the smoke has cleared that you can see the extent of the damage: the hose snaking along the smoke-stained corridors, the blackened shell of the rooms and the smudges left by the firemen caused by their hands finding their way along the walls.

It's not like you see on the television where the contents of a room, which is supposedly on fire, are visible. In reality you cannot see a thing and you stumble over everything in the room.

Most of the hotels in the West End were regular calls. The problem wasn't only restricted to the tourist hotels, which were full to the rafters with foreigners, the more exclusive also had their fair share. In some cases we were called several times in the same shift – the guests became 'best friends'! It got so bad that at one hotel, we were having regular meetings with the managers to improve their evacuation and response to the fire alarm. One of the problems was that there were so many non-English speakers staying in the hotel. We tried to get them to broadcast a multi-language message over their tannoy system. That was successful for a while, but it soon lapsed as the staff were constantly changing. We were then back to hundreds of people leaving their rooms and crowding into the foyer, which we then had to control as well as check out the alarms. (Next time you stay in any hotel, try and take a look at the night staff and decide whether you think they are capable of looking after your safety.) At one hotel I was called to an alarm indicating the roof. I asked the night manager, 'Where's the roof mate?' He said, 'I don't know.'

We did get regular fires in the hotels. I could never discover the reason, but there were many fires involving the laundry rooms. These massive buildings with several entrances have major security problems. There are cameras everywhere, but still intruders get inside to set off the fire alarms in the hope that rooms will be left open for them to steal. Guests responding to the alarms would leave in a hurry without locking their rooms, and the thieves would then do their evil. There were even guests who had evacuated in their nightwear and were mugged out in the street! Intruders and intoxicated guests would also set off the alarms deliberately by squirting aerosols into the smoke detectors, either just for fun or to steal.

I always dreaded the 0300hrs call to the Regents Palace. Heart in the mouth stuff as you charged down the avenue, I considered this place as the greatest risk on the ground. Other stations have industrial or chemical risks; Soho has massive hotels each with over 1000 guests sleeping in one building. When it's full, the Regents Palace has 1500. That's some risk. There only had to be a fire in a basement to cause a major catastrophe. During the week, we would be met by bewildered guests concerned for their safety and for that of their families. It was quite understandable, but when you have hundreds of them all asking, in some cases demanding, to know what is happening, it can develop into its own kind of hysteria. At the weekend we would, more often than not, be met by a rowdy throng of drunken young people. One night it was a young farmer's jamboree! Of course they were totally unconcerned for their safety, and their ladies showed more interest in the big city firemen. I used to have to shout at the top of my voice to get some kind of calm and control.

Another risk at the Regents Palace was the staff annex, which was joined to the main hotel by a high level walkway. Until there was a permanent security guard on the entrance, I'm sure that intruders entered the main hotel via this entrance. I had several fires in this annex, which were always at risk of spreading to the main hotel.

In fact, the whole of the area around this hotel gave us a lot of business – Glasshouse Street, Brewer Street, Sherwood Street and Air Street all had more than their fair share of incidents.

During one of our nights of multi-rubbish fires, we were called to Sherwood Street, where a pile of burning refuse had spread fire, not just to one parked car, but three, and part of the Piccadilly Theatre. Rubbish is often stored in doorways and it is a natural consequence that when the arsonists have their wicked way, the fire spreads into the building. Even if it is only smoke, we still had to gain entry to make sure it was safe.

Early one morning in Air Street, I dealt with a truck, which was full of hotel laundry. The whole vehicle was alight with flames shooting upwards through its Perspex roof. The driver was looking on in shock and amazement. He had bailed out when he saw belching smoke in his rear-view mirrors.

Another regular occurrence that is characteristic to the West End is multiple calls to a smell of gas spread over a large area. When this first happened to me, I went through the whole procedure of searching premises, calling out the gas authority and sniffing the air. I soon realised that this smell was not in fact gas, but fumes from a London bus that was leaking oil onto a hot engine and exhaust. Not just dripping oil, but the entire contents of the engine emptying through a broken seal. The fumes are heavier than air. While the bus follows its route, the fumes flow down into the shop basements and the occupiers start making their calls. On any similar calls it was great to be the one with the experience to be able to pinpoint the cause straight away, and be right!

I tried my best to take the operational side seriously, but there were times when to relieve the repetitive, nonsense calls I did try to have a bit of a laugh on the radio. When incidents needed a serious approach, I would never make light of the happenings, but there were times when I could not resist. I remember from when I was a mere buck, 'Turk' Manning sent a message from a call to smoke issuing. I was his temporary Leading Fireman on the Green Watch for a while and we were called to Sloane Street on Knightsbridge's ground. It was deep winter and after scouring the area and finding nothing, he sent a stop message, which read: 'Alarm caused by light reflected on falling snowflakes'! He was such an experienced officer; if he could get away with it then so could I. If the occasion arose, I would formulate the most creative messages and once I was established as an officer, there was no one who could question my inventiveness.

I remember being called to a smell of burning in Wardour Street on a Saturday morning. There was a strong smell in the area, but with all the Chinese restaurants in the vicinity, it was hard to decide what was cooking or what was burning. After a thorough search, we discovered a kitchen that was cooking the strangest produce. I sent a message that I can guarantee no fire officer has ever sent, 'Alarm caused by fumes from burning sea cucumbers!'

Alarm calls were always coming into Le Meridian Hotel, Piccadilly. I did my best to send any messages from there in a French accent. At one time we had an American lady working as a control officer and if anything came in with the slightest possibility of being pronounced in the American vernacular, I would give it a go. But the best, the very best, was the singing stop. In the early hours, when no senior officers could be listening, I would sing a 'stop'. The Toreadors' song was only one that matched the word rhythm of a 'stop' message. Most times I could not get through it without laughing, but it gave the poor overworked control officers a laugh and it made routine calls, in the early hours, tolerable.

All the firemen were amused by the 'radio wave romance' I was having with one particular control officer. This went on for about twenty years. We only ever met a couple of times, but when I heard her voice I knew we were in safe hands. Sometimes, if the time was right, we tried to disguise personal messages within the official jargon.

Her name was Mary. I never knew her surname but I hope she is well.

*Chapter 29*

## THE ALDWYCH BUS BOMB

We had a theory that the real excitement came, not when we were really busy, but when we were really quiet. That was how it was on a bitterly cold Sunday night on 18th February 1996. The station was quiet; the avenue was quiet. The men were quietly tired. Sunday night shift has a subdued atmosphere of its own. Leaving the comfort of a nice day at home with the family was a wrench. We had already worked one night shift; perhaps we were heading for a rare and peaceful night?

At 2200hrs, in the mess, drifting away in front of the telly, we were rudely disturbed by an explosion. We all looked at each other and waited for the bells to go down. Sure enough within seconds they clanged into action. 'Explosion on a bus, The Aldwych, WC2'.

I had already formulated an action plan in response to bombs. Normally we would turn out with the pump going first, followed by me in the pump ladder then the TL. For bombs, I decided that the pump ladder with me in charge should go first, followed by the pump. That way I could decide how close I wanted to get to the incident, and the pump and TL could park away from the location and await instructions.

As we entered the Strand, there was an eerie emptiness in this normally busy thoroughfare. In the street-lamplight, the far end of the Strand was obscured by black smoke. At any incident when an explosive device is suspected, we are not allowed to use our personal radios, but we can use the main radios on the fire engines. I quickly contacted our control and requested 'talk through' with the officer in charge of the pump. Sub. Officer Steve Johnson had been with me for several years and was a trusted, experienced officer. I told him to park on the approach to Waterloo Bridge and we would set up a restricted zone. I stopped at the beginning of the Aldwych. The sight before us was incredible.

Two thirds of a Routemaster bus was spread over the roadway and parts were hanging off the surrounding buildings. With the exception of one police officer, we were the first emergency service on the scene so it was down to me to get on with it. The chassis, the driver's cab and the back section of the bus had remained partially intact. Although the top deck and back of the bus was open to the sky, there were still some seats in one piece. I had to get close enough to see if there were any live casualties. The firemen were already in action; they were giving first aid to the driver who was, miraculously, still alive. He had escaped from his cab and was sitting on the roadside. A couple of pedestrians had been injured and were being cared for by the firemen. Remarkably, a quick-thinking motorist had turned the engine off and left the scene.

Three of us moved towards the bus, with our boots crunching on shattered glass from the bus and nearby buildings. I had asked my giant Leading Fireman, Geoff Cummings, who had served in Northern Ireland, to bring a ladder. Geoff was promoted in the field to 'advisor to the Guvnor on all things military!' We had to get a look into the top of the bus to be sure that there was nobody alive inside. I would have been surprised if anyone had survived. Geoff volunteered to go up; although it was dangerous. We had to use the ladder; there was no other way to make sure that there were no further casualties. To our relief, the bus was clear. When Geoff got back down he spotted something on the ground. 'Guvnor, look, there's a gun!' Sure enough there, lying amidst the debris was a big black revolver. We had not had any bombs in the West End for a long time and you always hoped that this sort of thing had come to an end, but that gun confirmed that we were dealing with a terrorist attack.

Then we began to inspect the lower deck. Here was what I now know to be the body of a man who was an IRA bomber. He was welded to the bus in a sitting position, transfixed, his hands in the air, as though praying. The body was completely black but mostly intact. I was surprised that he hadn't been blown to pieces. Now it was time for me to get everyone away from the scene and wait for the bomb squad.

I had sent my messages and it wasn't long before the whole shebang arrived – the bomb squad, senior fire officers, senior police officers, forensic experts and loads of coppers. There is always the suspicion that there may be another device, so as the police searched we were withdrawn. The bitter cold of the night was starting to penetrate the uniforms. We were standing by just in case we were needed, getting shelter in shop doorways. Eventually we were transported back to the station. The fire engines had to remain in position until the police gave the all clear.

This was an incident that affected a few of the blokes. It made them think about their own safety. Was it worth all the extra risk to life and limb by working in the West End? I cannot be sure because it was hard to get them to express their feelings, but I suspect that a couple made up their minds that it was time to get away to quieter stations.

Later on that year I made a mistake. I admit it and I have no excuses. I suppose I could have gotten away with it if it had involved any other building but The Houses of Parliament!

In the middle of the afternoon on 15th May 1996 we were called to a smell of burning. It had been one of those days. We were just going from call to call mostly being ordered on the radio. At that time we were getting three or four calls a shift to the Underground to their newly-fitted fire alarms. Perhaps I was a bit blasé, even negligent, or just too knackered to think straight. You can judge for yourselves.

The Houses of Parliament are protected by Westminster Fire Station, but they were out on another call. When I arrived at the scene, an appliance from Lambeth was already in attendance. We had taken a long time to arrive because of heavy traffic. Once we had gotten through the security and found the location, a Leading Fireman was coming out. He told me that he had inspected the area concerned, which was a kitchen, and could find nothing. He could only detect normal cooking smells. I took his word for it and sent the appropriate message and got the fire engines away. I should have taken a look myself; I should never have taken his word for it. How could I know how efficient the Leading Fireman was? I was the OIC and responsible for the safe completion of the incident; God, how I hated making mistakes.

We were half way up Whitehall when we received our next call; back to the Houses of Parliament to a fire alarm actuating. This is the point when your pounding heart slides into your boots.

When I got back and went inside, I discovered a faint smell of burning wood and a slight haze in the kitchen, but no fire showing. I set the blokes to search, bearing in mind that this is an ancient, complicated building. I get crews to look in adjacent rooms, above and below the affected area. Nothing. Now I'm really scratching. I suddenly had a brainwave and felt the floor; it was really hot.

This was a kitchen that had been very recently refitted. There was a central range of striking scarlet and stainless steel cookers and hot cupboards on a brand new lino floor covering. Instead of leaving the required gap between the appliances and the floor, they had been installed directly onto the wooden floor separated only by the lino. Over what can only have been a few days, radiated heat had gone undetected, heating the floor timbers to such a degree that they were charred and smouldering beneath our feet. There were no gaps where smoke could escape, other than at the extreme edges of the floor.

I quickly realised that I needed to move the gas-powered appliances and get the floor up. I would need more manpower. I knew that senior officers would have already been monitoring the incident and there was no way I could cover things up by keeping it low key so I called for assistance. Fortunately, Westminster's trucks came on the 'make up'. Their Station Officer, Peter Simpson, was an ally and between us we sorted it out. A large area of floor had to be lifted and the charred floor joists cut away.

The place was crawling with senior officers and politicians. Even Sir Willie Whitelaw, who was Deputy Leader of the Government, put his head round the door. I thought that this would be the end for me. I imagined the Chief Officer looking out of his office window planning my downfall. (Lambeth HQ overlooks The Houses of Parliament.) I knew that one way or another 'they' would get me. It was ironic that the Divisional Officer who ended up in charge didn't know how to formulate an appropriate 'stop' message. I had to prepare it for him! 'What should I send, Ray?' Oh, do me a favour, as if I needed that!

When it was all over and I was back at the station, the 'black macs and briefcases' arrived. Both of them had served under me at some time or other and, with our Station Commander, they started the interrogation. I decided that the best policy was attack! I ripped into them. How dare they question the mighty Chilton? If it weren't for people like me, and others like me, the Brigade would be on its knees! It was a complicated fire situation in a complicated building and without the skills of Peter Simpson, myself and the hard work and determination of the firemen, the outcome would have been far worse. They backed off and, to my relief, I heard no more.

Here's one funny story about that Station Commander. He was always having trouble with the radiator in his office and one quiet day he decided to fix it himself. It was either a Sunday or a Bank Holiday because we were all up in the mess when we heard his shouts for help. He had loosened the radiator valve so much that the water pressure had pushed it out of its housing and boiling hot water was shooting up to the ceiling! Everybody who had heard him rushed to his room and we would have helped him, but the bells went down! As we left, somebody told him to stick his foot on it.

So there he was holding back some of the flow, but his room was flooding and he couldn't quite reach across the room to the phone to call for help. Our call turned out to be a little job and we were away for some time. In desperation, he eventually managed to reach the phone and called another Station Commander to come and save him. It was a good job that the floors were concrete or the whole building would have been flooded. Now that would have been embarrassing! As it was, he only had to claim for a new carpet.

This was not the only Station Commander who came to Soho and quickly found himself out of his depth. One day I was called to The Royal Opera House to some workmen trapped in a cradle. This was when the Opera House was being rebuilt and they were working on the ceiling at least 70ft above ground. Their hoist had broken down and they had no alternative means of returning to ground level. We had no way of reaching them and it was just a case of reassuring them and waiting for engineers to arrive to repair the winding machinery. The Station Commander decided that he wanted to come and have a look at what I was doing. When he arrived I said, 'Thank God you're here. I don't know what to do.' 'Oh,' he said. 'I was just passing and thought I would just look in. I'll leave it to you Mr Chilton.' And with that he left!

While the reconstruction of the Opera House was in progress, it gave us a lot of business. All the types of incident you would expect with major building projects: fires, workers falling, and floods. On 1st December 1998, on another bitterly cold evening, we were called to a crane in a precarious position; a sight beyond belief. Perched precariously on the highest part of the roof, a seven-ton mobile crane with its load still attached, was resting half on and half off the roof. It had somersaulted; its wheels were in the air, and it was only prevented from tumbling 150ft onto the Piazza below by part of its jib caught on the scaffolding.

We made our way to the roof, but there was little we could do; our meagre toolbox had its limitations. It was simply a case of closing the surrounding streets and waiting for three hours while our crane's big brother was driven into London from 40 miles away. It was so cold with an icy wind chill that we had to wear our newly-issued smoke hoods to prevent frost-bitten ears.

## Chapter 30

# TRAINS AND REGRETS

Of all the things that happened to me and all the decisions I had to make, I can truthfully say that I have only one real regret. I made mistakes, took wrong decisions, but one thing has burned its way into my brain. I wish it hadn't happened; it tore me apart at the time and still hurts.

On 1st June 1996, I think it was a Friday, I know we were busy. It was about 1930hrs and we were returning from a call up near Bloomsbury. I was riding the pump ladder and the pump was also returning from a separate call elsewhere on the ground. We were both ordered to: 'Smoke issuing, Tisbury Court, W1'. Tisbury Court links Wardour Street and Rupert Street right at the heart of the 'red light' area. It is a pedestrian walkway full of peep shows and seedy cinemas, and the actual address could only be reached on foot.

Both trucks approached from different directions. I was stopped in Wardour Street and the pump was in Rupert Street. There was smoking issuing from a hoarding above a cinema. Fires like this are a regular occurrence and are usually caused by rainwater entering wiring causing a short circuit, and sparks catch the timber facia alight. As we had to leave the truck and walk to the fire, the two firemen with me had rigged in BA. Once I saw what was involved, I found that BA would not be needed. One of the firemen went back to the truck, took off his set and got a ladder. In the meantime the pump had arrived at the other end of the walkway. They could see the smoke and pulled off the hosereel tubing; the driver engaged the pump and opened the nozzle to check that he had water. Not much, but some water flowed along the ground down the walkway, so the ground was wet.

Not only have I got to organise the firefighting I have to keep the inquisitive public away. The Leading Fireman, Big Geoff, still had his set on. The man who had gone back to the truck came back with the ladder; it was pitched and Geoff went up. The electricity supply had already been isolated at the fireman's switch. Now the fire can be extinguished and the wooden surround cut away. The man who had fetched the ladder was footing it. This is an essential duty when someone is working aloft.

Suddenly the foot of the ladder started to slide away from the building! I was close and tried to help stop it sliding but the two of us could not prevent Geoff from falling from about 10ft. He fell directly onto his back and he was wearing a BA set.

It was just something I had not considered. Geoff was much heavier than the man footing the ladder and once the ladder began to slide, nothing would have stopped it. Nothing in my training had ever told me that men of similar weight should work in this way, but I should have thought of it. If I have anything, it's common sense. Why didn't I use it?

I called for an ambulance, but when a fireman is injured on the fireground you don't send the details over the radio, you have to use a landline. Where can I find a landline when I'm surrounded by clip joints? Eventually I'm shown to a payphone in a strip club by a topless hostess. I have no money and she has no pockets. There is a procedure whereby a fire officer can use a payphone by using a coded message and the operator will connect him with control, but it happens so rarely that the operators don't know what you're talking about. I eventually got through, gave the details and asked for a Senior Accident Investigator to attend. This is a senior officer with specialist training in health and safety.

How did this happen? There were other aspects to be considered other than the men's weight difference. The ground was wet and greasy. It was noticeably slippery from the grease dropped from the fumes extracted from all the surrounding eateries.

Later I found out that there was no official specification for the ladder we were using. Throughout the Brigade they all had different types of feet. In this case, the ladder was the most unstable, having plain, squared-off plastic feet which had hardly any resistance to sliding.

There was an investigation, and although no blame was directed at me, it was no consolation. Geoff injured his back so badly that he had to retire and the Brigade treated him ashamedly. He was desperate to stay attached to the station, but they transferred him into HQ. Then they found out that he had something wrong with his back already and used this as a reason to reduce his compensation. The investigation into the safety and stability of the ladder was washed away, but miraculously all the ladders were suddenly fitted with the most stable type of feet.

None of this improved my conscience. Geoff was a good man. He had served me well at the Carlton Club and the Aldwych. Nobody gave me any trouble when he was standing behind me; he had his heart in the

Station, not in all the old bollocks of the Fire Brigade, but in what he respected as the tradition of the Fire Brigade.

It was a sad loss and one that I have never gotten over. If my opinion of the Brigade's internal workings could be any more soured, this was it. I had always had a low opinion of anyone who took advantage of the job for whatever reason, but I changed my mind. I previously felt aggrieved by anyone who took advantage of their last years in the job by jumping up a few ranks, just to improve their pensions. Or those who took jobs at a higher rank without having to sit an exam just because it suited the Brigade.

'Get as much out of them as possible', was now my advice.

1996 was nearly out but it still had a little sting in the tail for the White Watch. On 3rd December we were called at just before midnight to a 'Derailed Train. Bakerloo Line. Piccadilly Circus Station, Regent Street, W1'. Seven pumps, a Heavy Rescue Unit and two Control Units were ordered on the initial attendance. The standby appliances were being ordered into the empty stations before I had confirmed the seriousness of the incident. I realised from all this preparation that this was no false alarm. My initial investigation confirmed that I had an eight-carriage train with the rear carriage detached and it had collided with the tunnel wall. I had one person with injuries that were serious enough that he needed to be removed from the train on a stretcher. As the rear carriage was wedged in the tunnel I had to get the remaining passengers out of the train and assist them through the tunnel to Oxford Circus. Later on in the incident, I found that I had a total of four persons injured who needed hospitalisation and 72 passengers that had to be removed from the tunnel.

I had to order four further appliances to Oxford Circus, as manpower was needed to assist the passengers from the station. A total of 24 appliances were involved in the whole operation.

This was the first time that I had been involved in any form of train crash, and I was thankful for all the assistance I received from all the officers and firemen from the surrounding stations, especially Station Officer, Ron Beer. He had been a long-time friend and his help and advice had always been valued. Ron later moved to Paddington and was one of the first on the scene of the Ladbroke Grove train crash.

It's impossible to relate all the bravery and thoughtfulness that goes into an operation like this, you just know that it is going on and that the people of London are being looked after in the best possible and safest way. Treasure the firemen!

The White Watch were on duty, nursing bad heads, on New Year's Day 1997. In the middle of the afternoon we were called to a fire in Sutherland Terrace on Paddington's ground. Three four-storey terraced houses, converted into flats, were involved. The smoke could be seen from miles away. Four buildings either side of the premises had to be evacuated. The occupants were sheltered in a local church hall.

When we arrived, the buildings were well alight and looked as though they were in danger of collapsing. So fragile were the buildings, that all the firefighting was taking place from outside. There were flames bursting out of all the top floor windows and a halo of smoke and flames obscuring the sky.

Paddington's hydraulic platform was working at the front, but it was seriously restricted by trees. There was hose everywhere and several ladders were pitched to windows on the lower floors. The Brigade had received 61 calls to the incident and it was clearly out of control.

On all operational fire engines, there is an item called a nominal role board. This is a register of the names of the riders and it is completed at the beginning of the shift and any changes are entered immediately. When you arrive at a large fire, the first thing that the OIC does is to take the nominal role board to the control unit to be registered and monitored.

While I was doing this, the men would stay with the trucks and wait for me to return with instructions as to what was required. I had been asked to get a jet from the ground floor up to the roof to see if we could make any headway from an adjacent property. Our efforts were being hampered by the bitter cold. The water was freezing as soon as it touched the ground, and hose was being frozen in position. There was a 135 ladder pitched to the second floor with hose frozen solid onto the metal. We managed to get a jet right up onto the flat roof of a loft extension and were doing some good work, but the surface beneath our feet was becoming icy. It was judged to be too dangerous and we were eventually withdrawn.

I had seen pictures of it in the old days, but this was the first time that I had ever seen the firemen with icicles formed on their helmets. The air was even freezing on the firemen's moustaches! Any water, which had rested on the ground, was turning to ice and the whole area became a skating rink. Equipment had to be left in position for several days before it could be made-up and the job closed down.

I found working on any of the Bank Holidays a bind. Especially Christmas, but the worst night for me to work was New Year's Eve. Due to all the activity in the West End, we were restricted to calls on our own ground. Any calls to Trafalgar Square and its surrounds were monitored by a senior officer who was detached to Scotland Yard.

Understandably, on New Year's Eve, Soho goes ballistic. The streets are filled to bursting with revellers. The fire station is not included in the celebrations. We are shut up in the station, all the jollity passing by.

Before the Brigade decided to monitor our calls, there would always be a malicious call to Trafalgar Square close to midnight and, of course, this caused a number of problems. Firstly it was nigh on impossible to reach the location because of the crowds and the sight and sound of fire engines increased the excitement of the revellers. All the girls want a lucky New Year kiss and all the young men want to climb on top of the fire engines. It all becomes very dangerous. Even when you were able to get moving, you had to be careful that there wasn't anyone hanging onto the back.

One year our Red Watch did some sterling work, when several members of the public were crushed by the crowds and had to be resuscitated. Some of them received bravery awards for their actions.

As soon as midnight passes we go back to out regular mobilising routine. The crowds start to move up into Soho and the cars start blowing their horns. All I want to do is get my head down! Every passing drunk rings our front door bell, or opens the running call telephone box setting off the call bells. No wonder I always tried to get the night off.

As soon as the main crowds start to disperse, the regular calls start coming in. One year there were several cars alight in Spring Gardens. We still could not get down Haymarket, and had to leave the fire engine with the driver and proceed on foot with some firefighting equipment. There was nothing unusual about this call, but I remember walking on smashed beer bottles all the way to the incident.

This was the year of the famous walking race. The gauntlet was thrown in the mess and the challenge was set. Steve King, The Victorian Strongman, reckoned that he could walk faster than, wait for it, Fireman Robert Walker! – known to all as 'Mary'. I don't know why he was called Mary; sometimes the origins of the nicknames went over my head. I do know that at one time they decided that the next bloke to come on the watch would be called 'Ginger' just because we didn't have one and every watch should have one. The next man to arrive had a shaved head; he was still called Ginger. I supposed it had its own little bit of irony. Anyway Mary had boasted that while at school he had been quite a useful walker, and that was how the challenge came about.

The course was to be the length of The Mall. Both fire engines were booked out of the station on false missions, available for calls via the radio. Both participants were riding my fire engine, which stopped at the starting point, and the other was parked on the finish line at the other end of The Mall.

I started the event and then drove alongside the racers, just in case we were called, shouting out encouragement. Mary soon established a fair lead and Kingy was starting to puff, soon to retire, faking a dodgy knee. At the finish line the crew had stretched out a length of pink toilet roll as the finishing tape. The finish zone was soon surrounded by excited Japanese tourists who all wanted to get a photo of the winner of this illustrious sporting event! Mary broke the finish tape to the cheers of the crowd and the flash of cameras. All this was in the cause of improving morale, you understand. By the way, Mary later transferred to the Devon Brigade, and was quickly re-christened 'Punchy' because he had a dust-up on his first night in town.

Sometimes there were visitors to the station who were, to say the least, unusual. On one occasion I arrived for a night shift to find a minibus parked in the yard. The OIC of the watch on duty told me that it belonged to a group of firemen from Chernobyl!

Apparently, they had been invited to the country by another Brigade, who now wanted to show them the bright lights. They had been told that there was not enough room for them all to stay at the station. That wasn't a problem; they would sleep in the bus. After they had sampled the delights of the West End, they returned to the station. A very strange atmosphere descended on the place. None of these men could speak English, but they came and sat in the mess with us and it just went very quiet. It was as if we had been invaded by aliens. From time to time they would return to the bus where they had an endless supply of vodka.

They were gone by the morning but left us with a quantity of 'Welcome to Chernobyl' lapel badges!

That is what visiting firemen do; they want to swap badges or any kind of uniform. But the only things we have to swap are T-shirts marked with 'London Fire Brigade' and cap badges from our personal issue. The Americans come loaded with home station T-shirts, badges and shoulder patches, but we are very much the poor relations and can't reciprocate. I did exchange a couple of letters with an officer in New York. His wife had visited the station with some swapsies and he wrote sending a very prestigious NYPD tie clip. He must have been about the same age as me with the same pressures. I hope he had retired long before the twin towers fell down.

One day I returned from a call to find a uniformed oriental gentleman standing in the appliance bay. As usual, at the sight of a visitor, all the blokes disappeared. I was left on my own to deal with this man who stated that he was a pilot with the Chinese National Airline. He was based in Shanghai and was on a fact-finding mission for his Government, and had been given the responsibility of buying some new fire engines for the Shanghai Fire Service. I had read somewhere that Shanghai was one of most rapidly developing cities in China.

He was a very well spoken and polite gentleman and seemed not at all mad. Pointing to our trucks, he told me that he had to buy six fire engines just like these, fully equipped for his Government. All this with a straight face. There was no way it could have been a wind-up; it was so ludicrous that it had to be straight up. I told him that nobody could just buy a fire engine. The usual method is to put your requirements out to tender with the various manufacturers.

He told me that he did not have time to do this, as he had to fly home. He asked me if I would do some research for him. He would be back next month and he would pay me some commission!

What should I do? I could make a bit of money. I'm no monkey and this man was so convincing. So I went for it. I went home and made some enquiries with the fire engine manufacturers. They must have been laughing behind their hands, putting the phone on speaker so their mates could listen. What an idiot! He never came back – I wonder where he got the uniform from, or on the other hand, will you now ever get on a plane to China!

One Sunday morning at about 0630hrs, I was resting in my bed and the front door bell rang. When this happens, the dutyman who is also resting in the watchroom will answer the door and try his best to get rid of the caller. If it is a genuinely urgent situation he will call me or put the bells down. 'Candy' was the dutyman. He phoned my room and told me that he had young lady in reception in a state of distress. I asked him if she was good looking. He said beautiful, so I went down to see her! She was beautiful, and she'd had her purse stolen as she was coming out of an all-night shop in Charing Cross Road. She had been buying food for her cat and was stranded. She was also being followed by one of the scummies and was scared stiff.

I asked what she was doing shopping at 6 o'clock in the morning. She told me that she was returning from a party, which had been held to launch her taking part in the Sahara Marathon. I know it sounds absurd, but I'm not making it up. Candy had already got her a cup of tea, the firemen's stress cure for all situations. She made a phone call on her mobile and asked me to talk to the man on the other end of the phone.

He said, 'Do you know who the girl is? She's Kate O'Mara's daughter.'

I said, 'Who are you?'

'I'm her bodyguard.'

'So why aren't you guarding her?'

'I'm in Peckham…'

As if that was some sort of excuse. Does a bodyguard ever go off-duty? Now, me being a gentleman of a certain age, I know what Kate O'Mara looks like and this girl was the image. However, it would not have mattered who she was, we would've helped her. Both Candy and I are fathers of daughters, and imagine how we would have felt if it was one of our girls who were stranded.

We did not have much cash but we managed to scrape together £10 and Candy went out into the Avenue and persuaded a cab driver to take this girl home to Islington. She was eternally grateful; there were lovey kisses all round. She said she would get the money back to us that night. She never came back. One of the blokes checked on the internet and Kate O'Mara doesn't have a daughter! But she was the image: the eyes, the cheekbones, everything. Why go to those extremes just to get your fare home?

On a typical shift in Soho it is quite common to see, and come into contact with, famous people. While the fire engines were driving around, or they would be walking past the station, you would see actors and celebrities heading for their appointments or auditions. We called this activity 'spotting' and the best of which were recognised by a general scrabbling to get to the windows. Incidentally, the same happened for every attractive woman.

There were a number of times I bumped into well-known people, and although I recognised them I often forgot their names. On one call to St. Anne's Court (once one of the seediest alleys in Soho), I came face to face with the highly recognisably character actor, Jim Broadbent, when he was walking down Wardour Street. I said, 'You're, you're, er, a very good actor.' His reply was, 'I'm sure you're a very good fireman!'

We were putting out a car fire in Shaftesbury Avenue when the romantic novelist Jilly Cooper came up and told us that she thought that firemen were wonderful. I knew who she was, but do you think I could remember her name? The car was a Triumph Stag in pristine condition and its owner was in despair as his pride and joy went up in flames. Characteristically, one of the firemen who was interested in cars made him an offer for the wreck!

Amongst other calls to famous people, we attended to a smell of burning in Brian Cox's luxury flat that turned out to be the lady downstairs smoking very strange tobacco, and a flood in The Eurythmics' Dave Stewart's home/studio, which is a converted hospital in Covent Garden.

Here are a few of my best spots. The theatres were very kind to us and if you spoke to the right person, if they could, they would let you have complimentary tickets. El and I and a couple of our friends wanted to see a play at the Wyndam's. I approached the theatre manager, who was surprised that I wanted to see the play, as in his words nobody could understand it, even him. I hoped he wasn't implying that a fireman was too dumb to understand a bit of Harold Pinter. As we came out of the theatre, the late Richard Harris was standing there dressed in a long black overcoat with a hat partially covering his face (probably trying to avoid the attentions of star-struck idiots like me). I had just seen him playing English Bob in 'The Unforgiven'. I said, quietly, 'You're The Duck of Death!' He put his finger to his lips and disappeared into the theatre.

On one of our many nights on the doors, we were collecting for some worthy cause and up walked Chris Eubank. Now he is barmy! Not only did he put a load of cash in the pots, but he stripped off his sheepskin coat, which weighed a ton, and joined in the collecting. Who could refuse the Middleweight Champion of the World? He shook my hand; it was like holding a lump of granite.

But the best, the very best, was when we were returning from a call and driving down Berwick Street through the market. As we approached the junction with Broadwick Street, I felt an extraordinary presence to my left. Standing on the pavement, level with my face, I turned to look into the dark eyes of Tony Soprano!

What! There he was, James Gandolfini wandering around Soho. This was before 9/11 when I heard that he was in the crowds of people lining the route and cheering the firemen as they went into that hell hole. At the time his wife in the show was appearing in a play in the Avenue. 'How ya doin?' He didn't need to say anything more and that did for me. I didn't need to see anyone else. Nothing could top that!

*Chapter 31*

# THE ROYAL ACADEMY OF ART

The 3rd May 1997 was a date that was to go to the top of the list of spectacular Soho fires. The bells went down shortly after 1900hrs. Saturday night again! 'Fire, The Royal Academy of Art', located in Burlington House, Piccadilly since 1868. The Academy was first established in 1768, and houses works of art contributed by its members and many of the greatest artists from around world. It holds an annual Summer Exhibition when 10,000 pictures are submitted to be selected for show. It also stages Loan Exhibitions, and some of these have been so popular that the queues stretch far down the road.

I was very familiar with the place. Like all big public buildings, it was my job to have a basic knowledge of the layout and we were often there answering calls to their temperamental AFA.

Apart from all the offices, art stores and workshops it has 17 galleries. To reach the main building you have to pass though a narrow arch just wide enough for a fire engine. You then enter a large quadrangle. From here you can access the main entrance.

I looked at the call slip and instead of ordering us to the usual front entrance in Piccadilly, we were to go to the rear entrance in Vigo Street. I didn't really need a call slip!

The doors opened and the trucks turned left into the avenue. The Academy is about a mile from the station and, even though surrounded by high buildings, I could see a dark shroud of thick smoke rising into the evening sky. It could be seen all over London. The nearer we got, the thicker and blacker the smoke became. The entrance in Vigo Street is another narrow archway and a security guard was waving us in. Even though the building was at least the height of three storeys, we were being showered with embers and ash. The pump ladder went in first and I quickly realised that we were going to need the TL, which was on its way, returning from an earlier call. As the firemen were laying out hose and setting up a water supply, I got the driver to reverse out to allow the TL to get into the face of the building. I also knew that back-up appliances heading towards the fire were coming from Knightsbridge. I sent a message that they should go to the main entrance. Station Officer Ron Beer was in charge at Knightsbridge, and as soon as he arrived I established radio contact and asked him to handle the operation at the front of the building. If we could attack the fire from both directions, we would have more success.

The most direct access to the fire was from the roof. This had already been breached by the fire. It was as if we were working in the middle of a total eclipse – surrounded by smoke and yet the sky was still bright. I didn't discover until I got the TL into position, and the men were taking jets up the ladder to the roof, that a section of the roof had been removed by builders. At the front, Ron also had to get ladders pitched to the roof. BA crews had been sent to investigate the inside of the building from the front main entrance.

Not only did we have a major fire; we had a massive salvage operation. I had already 'made pumps six' and quickly increased this to eight. There were national treasures inside that had to be removed to a safe place – paintings that had not only to be protected from the fire, but from the damage the firefighting operation was going to cause. It eventually went to 15 pumps and most of those men that arrived after the initial attendance were involved in the salvage operation. Academy experts were called in to advise and assist in the removal of the paintings.

The seat of the fire was in an area which was being prepared as a new exhibition space, and was screened from the remainder of the gallery by a builder's hoarding. It had started in the temporary wiring. It had soon got a strong hold involving two floors and was now through the roof in several places.

My boys were working like dogs on the roof and it was their efforts that saved the building. By getting water directly onto the fire without having to wear BA, we were able to restrict the fire. If we had been dragging hose through the building, even more damage could have been caused.

I never felt that I had to thank them for doing something that they enjoyed, but on this occasion I did. I was so proud of them. Not a hesitation; there was the job and they got on with it. My current new boy was at his first big job. I slapped him on the back saying, 'This is what it's like to be at Soho!'

A local senior officer was soon on the scene, a man called Nick Ginty. I knew him to be an experienced and trusted officer. I was glad to be able to hand overall control to him and concentrate on the firefighting.

I moved from one firefighting location to another organising and encouraging the men. The work going on inside the building was hard and dangerous. The fire had managed to find its way into many concealed areas. The firemen had to cut away large sections of timber to expose the burning. There were some tight spaces and only by crawling inside could they attack the burning. At the same time, there was a daisy chain of valuable paintings being passed from hand to hand away from the danger area.

We were there for several hours and the reliefs went on through the night. It was several days before the job could be closed down.

The next time we were on duty something happened to me that touched my soul. One of the firemen came to me – a senior man who was not easily impressed. He said to me, 'You know when we do a good job you give us a pat on the back. Well, who pats your back?' I told him that although nobody did, I knew that as my own hardest critic, I got my satisfaction knowing that the job had gone well.

The next thing I knew he had put it in writing. Not an easy thing to do as he had typed the report and his fingers were so big that they must have hit two keys at a time! Normal circumstances were such that I would forward both copies of his report to the Station Commander. But this was far too important. One copy went straight into my red lever arch, and there it will stay. That was one of the best compliments I ever received.

At the end of 1997 we got something that was well overdue. We had not had a Station Commander who came up to my expectations since the time of Kings Cross and Ray Firth. Graham Ellis had recently been promoted; he had served at Westminster and had been a Station Officer at Whitechapel. At last someone I could talk to, someone who I knew cared about the station and the men. Not just there for self-advancement. Some officers just wanted to get an attachment to Soho on their record. He looked after me until I retired, and deserves the greatest of respect from all of us. How he coped with it all, I'll never know. Not just my problems but the same magnified four times. And didn't he have some managing to do. Not as if all the problems with personnel weren't enough, there were all the problems with the building and the cooks. There were times when I'm sure he wondered what he had taken on, especially as he was also one of the Station Commanders who worked his on-call hours from quarters provided by the Brigade. They are the first to be called out operationally. I know that his 72 hour week didn't involve much rest.

The Soho firemen cannot hide; they are always in the public eye. Every time we were called out, our actions were under scrutiny. Once, Graham phoned to ask if I had attended a call in Charing Cross Road on the previous night. We had been called to smoke issuing from the Angus Steak house at about 1900hrs. Why was there a problem? Apparently, the Leader of the Fire Authority, Councillor Tony Ritchie, had made a complaint to the Chief Officer that he had witnessed one of my drivers making a racist remark. Now, if this was true and knowing the Brigade's policy on such things, we were in big trouble.

I found this very hard to believe but I had to investigate the claim. I could remember that at the start of the shift the pump had been off the run because we were short of personnel and I had been out on a call and then been ordered over the radio to Charing Cross Road. In the meantime, the pump had gone on the run in time to attend and turned out from the station. Consequently, we approached the call from opposite directions. I knew what Councillor Ritchie looked like. I spotted him standing at the side of the road, and he was hard to miss being a large man wearing a white suit.

I got the driver into my room and he emphatically denied making any such remark. While the OIC of his fire engine and the crew had been inside the steak house, he had been outside. A mate of his who was a cab driver pulled up and asked him what was happening. The conversation was short and congenial, but at no time had any form of racial remark been made. My driver even offered to bring his mate forward as a witness.

I put all this into a report and gave it to Graham, and fortunately it went away. There were no other witnesses. Anyway, if you have been in Charing Cross Road at 1900hrs on a busy night, with fire engines approaching from different directions with horns sounding, how could you overhear anything that was being said? The world was going mad!

While on the subject, Angus Steak Houses. What are they all about? They are in prime sites around the West End and must be paying high rents, and yet they are nearly always empty. The only customers seem to be smartly dressed out-of-towners, country folk up to the big city having a pre-theatre dinner. Then they were empty again. We had a theory that they were a front for the Russian Mafia! All the staff suddenly became Eastern Europeans. Once every six months, the one in the avenue caught fire. It was the sign outside which I kept telling them to get replaced. Ahhhh Soho!

That year was good to me in another way. A man called Michael Herschell transferred to the watch. He was a Leading Fireman and was the replacement for Big Geoff. Another big man who was later to become the Sub. Officer. A great assistant in my time of need. My time of need? My time of need came when my, long time, Sub. Officer, Steve Johnson decided that he had had enough and needed to be closer to home for the sake of his family. Being the Station Officer at Soho was difficult enough, but it was made much easier by having a reliable and experienced deputy, not only to help with the running of the station, but with whom you can confide and discuss problems. As I have said before, the Station Officer's room, at times, is a very lonely place.

For a long time I had no help at all. Mainly because I would not ask for it and I started to pay for it with my health. I never foresaw that the job would get on top of me, but it did.

I had come home from nights and it was a nice, dry day and I decided to do a bit of gardening. I wasn't feeling wonderful; I put it down to tiredness. If tiredness stopped me from doing anything, I would do nothing! I took little notice of it. I thought I was getting a cold. That evening, part of my tongue went a little bit numb. When I woke up in the morning I felt very strange; the right side of my face had no movement. Very distressing; I thought I'd had a stroke. El took one look at me and with her famous matter of fact manner said, 'You'd better go to the doctor with that.' My doctor told me that I had a thing called Bell's Palsy. This is caused by the facial nerve becoming restricted. The eye on the affected side continuously waters and you are prone to dribble. The blokes said that I looked little different!

Apart from feeling rotten, it does nothing for your state of mind. The doctor put me on a high dose of steroids. I was off work for a month. It wasn't until later that I found out that one of the main factors contributing to this condition is stress. This was just the beginning of my trip down the slippery slope to general bad health.

When I got back to work I could feel that the atmosphere had been disturbed. Both the junior officers and the men were disgruntled. There had been an officer posted in on a temporary basis and there been some unconventional management decisions.

Soon after, Mick Herschel took on the job of deputy by acting-up, and Graham was able to divert the efforts of management to send in someone and deny any requests from more qualified Sub. Officers who wanted to take the job. Mick was good for me, both at the station and on the fire-ground. He was great with the men. His development from fireman to junior officer had all been gathered in the central area, and with this solid background, it could not help but attract immediate respect.

I reached a major landmark in 1998. I reached 50 years of age and achieved 25 years' service. It marked a time in my life where I was forced to make some decisions about my working life. My retirement was only five years away and I was not as fit and healthy as I would have wanted. I decided that I was making life too hard. For the past 15 years I had been cycling from Croydon to the West End and it was time for me to stop. Cycling had been a great way of getting to work but it had to go. I had always been careful and aware that El was concerned for my safety. I always rang to let her know that I had arrived at work and called to let her know if I was going to be late home. At first I stopped using the bike on days and only rode in on nights, and I stopped going home between the two nights. I started to ride gently around London looking at the sights, visiting the museums and galleries or, if I was too tired, I just rested in my room, sat in the park or went to the cinema.

Not caring for public transport, I was fortunate to be in the position where I could share the driving with two of the firemen who live near to me. It's not very practical sharing a car, as the risk of being delayed in leaving the station increases when your travelling mates are on different appliances to yourself. When Cheesy was driving the ladders, he would often be out on calls and Candy, who was not a driver, ran the possibility of having to stand by at another station. So sometimes we got home very late indeed.

We had to leave Croydon by 0630hrs to miss the bulk of the traffic and to be sure that we would be ready to start work at 0900hrs. This meant that we were in the West End by about 0730hrs with time to waste. We took to either going swimming at the Oasis or running around St. James's Park. The nice thing about this was that you had a choice; you could exercise or you could just have a cup of tea with the watch on duty or wander over to Bar Italia in Frith Street, sit outside, drink coffee and watch the world arriving for work. What a place to work. What could be better? People would pay to do what we were doing for free. For some strange, weird and wonderful reason, we once entered an early morning piggy-back race sponsored by Capital Radio. What was I thinking of? Years earlier we entered a team for a pancake tossing relay race organised by the same people in Carnaby Street. We won by a mile but got disqualified for cheating. It was an injustice. A team of beautiful models were promoted to first place over a bunch of ugly firemen. I wonder why?

Piccadilly Circus must be the busiest and the slowest moving road junction in the world. The Circus and its surrounds provided me with a lot of work and amusement. All the stores, shops, offices, restaurants and the Underground Station were regular customers.

Being located at the other end of the Avenue, any calls to the south and west of the ground involved negotiating the Circus. Either going at speed when proceeding on calls or our leisurely return, it provided a miscellany of sights. There is not an hour of the day or night when it is free of traffic.

The whole of the West End is rock-solid during 'the burst'. This is the time when the theatres and cinema turn-out at about 2230hrs. When the trucks have to turn-out at this time, it was often the case that we would struggle to get further than the forecourt. The fire engines just added to the general chaos – double-parked cars, coaches picking up, plus any vehicles that were stupidly trying to traverse the area.

At one time I had a really dodgy driver. He was a man who had transferred to us from Euston. A good fireman but, he admitted it, a lousy driver! He won't mind me mentioning his name, Brian Still. He was eventually taken off driving at his own request.

The avenue was the site of his greatest driving accomplishment – he went straight down the side of a stationary car. Nothing ordinary; a brand new Bentley. The petrified driver sat looking up at a 10-ton fire engine wedged against his sparkling olive green treasure, which was only a week old. In one fell swoop 'Hank' had reduced it to scrap!

Before the traffic management's attempt at improving the flow, we could drive straight down the avenue, into the Circus and treat it as a roundabout. Once it was improved we had to negotiate one left and two right turns to get to the same place, drastically increasing the attendance times.

While traffic management proposals are in the consultation stage, the Council ask all the emergency service providers for their opinions and then they go ahead with what they wanted in the first place. This was so with Piccadilly and, later, the Strand. The changes around the Strand were unbelievable. All but one of the roads leading into the Strand, from the north, were blocked with bollards and the new central reservation prevented any emergency vehicle from overtaking. The congestion was at its worse when coaches were dropping off at The Stand Palace Hotel. Even the 'old bill' disagreed with this proposal but, of course, it went ahead.

There were occasions where they did take notice of us, but only after the scheme was put in place and found to be totally impractical.

The East Soho traffic project proved to be a nightmare. Certain streets were pedestrianised at certain times of the day; locked gates stood in our way in Old Compton Street! Although we had keys, ambulances, police, and fire engines from other stations did not. If there was an accident or a crime was committed, the police had to leave their vehicles as close as they could get and run; ambulances just had to stand outside and look! Eventually the Council saw reason and made appropriate alterations to the project. But not being satisfied with making the mistake once, they only tried to do the same sort of thing around Seven Dials, which would have created another no-go area. The old bill and the Fire Brigade protested against the proposals and, unbelievably, the council relented.

Seven Dials was once a very squalid part of the area being near the Rookeries of St. Giles and named so because at one time seven streets formed a star out from the Doric Pillar in its centre. It was a rendezvous for local criminals and footpads. Now, although it is ominous and echoey at night, it is more noted for its shops, restaurants and street markets.

At the far end of the avenue on the left hand side is The Rainforest Café. In the windows that front the street there is a simulated jungle with a stream running through. When it caught alight, it wasn't something you would expect an inner city fireman to have to deal with. Although we train for the most diverse of scenarios, we had not been skilled in wading through undergrowth avoiding crocodiles looking for a fire! As you can imagine, the pavements outside were soon crowded with onlookers. We had to set up barriers and call the police to control the crowds. To the delight of the crowd, the firemen were soon increasing the absurdity by attaching camouflage to their uniforms and being dragged further into the undergrowth.

The Trocadero shopping and leisure complex has been on its site in the avenue since 1851, and has been the scene of many electrical explosions, floods and fires. It was completely re-constructed in the '80s and included 'The Rock Circus'. An electrical fire filled it with smoke. With no lights, working in the smoke with just torches bumping into Jimi Hendrix and Michael Jackson was just run of the mill to the Soho firemen. Like a lot of these massive buildings, it had its own electrical sub-station. When it caught alight the whole place was out of action for several days.

Fires in electrical sub-stations were a part of life. Sub-stations are such dangerous places that even when they are not on fire, we are not allowed to enter. They are all heavily secured, and you have to call the electrical authority to make the place safe before any firefighting takes place. Usually there is a lot of thick, black, choking smoke but they eventually burn out. The Fire Brigade just has to prevent spread and protect the surrounding area. Once it is safe, we can enter to make sure there is no remaining fire.

*Chapter 32*

# EMBASSIES AND AUSSIES

On 7th January 1998 at 0805hrs we were called to smoke issuing from the first floor of a building, Piccadilly, W1, just off the Circus. As the trucks were proceeding, additional information came over the radio: next to cinema and Clydesdale Bank, then above Ponti's Café Deli.

The scene: Piccadilly, just opposite a big hotel, at 0800hrs, full of traffic and people on their way to work. Smoke and flames were bursting out of the windows at second-floor level and shooting up the front of the building. The ground floor housed the restaurant and was of almost double height. As we pulled up, a man blackened from smoke stumbled into the street from the ground floor doorway with his clothing alight.

Through his terror he told me that there were two more people inside. The firemen got to work. A hosereel was being run off, the BA sets were already donned and the drivers were getting water. The TL was going up with a fireman at the head of the ladder, being held away from the building, waiting to swing in just in case the occupants needed to come out of the windows. I'd given no instructions!

I'm up the stairs following the BA men just to have a look; I've already sent, 'Make pumps four, persons reported'. I knew that Knightsbridge were on their way and an ambulance had been ordered. I only reached halfway up the first flight of stairs and I had to retire and let the BA men do their work. It was too thick for me to see anything, so I went back outside.

As I reached the doorway, I turned around to see another smoke-blackened man being dragged out. One of the BA crews had located him on the fourth floor, which was now also smoke logged. This man had tried to escape by going upstairs, came up against a locked door and very nearly lost his life.

I then received a message over the hand-held radio; a further casualty had been found inside the flat. He had been dragged to a relatively smoke-free area and was being resuscitated by the firemen. As I prepared to re-enter, the ambulance arrived and the paramedics came with me to take over the life saving.

Everyone's efforts were in vain, as the man died from burns and smoke inhalation before the firemen could get their hands on him. Poor creature was found naked, but the firemen soon covered him so at least there was a little dignity in his death, although not much. Lying naked and dead on a cold, wet, stair landing – not a fitting end to anyone's life.

As with all fatal fires, the OIC and the men who find the victim have to complete statements for the inquest. No longer did we have to go through the ordeal of attending court; that was now left to the Fire Investigation Officers. The fire had started in the dead man's bed, probably caused by smoking.

The next year on 14th July 1990 at 2031hrs, supper had just gone on the table. We were back to almost the same spot to another fire with a different set of complications. This was to be the start of a sequence of events that ended a couple of months later.

The call came in: 'Automatic fire alarm, Duke of York Street, St. James, W1'. This is located off Jermyn Street, just behind Piccadilly. As the fire engines entered Jermyn Street from Lower Regent Street, there is a man standing on the corner waving us in another direction. I noticed that there was a small group of people on the corner of Piccadilly looking upwards, pointing and looking aghast when the fire engines turned left away from them. I could take little notice, as once ordered, appliances cannot be diverted from the original call. As soon as we pulled up at the address, I verified with the occupier that there was no fire, sent a stop message and left the incident in the capable hands of Leading Fireman Blakeman 'Carrots', who later told me that there had been a small fire but that it had been put out before we arrived. I just had the feeling that there was a real job waiting for us in Piccadilly. I got on the radio and told control that we had been 'Called by stranger to a fire'. Carrots knew what I was up to and booked his fire engine mobile so that he could also get on the call. No one likes to miss a fire on their ground.

It was a beautiful evening, still hot and sunny. Just the sort of day when London has its hat on the side of its head looking its best. It was just the sort of night when you knew you were going to be busy. When the weather is hot, crowds stay longer, drink more and it is always likely to be livelier. The whole place was buzzing. The weather, the circumstances, the whole thing seemed surreal. As I try to recollect, it might just be that I'm getting reality confused with one of my frequent dreams. It was just one of those times, I felt great. The job was great. It went smoothly and I felt right on top of my game. Well why shouldn't I! I was probably the most experienced Station Officer in the London Fire Brigade, well, at least the longest serving.

As the fire engines turned into Piccadilly, there were little signs of a fire. There was a lot of police, some on motorbikes, looking up and obviously surprised to see a fire engine. Although they had been in attendance for about 20 minutes, they had only just called the Brigade and we arrived as though by a flash of magic. Once out of the truck, I looked up and saw smoke issuing from a small vent high up on the outside wall. The reason that the police had taken their time in calling us was that, unknown to me, this was a building of diplomatic importance belonging to the Chilean Government.

Fires in Embassies and the like can prove to be very tricky, as the police and the Fire Brigade can be refused entry. The police had been trying to find out if this was a legitimate fire or something more suspicious. In reality, they should have informed the Fire Brigade and got us to attend, if only to stand by. All diplomacy went to pot as soon as the firemen sent their size tens marching up the stairs.

There was a whole suite of offices blazing away quite merrily and unseen on the second and third floors. It was dangerously bottled up and could have spread to the whole building. Carrots led the first BA crew inside, and he was talking to me via his radio letting me know the conditions. It was easy.

A high ranking naval officer soon arrived, and far from being guarded, he was very cooperative and complimentary about the firemen's work. All naval officers are fire trained and I think he would have got his hands dirty if I had allowed him.

To help illustrate the next part of this story, I should remind you that the firemen who ride the Fire Rescue Unit are the Fire Brigade's version of supermen. Not being at all flippant, they are just the same brave men but with a lot more training. The FRU was re-titled some years ago; before this it was called the ET (Emergency Tender) and that is still what firemen of a certain age call it.

The fire is now under control and I'm at a stage where I can relax a little, when my trusty driver Cheesy approaches me and nods to the sky, 'Did you ask for the ET Guv?'

Overhead, skydivers were parachuting from the sky trailing red, white and blue smoking flares. For the first time the Military Tattoo was being held in the open – Horseguards instead of Earls Court Exhibition Centre – and this was part of the display, gatecrashing our fire!

It took forty firemen using BA with two hosereels and one jet to get it out. Reliefs went on through the night. But it didn't finish there; the tale goes on. Once the fire was out and the relief trucks had arrived, I got the boys mobile. We were anxious to get away as it was now nearly midnight and we were starving.

While stuck in traffic in the avenue, all of a sudden there's a man hanging onto my door, 'Hello mate, I'm a fireman from Sidney, Australia!' He had his luggage with him; he had come straight from the airport to the West End and was on his way to his hotel when he saw us working in Piccadilly.

He seemed a jolly chap, so I invited him back to the station for a cup of tea. We got him into the truck and headed home. No food for us though; supper was welded to the plate. Sometimes I lived to regret my impulsive offers of hospitality and this was one of them. Boy, could he rabbit.

That night it was still hot and we were drinking tea outside in the partially complete 'Home Front' garden. He told me that as well as being a fireman, he was the official photographer for his Brigade. The boys listened politely for a while then, unknown to Aussie, who was not very worldly, they started the wind up. After a while I decided it was time for me to intervene and get rid of him.

It was apparent that this man was a real Fire Brigade nerd. He was over here on his holidays at the invite of our photographers to take pictures of London's work.

The next time he bumped into the White Watch was at another four-pump fire in Panton Street, W1. All the students in London will know of a restaurant called The Stockpot – lots of good food at a reasonable price. The owners went home leaving a gas stove burning. Whoosh up it went, all three floors damaged. I didn't ask for the Brigade Photographer but he arrived with our 'old cobba' in tow. Of course all the boys are now speaking with Aussie accents giving this poor bloke lots of stick for taking photos when he should have been sitting in the sunshine on a beach in his shorts swigging tinnies of Fosters. Instead he's scratching about in a burnt-out restaurant in foggy old London town.

I did not witness his next appearance as I was away on holiday. The Brigade, in their infinite wisdom, had organised a major exercise on, of all nights, a Saturday, which was supposed to test our reaction to a release of poison gas in the Underground.

Typically, on a hot Saturday night in September, everybody wants leave, especially those at the stations which are going on exercise. At 1800hrs our pump, which is on the exercise, is off the run due to a shortage of riders. The pump ladder, with Mick in charge, is chasing calls around the ground. Control gets on the radio wanting to know why the pump is not at the exercise and, thinking that we are working a fast one, will not accept any excuses and orders the pump ladder to attend.

When there was warm weather and because the new uniforms were so hot, I didn't worry what the men wore under their firegear. This night they were all wearing shorts. Now this would not have been a problem to a normal human but, don't forget, we are dealing with Fire Brigade senior officers and the men have got to get changed into chemical protection suits out in the street. They might have gotten away with it but up came our 'old cobba' and at the top of his voice he said to Mick, 'Strewth! Some of your guys are wearing white boxer shorts!' That was it. Mick had a hell of a job diverting the flack. In fact, it took some strong words at the back of the fire engine with a man that was intent on making a lot more of it than it deserved.

'Strewth! Some of your guys are wearing white boxer shorts!' went down in the White Watch annual of best sayings.

Back to '98. They took me out for my birthday with lashings of beer and a night in the 100 Club. Bob Walker, 'Mary', had a mate who was playing in a band and we got in at a special rate. I was introduced to Eric Delaney, an old jazz band drummer who was quite famous in the fifties and sixties. Not that he was anything special to me, but it was nice to talk to him, although I don't know if he was impressed by or understood many of the words I was slurring.

The year progressed and Soho not only made the front cover of the London Firefighter magazine, but also the back cover. Whites on the front, Blues on the back – as it should be! The Blue Watch job was a six-pump fire at The Freemasons Hall in Great Queen Street, and ours was the rescue of some injured building workers who had become trapped when part of a building in New Oxford Street collapsed.

I had been involved in the removal of injured building workers on several occasions, the worst of which was when an electrician fell three floors down a shaft and landed flat on his face. Ron Morris was in charge and I will always remember that he took off the scarf, which we wore under our tunics to stop sparks from getting inside, and slid it under the man's face. We managed to get him to the ambulance cradling his face in the scarf.

If it were possible, we would carry casualties downstairs on a stretcher. If that was impossible or too dangerous, they had to be lifted off the building using an aerial appliance. The advent of Hydraulic Platforms in the Brigade made this type of job a lot easier. Previously, when there were only TLs, this was a very tricky operation.

The first time that this happened to me was when I was a Leading Fireman riding in charge of the ladders. We were called in the early hours to a man who had been wandering around in a building under construction looking for somewhere to sleep. He had fallen, broken a leg and fractured his pelvis. It was a good job that a passer-by heard his cries for help as it was a cold night and he might have died from exposure and shock. With the help of the paramedics, we got him onto the ambulance 'scoop' stretcher. We then had to tie him to part of one of our ladders and then attach the ladder to a rescue line. This line was passed through purpose-designed pulleys fixed to the TL and then lowered to the ground. Before the casualty was lowered, you made sure that all your knots were good and that the casualty, once raised, was in a level position. The ladder needed to be balanced before it was lowered. Prior to the rescue line being played-out, a guide line was attached to the ladder being lowered. The other end was held at ground level by a couple of firemen to stop the ladder from swinging around or crashing into the building. The whole operation took a lot of time, skill and manpower.

There was always a hairy moment when the casualty was first swung out from the building. It was a good job they didn't know what was going on; it was even better for them if they were unconscious.

At the job in New Oxford Street we had the benefit of a hydraulic platform. It was just a matter of freeing the casualties, getting them onto the scaffolding and then onto the HP. The paramedics made sure that it was safe for them to be moved and we got on with the job.

Towards the end of the year, we were back in Piccadilly Circus to a man who had climbed the statue of Eros to protest about his disabled son's medical treatment. He had a knife and was threatening to stab himself if anyone attempted to remove him. Poor man, all I could do was extend a ladder so the police negotiator could talk to him. I tried talking to him but he was not interested. The poor man was eventually persuaded to come down, but not before slashing himself across the stomach.

In October 1999, the Blue Watch had dealt with a massive fire on the ground. It went to 20 pumps and it involved a range of buildings in Covent Garden, the most well known of which was Belgo's – a Belgian bar and restaurant on two floors: ground floor and basement. About two weeks after the Blue's fire, we were called on a Sunday evening to smoke issuing from the same building, part of which was now under demolition.

Firstly, we were obstructed by a massive crane and had to go around the block to get to the fire. By then the crowds were gathering, obstructing our attempts to reach the place. The smoke was increasing and the fire developing. The fire was above Belgo's, which was full of customers unaware of what was happening and were reluctant to evacuate. People seem to prefer dying than leave a meal they have paid for. After taking no notice of the staff, I had to go in there and start shouting to get them to leave. They were mostly tourists who must have thought that this was part of the cabaret!

Meanwhile, the firemen have had to find their way into the building where they can. It was scaffolded and most of the ground floor was boarded up. Mick was directing operations at the opposite side of the block. We eventually found four seats of fire, deliberately set by some loony.

When a fresh-faced senior officer arrived to take control, instead of helping me, he started to complain about the way the fire engines were parked! My original Sub. Officer, Steve Short, was now the Station Officer at Clerkenwell and you should have seen and heard us lay into this man. We pinned him to the wall and really read him his rights!

If you weren't there at the beginning of the fire, you wouldn't have known the difficulties that plagued us from the outset. It's all very well to turn up when the building has been evacuated and the crowds have dispersed. But in the beginning you have to do what you can with resources at hand. It's like coming home after the party's finished. To his credit, this man, once educated, did apologise, saying that he was new to the job.

During this fire I felt a sharp pain in the side of my face. I did not realise that this was another symptom of the gradual deterioration in my health. I worked the rest of the night but had to book sick before the next duty.

I didn't know what was going wrong with me; neither did my GP. I had headaches, stomach upsets that went on for days and a general feeling of being unwell. It wasn't until much later, and after undergoing a series of hospital tests, I was told by a specialist that he thought I was permanently damaged by overwork. 'Burn-out' was how he described my condition. I never really believed that such a thing existed – the stuff of chancers and malingerers. He told me that the human body was not designed to stand up to what I had been doing for the last 30 years, and that the best thing I could do was rest and get into the habit of sleeping seven nights a week. In the meantime, I had a shift off and then went back to work. I still had about four years to go until I retired and I wanted to do them at Soho. Until I had the tests, I never considered that work might be the cause of my bad health.

The Brigade contracts-out its health care to a private occupational health provider. Once you reach the age of forty, you are required to attend periodic medicals. At these medicals your general fitness, sight, and hearing is checked. If you fail, you can be put on light duties, placed sick, or even retired. I never had any problems with the medicals but once you had been examined, you were asked if you had any medical problems. At my two previous medicals I told them that I was having difficulty sleeping. They had no answer to this and just shrugged their shoulders as if it was something I should expect – part of the job. So I just carried on as usual.

We were being run off our feet; the station was so busy. Not just with the work outside, but the administration was driving us mad. There was always some new study into the Brigade for which we had to provide the statistics. We were filling in forms providing figures, that I was sure were cutting our own throats, voluntarily offering up the ammunition for them to cut stations and fire engines.

All the mundane calls to AFAs shut in lift, etc. were increasing to a point where the efficient running of the station was suffering. I tried to look on these calls in a different way. I decided that they were all training. Training for me to expect the worse and not expect everything to be a false alarm. Training for the drivers – they still had to find their way to the address through the congested streets. Training for the crew in the back of the truck, getting them to think about what equipment to get ready, keeping up their knowledge of the ground and not leaving the topography to the driver and me. I know that they thought I had finally cracked: 'The old man's gone barmy!'

On 20th June 2000 we were called to a fire in Greens Court right in the middle of the red light zone. It is a narrow alley that sells sex in all its guises. We were met by a provocatively dressed woman and two other ladies dressed only in dressing gowns. Smoke was drifting out of the doorway. I asked the usual questions, started up the BA and sent the blokes inside. They soon reappeared dragging a smouldering mattress. The fire had been started by a punter, who had dropped a cigarette whilst a live bed show was in progress.

Fires in emporiums of sex were not that regular; we were much more likely to be called when a peeved customer started complaining about the lack of fire precautions. It was the same with some nightclubs that were started up in empty premises without planning and licensing permission. Before we went to inspect them, it was necessary to have a police presence.

That isn't to say that we didn't have any fires. My first experience of such an occurrence was when I was a Leading Fireman and we were called to a topless bar in Rupert Street. It was only a tiny place, but there were enough firemen forcing their way inside that they could have sucked the smoke up in their lungs and taken it outside. From then on it was more usual that the fires started either deliberately or accidentally after the places had closed for the night.

It seemed that the favourite method of arson was candles placed near or on something flammable. In one adult book shop in Berwick Street, we were called before the fire got going. We found lit candles tilted downwards and wedged between the books. That was the same night there were two fires in Walkers Court, another alleyway where the Raymond's Revue Bar is located. One of the suspicious fires was in a very strange, and out of place gift shop, the other in a place selling sex aids. Both were cases of arson.

The whole of the area has changed over the years. At one time you couldn't walk for more than a hundred yards without being solicited. Illegal clubs would open and close like clockwork. Then Westminster City Council had a major clampdown and all the premises had to be licensed; then the area started to clean up. Now there are more coffee bars than sex shops and most of the 'models' are off the street.

## Chapter 33

# LIBERTY AND COINCIDENCE

On 9th September 2000 we were called to a fire in Liberty's, the jewel of Regent Street. This a beautiful and historic department store that has been in existence since 1875. Just imagine if I became known as the man who lost Liberty's! I knew that the store was housed in two separate buildings and separated by Kingly Street. That was also where the entrance to their offices were, and where the security staff could usually be found. So without a more definite location, that was where we headed.

On arrival, it was quite apparent that a serious fire was in progress. The store was in the process of evacuation and hundreds of people were spilling into the street. The part of the building on fire was under development, and contained all the things that can add to the complications of a fire. Asbestos was being removed and oxy-acetylene cutting equipment was being used. Both of these involve individual operational procedures.

The asbestos is the least dangerous; the firemen are protected by wearing chemical protection suits and BA. An exclusion zone has to be established. When the firemen leave the building, they have to be de-contaminated before they remove their BA by uncontaminated BA wearers. Asbestos doesn't prevent them from entering the building and firefighting. Acetylene cylinders in an enclosed area present a very different problem. They can explode and cause devastating injuries, so their location is of the utmost importance. I have to treat all reports as the real thing. There is no sense in introducing the procedure after something has happened.

When you are dealing with a building which is undergoing some reconstruction, there is often a problem in getting accurate information. It's a case of the left hand and the right hand. The builders have one set of priorities and the Store has others. I eventually discovered that there were cylinders on the site but that they were away from the affected area. This made it a lot easier, as I could send the BA men into a less dangerous situation. Then I was told that the asbestos had been removed, although the notices attached to the building had been left in place. Thank goodness. Now I could treat it as a normal fire.

Once inside, two junior officers started sending me information from the basement and the third floor. These were the two points where the smoke was at its thickest and where the seat of the fire was going to be found. The problem was that it could not be found! The BA men were running out of air and had to be replaced without even doing any fire-fighting. The second pair of crews both reported that they could hear small explosions, which sounded as though they were coming from within the walls.

It must have taken at least 45 minutes before we actually got water on the fire. After an exhausting search, the seat was located in a disused lift carriage, whose final descent had been into the basement and all the doorways had then been disguised by plasterboard walls. To make matters worse, the entrance in the basement had been further concealed with a shop display.

The firemen had to break down the walls before they could get to the lift carriage, which was three-quarters filled with rubbish and discarded aerosols. This was what had been exploding. Water had been directed though the smoke into the lift shaft from above, but it wasn't until the basement lift doors were opened that the actual fire could be extinguished. With the help of the Fire Investigation Officers, we decided that the fire had been started by sparks falling from much higher up the shaft where the builders had been cutting out old steelwork.

There were so many additional officers and appliances in attendance that I was never more pleased to hand over control to Graham. It was so good to have a senior officer to work with who understood what was going on and appreciated the complications.

It is a pure fluke that things happen in the same location, on separate occasions and within a short space in time. In 2000 we went through a very busy time all in the same area. The streets north of Oxford Street are an eclectic jumble of one-ways and rat runs; very much a commercial area, with many offices, shops, and workshops dedicated to the clothing trade. The whole district is bustling during the daylight hours. After dark, the streets empty and crowds can only be found in the limited entertainment spots.

A major portion of the area is taken up by two sprawling hospitals: The Middlesex and University College. We were called to these buildings at least once a shift. They both have antiquated and sensitive fire alarm systems, being set off day and night by either smoking in the wrong place or by the nurses and students burning toast.

We were always met by a cluster of patients and staff waiting outside, some in dressing gowns, some in wheelchairs. It wasn't realistic to evacuate the whole hospital; these were just those who were mobile and close to the exits. The hospitals have emergency action plans unlike many addresses. I was always met by a safety officer who would lead my crew to investigate the origin of the alarm. I was keen to give the all clear. As soon as the men told me it was safe, I would get the evacuees back into shelter and warmth.

On one call to the Middlesex, we were approached by a damsel in distress. Her car had been blocked in on all sides after she had brought her husband to the hospital. I had never seen the firemen so enthusiastically bump and push stationary cars out of the way to allow this lady her freedom. I wondered what the response would have been if this lady were not so attractive?

Surrounding the main hospital there are various research units, medical colleges and nurses homes, which also kept us busy. All the nurses' homes in the area were regular calls. The nurses would evacuate the buildings and wait for the all clear in all states of dress, half of them straight out of bed having just worked a day or night shift. It must have been a curious sight to the unfamiliar.

The main hospitals are such large and complicated buildings that I was glad not to have ever been called to take charge of a serious fire. I only experienced one complicated and drawn-out fire involving electrical equipment in the warren of tunnels under the Middlesex, which contained all types of services.

Our main route to this part was along Oxford Street, then right into Newman Street and then into Mortimer Street. From there we could reach most of the remaining area. The whole route was fraught with incident and danger to speeding fire engines: cars and buses blocking our way, people stepping off the pavement in front of the trucks, or walking in front of us while we were temporarily halted. Nothing could stop the progress of head-down shoppers.

In fact, pedestrians were the greatest hazard. On one call in the early evening, we were turning left from Charing Cross Road into Oxford Street when a man walked straight into the front of my truck. Bomp! He was knocked a few feet up the road. We stopped to see if he was all right but he refused treatment and just walked away! Suicidal cyclists and people walking between buses into our path were simply occupational hazards.

If any kind of accident happens on the way to a call, a fireman has to be dropped-off to get the details and the fire engine has to proceed. That's if the truck can still be driven and there are no injuries. Every fire engine carries a supply of forms to record the details of an accident. Once the incident has been dealt with, we would return to pick-up the stranded fireman.

The street adjacent to the station, Gerrard Place, was originally called Nassau Street. I don't know why it was renamed, but Nassau Street was relocated on the west side of the Middlesex at its junction with Mortimer Street. A quiet, little place, which was just a continuous row of terraces opposite the hospital. It was in this street that we were called late at night to a smell of burning in a flat. After searching the place and doing the usual sniffing of the air, I began to suspect that the two lonely young lady occupants, in their best clothes with fresh make-up, had called us just to get the handsome firemen into their flat. It must have been a real disappointment when my surly bunch arrived! Unable to prove my suspicions, there was nothing I could do except warn them that it was an offence to falsely call the Brigade. Anyone can say they thought there was a smell.

I blame all the interest in the firemen on the television programme 'London's Burning'. It was the first such programme to give the public an insight of our previously confidential activities. I much preferred it when nobody knew what went on behind the big red doors, especially when they thought that all we did was play snooker and watch television. I also blame the programme for giving a false impression of the Brigade and causing young men and women to want to join a job that is far less exciting than the one portrayed. Not everyone can work at a busy station, and unfortunately it will become clear that although not an ordinary 9-to-5, London isn't burning and none of us has excitement every day. Thank God, say the general public! The pay is all right if you're single; the problem starts when you need to get a mortgage or want to start a family life.

I did watch the first episode and there were so many operational mistakes that I felt embarrassed and left it alone. The programme got permission from the Brigade to film at my station on several occasions. As you probably expect, I was very put out by anyone taking advantage of my station. These people did not understand that Soho was no ordinary workplace; to me it was the centre of the universe, the jewel in the crown!

On one occasion, a writer was given permission to ride with us to get a 'feel' of a busy station. Of course, by the time the details reached me they had been misheard and misconstrued and I was expecting the soap star Anita Dobson! The lady who arrived was a very different prospect; charming and polite in her fire gear, which consisted of a Barber jacket, green wellies and a bump hat. She was due to stay for two nights, but after the first she bailed out and called it a day. We had a stinker; after about the fifteenth call-out she asked if it was always like this? Yes, mostly it was!

My next brush with the crew of London's Burning was when they were filming an episode which involved the Soho area. I knew they were coming, but that didn't make it any easier when I arrived for night duty to find the yard full of their vehicles and nowhere for the firemen to park. It just went downhill from there. We did have a laugh though when I asked the actor who played the mess manager what he was doing in the watchroom, and why wasn't he upstairs in the kitchen preparing supper? He looked at me with a startled expression and said that he wasn't the mess manager any more; he was producing the show. Oh dear.

Later that night I really went into one. The Brigade provided an adviser to the show. At that time it was a man I knew and, although he had never taken an exam in his life or been in charge of a station, he was given the same rank and was getting the same pay. That wasn't really the point; I wasn't bothered about that. At one stage of the filming, a fire engine was required to leave the station on an emergency. They had their own truck and this prat of a man drove it through the station and out into to the avenue with the lights flashing and two tones blaring. Now this is a real no-no; it is against the law! If I were to charge around the West End in the same fashion, my guts would quickly become garters. Filming was cut very short after that, especially when he said that he had to do it to create some realism! As if we needed any more of that.

If realism was required, they should have been with us when we were called to a fire in Wells Street in the early hours. This is another turning off Mortimer Street, just past Nassau Street.

I was riding in charge of the pump that night, although I should have been riding the pump ladder. The Brigade, in its wisdom, had decided that it was better for the OIC of the station to ride the pump ladder. I wasn't happy with this and would sometimes ride the pump just to see how the blokes were getting on with the incidents that the pump would attend on its own – the shut-in lifts, car fires, rubbish fires, humanitarian services, etc.

Wells Street was a part of the ground where the Square would regularly reach before us. Their pump turned left into the street shortly before I turned right from the opposite direction. By the time my truck stopped, the men from the Square were slipping their extension ladder. As I got off the truck, I bumped into Carrots who was riding in charge of the ladders.

'Carrots. Why are they slipping the ladder?'

'Up there, Guvnor!'

It was so dark; I must have still been half asleep. Partially obscured by heavy smoke, up on the second floor there was a naked man standing on a window ledge. His body was already blackened by the smoke; he was in a very agitated state and looking as though he was about to jump.

I could see in an instant that the extension ladder would not reach the man and called for the 135. Good boys – it was already off and heading my way. I shouted as loud as I could at the man telling him not to jump – we would reach him.

Before the 135 was in position, the extension ladder had hit the wall and the man was onto it, even though it was about three feet shy of the sill. A Manchester Square fireman was straight up to the head of the ladder and managed to guide the man's dangling feet on to the top round of the ladder, and then assist him to the ground.

Fortunately, he was a young agile man and still able to walk down the ladder. As he came into sight, I noticed that he had blood streaming from deep cuts on his backside. He had done this climbing out of the window after smashing the glass. Old sash windows are usually so clogged-up with paint that they never open. He was given first aid until the ambulance arrived.

Meanwhile, the BA men had started-up and were making their way up the stairs to fight the fire and search for further casualties. The rest of the flat was person-free and the fire was confined to the sitting room and had originated in a television set. The whole of the four-roomed flat was severely damaged by smoke. Great work by all the firemen.

On the next night duty I took my truck round to the Square to thank them for their brave efforts. Their Guvnor, Gareth Evans, was another ally and a fine officer – well liked and respected for his experience and affable manner.

Mortimer Street and its surrounds continued to give us business. I had dealt with some unusual incidents but this one took the biscuit. It tested the teamwork and all skills of the firemen.

We were called in the middle of the afternoon to, 'Van fallen into basement,; driver trapped'. A Transit-type van, delivering supplies to a small print shop, had reversed onto the off street loading bay, gone back a little too far onto a goods hoist and was now in the basement. It fell the last few feet and the driver was sitting in his seat, unable to escape from any of the doors. He was quite calm and unhurt, but understandably shocked.

This was a category of incident where an FRU would automatically attend. I knew that they would soon arrive with all their specialist equipment. If the unit at Euston was busy, the next nearest would attend; it was coming from Battersea. We were already quite chummy with this crew, as they had quite recently helped us to free a schoolboy with his arm trapped in a revolving door at the National Gallery.

It was a really testing task. We had to release the driver and get the van back to street level. We also had the risk of fire from petrol spilling from the engine. The van was at such an acute angle that we had to devise a way of not only lifting it, but also tilting it at the same time. Just pulling it would only force the van against the lift wall.

Using air bags, we raised the van a little. Then we were able to open the rear doors, unload its contents and the driver scrambled out. Then with the air bags and the FRU's inboard winch, we were able to get it back onto terra firma with only minor damage. Ingenuity and pure know-how are not found in the training manuals; they come from good hands with a wealth of experience.

During the 2002/3 strikes for better pay, they decided that a fireman was not worth £30,000 a year. When comparing us to other workers, they didn't take into consideration that we might be worth some sort of bonus for bravery and ingenuity. It may never happen, but you have to be prepared to risk life and limb. I wonder what kind of reply I would get from my postman if I asked him to do that?

## Chapter 34

## '9/11'

Apart from all the operational duties, the station had to be managed just like any other workplace. Essential stores had to be ordered, equipment had to be repaired or replaced and records had to be kept. All these duties were split four ways; each watch had a reference. Mine was housekeeping. I was happy with this, as previously I was fed-up with running out of two of the most important requirements – tea mugs and toilet paper. At one time we were given a budget and we overspent. The powers that be would not allow any credit and supplies ran out. At every fire station there is a supernatural creature that eats cups – the same creature that drinks washing-up liquid!

In the early days, we were supplied toilet paper that the firemen referred to as the 'skiddy stuff'. That never ran out! As soon as we got soft tissue, I could never order enough. The first time we ran out I had to convince the stores department that there was a need for a more flexible budget. I composed a long report outlining the fact that Soho was a special case; there was an imbalance. On a day duty, as most of the firemen lived far away they had to leave for work very early and would not use the toilet until they reached the station. But, after a night shift they would use the toilet *before* going home. Therefore, we were entitled to a further issue of toilet paper – and I got it!

On 5th April 2001 we were called to The University College Hospital in Grafton Way, WC1, on Euston's ground. This was a regular call. All hospitals get an augmented attendance because of the life risk. So our three appliances joined Euston's pair on the predetermined attendance. Up Tottenham Court Road, right at the end and back down Gower Street. There were so many calls to this location that if Euston's trucks were already in attendance, we would wait in Gower Street until their Guvnor gave the all clear. If we turned into Grafton Way, we would have to go all the way back round a convoluted one-way system to get home. Although it was dark, in the streetlights I could clearly see that a hosereel was being pulled off. Station Officer Mick Pinchen was soon on the radio telling me that we had a job. Mick had always been a good man on the fireground with an abundance of tradition and experience. He was once one of the Brigade's standard bearers – a voluntary duty, which he carried out devotedly until he was taken advantage of just one time too many.

Once you reach the age of 50, you no longer have to wear BA for training purposes. As I was nearly always doing my job outside the fires, to stay familiar with the equipment, I had to wear it around the station when the sets received their monthly test and service. Grafton Way turned out to be the last time that I would wear BA into a fire.

The fire was in the basement of a wing of the hospital where specialist treatment was being carried out and some of the patients were bedridden. One crew had already gone up to the fourth floor to assist the nurses to get the patients out. The smoke was rapidly increasing. Another crew was making its way to the basement. Mick Pinchen asked me to go to the basement and organise the firefighting while he dealt with the rescues and control.

I grabbed hold of Candy. We donned our sets, booked in with the BA control and made our way down a corridor towards the smoke and the basement. We were following the hosereel, which had been taken in by the first crew. We traced it down the stairs past the entrance to the basement and into the sub-basement. There was smoke down there but not very thick. I managed to convey to the other crew that we were in the wrong place and moved back up one level to a set of double doors. I crouched down and cracked the door. As I did, the smoke started to roll back into the room; a good sign that the fire was in need of oxygen and could flash.

I got onto Pinchen and told him that we were going to need a jet to be in place before we could open it up. Another crew came in with the jet and worked with the original crew. After about half an hour, those of us who were the first inside started to run short of air, and our low pressure warning whistles started to actuate. So we had to get out and change our cylinders.

Once outside I began to take in the extent of the rescue operation. Twenty patients had been carried down, through the smoke, from the fourth floor. The nurses were working in the smoke, disconnecting the patients from intravenous lines and monitoring equipment. One of the patients was a twenty stone man! The crews upstairs were a combination of Euston and Soho. Two of my men, Carrots and Kingy, The Victorian Strongman, worked so hard in such difficult conditions without BA that they were eventually overcome, and had to be given air while sitting exhausted in the street. Eventually they had to be taken to the casualty department, which was just across the road. Talk about having resources on hand. Kingy was straight back to work, but Carrots took a fortnight to recover; but then he was not really a White Watch man, having started out on the Reds!

Mick Herschel was working away at the front entrance; Pinchen had asked him to look after the BA control as there were so many men going in and out. In the meantime I had found a side entrance nearer to the basement staircase. I got a truck up to this point to supply water and equipment directly to the men firefighting.

Pinchen had made pumps eight and asked for two FRUs. The FRU carries long duration BA sets, which give about double the amount of working duration. They were going to be needed, as this fire just didn't seem to want to go out. The firefighting crews were working in relays, but there was one from Euston who would not come out. This was the same man who all those years ago had carried two people down an escape in Gosfield Street. I could hear his whistle sounding; I had to shout deeper and deeper into the smoke to get him out.

The fire was confined to an area where dirty laundry was stored. It was held in mobile cages about four feet high and the fire was really roaring. I couldn't understand its voracity until one of the men coming out told me that he could hear a loud hissing. I stopped people going down and got onto the maintenance staff. Was there anything dangerous down there? Were there any gas pipes? It was confirmed that there wasn't so we carried on firefighting. Once the fire was eventually extinguished, I found a burnt-through oxygen pipe. A lot of help the maintenance staff were. That's why it wouldn't go out. At the outset, the fire was starved of oxygen, and then it was fed in abundance

We were just getting on top of it when a security guard came running up: 'There's another fire round the corner.' Sure enough. Now we've got a four-pump fire in the nurses' home. Some of the men working on the original fire legged it to the nurses' home and a whole new attendance had to be ordered.

I was glad that I couldn't leave where I was working as I was out on my feet. I was knackered, black as your hat, hungry and wet. I had not noticed that night had passed into day. For some reason my nose was bleeding. I didn't know what that was all about.

Once it was all over, we went to visit the boys in hospital and saw they were receiving more than their fair share of attention from the nurses. We took the piss out of them, and then headed for the canteen van for, at least, a cup of tea. I cleared off all the people hanging around the van who didn't have dirty faces so that my men could be served.

The next week, old Pinchen got onto me. He was writing a report recommending that Carrots, Kingy and Mick be recognised for their meritous conduct. He wanted me to do the same to back him up. I did, but we never heard anything, so Pinchen had to chase it up. The next man up the line said that he had forgotten about it and that he felt that now it was too late!

How did the fires start? Yep, you guessed it; a bored, attention-seeking security guard. The police got him, thank goodness.

Later that year came the catastrophe that must have made every urban fireman stand back and take a good look at his vocation. When the first plane went into the World Trade Center, I was at my daughter's house helping the son-in-law with his bathroom. We watched for a couple of hours transfixed by the unfurling disaster. At that time, it was inconceivable that the twin towers would fall down, and that a building that size would crumple into the ground, along with 400 dead firemen. The only way I could get my head around it was to make comparisons. The whole of the night shift, and some more, working in Central London would have been wiped out – every fireman you knew, everyone who was close to you.

I am not exaggerating when I say that I felt heartbroken. I apply all these things to my life, to my wife, to my family. It was the same as when Colin died. All those kids with no Dads. Unbelievable.

What could we do that was positive? Not much, except raise money and that was what we did – the whole station, out on the door with the boxes. In the end we sent out £38,000 ($50,000). I hope it helped somebody.

A couple of days after the attack, I was due to fly out on holiday; that was a bit scary. Mick was left in charge and on our first night there was a ring at the door. A New York fireman was stranded in London with not much money and nowhere to stay; his flight home had disappeared in the aftermath.

Some of our Red Watch had been on a visit to New York and they had been to this man's station. That was why he headed for Soho.

Clever man, Mick Herschel. He realised that this would get some attention, so he did the right thing. We have to get permission from a senior officer to allow anyone to stay at the station. If Mick had let him stay without permission, he would have been in all sorts of trouble. Only they refused! Saying that they didn't think it was appropriate! But, good for Mick, he stuck to it and eventually spoke to the right man who agreed to let Bill stay. He stayed for about a week and I know that he will be eternally grateful to Soho. He was interviewed on local radio and television. The humane attitude of the London Fire Brigade's management was, of course, highlighted. Like me, he was in charge of a station and he lost a lot of friends. He has since been back to visit but I had retired by then.

Our next visit from a New York fireman was a very different affair. I can't remember his name, but he was a boxer, a Golden Gloves Champion. He was over here to box a business man in aid of the Widows and Orphans. After the fight at a hotel in Kensington, he headed for the bright lights and Soho.

Our mess room was off the run at the time and we had set up temporary camp in the dormitory. As daft as a box of monkeys, he couldn't understand a word we said. We had to explain all the slang and London fireman's talk. He had been off duty when the tragedy happened, had jumped into his car, got his firegear and went to help. That night some of the boys took him out on the town. When I saw him the next day he looked very much the worse for wear. Still that was it; back to Heathrow and home to do some more digging.

On 11th October I managed to get the pump off the run to go to a Commemoration Service for the New York Firefighters at St. Paul's Cathedral. There were hundreds of British Fire Service present. We stood outside and listened to the service being broadcast. It was very moving. One of the Brigades provided some pipers who played on the steps of the Cathedral. Later, being one of the local stations, we were also invited to a service at Westminster Abbey for the families of those who lost their lives.

Admiration, praise, recognising the loss; I don't really know how I feel now. It was something so big that there are no words to describe it. I do know that I was affected, and a shudder still goes down my spine every time I see pictures of those buildings. When I watched the documentary made by two French brothers and saw the first officer in charge in the foyer of the first tower, I knew what that man was going through and, unbelievably, holding it together. I could see the strain on his face. I know that you cannot compare it but, I've been there. You know that your men are in danger, but you can't do anything about it; you can't even raise them on the radio.

Graham Ellis got in contact with the OIC of New York's Soho fire station where they lost fourteen. When the time was right, some of the boys went out there to present them with the cheque and a plaque, which we had all contributed to.

I'll get there one day to pay my respects, but they'll probably all run upstairs and hide when I say, 'I'm an old retired fireman from...blah blah'.

Life went on much the same at the station until Graham did a really nice thing. He discovered that the two firemen who died inside the station when it was bombed in 1941 had never received any kind of recognition. A plaque was made to hang in the appliance room and he invited a lot of Soho veterans to an unveiling ceremony. It felt really good to see all those faces from the past.

The plaque was unveiled and Mary had a mate who played the Last Post on a cornet; that was real goose pimples stuff. Then we had a reception upstairs in the mess. That was when I first met Ernie Allday. He had been stationed at Soho and went on to be the Deputy Chief Officer. Ernie's great claim to fame is that he had been in the Brigade but left to join the navy during the Second World War. He was home on leave and was walking down Frith Street when the bomb hit the station. After the war, he rejoined and went on to achieve that lofty position. I believe that he was even Chief Officer for a short time. His nephew is one of my best friends, but unfortunately Uncle Ernie passed away in 2004.

Another real old character, Harry Errington, was also at the reception; he was awarded the George Cross for his bravery as a fireman during the Blitz. He has great tales of wartime Soho; as bright as a button and still ready for a laugh.

I had gone in early before a night shift. There was some liquid refreshment and we couldn't get rid of all the old boys until it had gone. I'm sure they were all a little wobbly by the time they finally left. They had to be taken downstairs in our lift – at last it had come in useful!

Graham invited Harry back to the station for another little ceremony early in 2002. We had recommended some of the White Watch for their brave deeds. Leading Fireman Michael Stanley received a letter of congratulations for saving a suicidal man.

It happened in Maiden Lane just behind the Strand. Michael was at the head of the ladder when the man jumped, and he managed to grab him with one hand while hanging onto the ladder with the other. This time he managed to hold on and the man survived.

Michael Herschell, Chris Andy and Steve Day received Royal Humane Society Awards for resuscitating a man collapsed outside the station suffering from a severe nut allergy. At first they thought he was a drunk, but then realised that he could not breathe.

It was at about this time that I was really feeling ill. I went off duty one day and just had to go sick. I thought that if I took a bit of time off I would be able to see it through to the end – 28th April 2003. It would have been my last day of service and I was determined to get there as an operational officer. I had some really black days during that time. How El put up with me, I'll never know. I was short-tempered, not sleeping and wandering around the house in the early hours, not really knowing what was wrong. I did go back to work, but I wish the circumstances of my return had never happened.

*Chapter 35*

## LITTLE CHRIS

Firemen come in all shapes and sizes; you need big men to knock a door down, but you also need them small to get through narrow spaces. Once the height limits restricting entry in the service were dropped, as it was thought that this was prejudicial to short people, it seemed that a lot of new recruits were on the small side. Not that this concerned me, as now I started to appear tall. Now I could stop making firemen stand in the kerb while I talked to them!

During my whole service, I had only supervised the development of five people that were sent to the station directly from training school. If ever there were vacancies on the watch, the holes would be filled by men who were waiting to get into Soho. My first recruit was an ex-Marine; the next was Lara and then Bob Edwards. You're not supposed to have favourites, but Bob was great; he had no trouble fitting in and he excelled at everything. After about six years we managed to give him enough encouragement to go on to get promotion. Now he is back at Soho as a Leading Fireman, and next I hope that he will be able shake off the bug and go on to greater things. As I told everybody – you can always come back!

Some time in 2000 a young man was posted to me. Chris Kirby was very quiet and unassuming. He was so well brought-up that he wouldn't even swear. He was able to resist all the provocation. He couldn't be broken for some time. You should have heard the cheers when he finally cracked. He was polite and respectful but, at the same time, I could tell that somewhere in there was a little devil waiting to escape.

I always got any newcomers into my room. Firstly to welcome them to the station, then to explain to them what I expected of them – the finer details of being a member of the White Watch. My theory was that you have to know the rules before you can obey them. The OIC has a special responsibility to new recruits and I took this role very seriously. Without strict guidance they could either be lambs to the slaughter or, especially at Soho, go wayward. They also need someone to turn to, someone who would clarify what was right and also to nurture their development.

At one time, recruits would be sent to stations with only the basic training and with no guide to direct their progression. In recent years the Brigade got its act together, and new boys now have to complete a laid down programme of achievements. This has to be monitored by the OIC and each element has to be signed-off. This programme has to be completed in their first year and if they manage to achieve an acceptable standard, they are then considered to have served their probation and their continued employment is confirmed.

Prior to this I used a programme that I had developed. Although the whole watch would advise and help, it was the Sub. Officer who would control the programme and I would monitor progress.

Soon to be christened 'Little Chris' and then for some reason, 'Sausage', it wasn't long before he hit my soft spot. How could I help it; I had started in the Brigade before he was born. I felt not actually fatherly but 'uncley'. He was such a good lad. I told him at the beginning that if there was anything around the station that had not been done, then it was up to him to do it. He took this literally; if the tea was late he would make it, and he always brought me a cup wherever I was.

His first year was full of incident and we made sure that he was in the thick of the action. His lack of height and size complemented our catalogue of talents.

Once we were called to water percolating into a porn shop from the flat above and he was stuffed through a fanlight to gain entry. A call was received to smoke issuing from The Red Door, Davies Street, W1. Until then, I didn't know that this was the trademark for Elizabeth Arden beauty spas around the world. Looking through the windows, it was clear that the building was smoke-logged. As the smoke was drifting rather than throbbing, I decided that we had time to get inside rather than smash our way in. The only point of entry was through an oversized, high lustre, solid, red door. It would have been a travesty to force it open. I got the men to neatly cut out a panel and Chris was again shoved through the hole. Once inside, he could open the door and the BA men could search. They found a burnt-out waxing machine in a basement treatment room, which had managed to smoke-damage two floors – another bizarre cause of fire to add to the list.

In most places, if we had to gain entry, the burglar alarms would actuate. This was useful if we were unable to re-secure the premises. The police would attend and we could then leave the security to them. I never failed to rub it in as we left the poor old coppers out in the cold and we headed back to bed!

Little Chris got through his probation with no trouble and with not a day's sickness to boot. In 2001 he got married; we were all invited to the reception. This was very brave of him, as he had already been regaled with stories of previous watch weddings. It was a big do, at the Piccadilly Hotel. Everyone was in their best bib and tuckers and with the ladies present, on best behaviour.

It was a great feeling to be welcomed into the celebrations, although the father of the bride soon realised that the free bar was no longer a very good idea!

About six months after the wedding, Chris phoned in sick with a bad back. I was a little suspicious that this wasn't on the level. On the previous duty he had an altercation with one of the watch. Getting leave at short notice was always difficult, especially at the weekends. Chris had booked this particular night off in advance; he didn't take the leave but failed to tell anyone. One of the others was desperate for the night off; it went to waste and there was a row. The reason he no longer wanted this night off was not discussed at the time. It was only later that it became evident.

The Brigade has what it calls an 'Absence Control Policy'. It was formulated to deter sickness. Even the doctor at our Health Service called it 'Dickensian'. It gives the OIC no leeway; no chance to use a little discretion and it has made individuals frightened of taking sick leave. One of the conditions of the policy is that the individual has to speak to the OIC on each day they are sick.

When Chris phoned me I questioned the validity of his bad back. He assured me that he had been walking his dog, which had suddenly pulled on its lead and jarred his back. I could only take that to be the case. Another part of the policy is that I have to hold a return-to-work interview. I was still concerned about the altercation, but Chris still assured me that his sickness was justified and that there was no other reason behind his sickness.

Once he had returned to work, he came to see me and asked for a transfer. The reasons he gave me for wanting a move were mumbo-jumbo and I still thought it was because of the altercation. But, I told him I would think about it and let him know next shift. He was very quiet and withdrawn; I knew something was wrong. I decided that, whatever the reason, I was not going to let him transfer. You can't sort out problems by shuffling them around. I asked Mick to talk to him to see if he could get to the bottom of it. Perhaps it was just that he wouldn't tell me, frightened of being thought a grass. Mick got it out of him; his marriage had gone down the drain. None of his fault. He was heartbroken, and ashamed to admit that his marriage had only lasted six months.

The next night he came to me and confessed. I really felt for the boy and I told him that the best place for him was here with the blokes that knew and liked him. Firemen have their own way of dealing with problems like this; first they are quiet, treating the individual with care. Then they start to gently take the piss. If that works, then the banter goes back to full-throttle. Within about six months we had him back to normal – well, at least, normal at work. Graham and I got him over to see our special people at Welfare and Counselling and they played their part in his recovery. I was really grateful to Mick and the watch for sorting him out because, for some reason, he didn't seem to want to bother me with his problems. See, what a good boy; he knew that I wasn't at my best.

On the day that would have been his first wedding anniversary, 6th April 2002, he went to a family wedding with some of his non-firemen mates. The next day, a Sunday, I was off sick, and the phone went. It was the Station Officer on the Green Watch, Jeff Hale.

'I've got something really horrible to tell you, Ray. Chris Kirby is dead.'

It really didn't sink in. I think it had something to do with being at home and still attempting to keep the two worlds apart. I booked fit straight away and went back to work, even though I was still unwell. It was a night shift. I have never seen a group of men so upset. Fortunately, the officer who was dealing with the whole affair, Trevor Browse, was an ex-Soho man whom I knew and trusted. He managed to get the whole watch off duty; there was no way any of us could have just worked on as though nothing had happened.

He had died in a motor accident. He had been at the wedding reception and one of his mates had a new car which he wanted show off. They went for a drive. There was no drink involved. The car went out of control. Chris and the driver's brother were killed.

As Chris was only carrying his ID card, the Brigade were the first to hear of the accident. Trevor was the duty officer in the Command and was sent to his parents' home, but found out that they were staying at a hotel near to the wedding. He then had to drive to the hotel to break the news. Officers have no training in this sort of thing, but fortunately Trevor is a very intelligent, considerate man.

As soon as we could, Graham and I went to see his family. Although I had met his parents, I was so apprehensive. I had never had to cope with a situation like this. My fears were completely dispelled as soon as I entered their home. The whole family were there and their neighbours, who were so close. They were like a second family to Chris. I don't really know how to explain how I felt; his mum and dad are from the same generation as me. It was back to applying the situation to my own life and family. I don't think that I could have coped like them. They showed such dignity at such a dreadful time.

Graham and I had to ask some difficult questions, such as what kind of funeral they would like – quiet and private, or a funeral with a Brigade presence. His Dad said, 'I want him to go out in a blaze of glory; I would like the full works.'

That gave us the go-ahead to do the best we could. The Brigade usually only provides a traditional Brigade funeral if a fireman has died during service. So we had to organise a replication. Working closely with the funeral directors, Welfare and Counselling, and the police, we set about giving him the best possible send-off. We also had to meet and make arrangements with the Kirby's local Catholic church in Paddington; Church of Our Lady of Lourdes & St. Vincent de Paul in the Harrow Road. The whole family had strong links with the church.

On my next duty I got all the men into the mess, including Bob Edwards, who played golf with Chris and was now a Leading Fireman at the Square. I was faced with another difficult task; I had to select the pall-bearers. I had already decided that I had to pick men who had known him from his first day of service and those who socialised with him outside work. There was also a practical consideration; the six men had to be about the same height. As you can imagine this was a very emotional meeting. I didn't think it to be anything but natural to see this brave, close-knit group of men with tears in their eyes.

Mirroring an official funeral, we managed to get a Cross of St. George flag to use as a pall. Damn to those who misguidedly look on this flag as an emblem of right-wing patriotism. Chris was a keen footballer who was passionate about his national team and nothing would have been more suitable.

One of the men stationed at Paddington owned a vintage TL, which he volunteered to be used as the hearse. Next, we had to scour the Brigade for six old-style tunics and white belts. Station Officer Mick Pinchen volunteered to come out of retirement as standard-bearer just for this one occasion.

Mr & Mrs Kirby had given me permission to speak at the funeral. I felt that it was my duty to put some words together expressing the feelings of the White Watch. I spent a lot of time trying to get that right, bits borrowed but mostly my own, knowing that anything I said would have to bring them some solace.

Thursday 18th April, the day of the funeral arrived. We all met at the station with our wives. Welfare had provided a coach to transport all the firemen from the four watches to the Church in Paddington and a minibus for our wives. The pallbearers had been taken to the funeral directors where the TL was being dressed with flowers. From there they rode, standing either side of the coffin to the church.

All the Soho firemen provided a guard of honour at the church. When the TL was approaching, in the distance along the Harrow Road, it looked unreal in the bright sunlight; it seemed shrouded in mist.

The Church was packed with family, friends and the Brigade. There was a children's choir from St. Vincent's School where Mrs Kirby was school secretary. The whole service was a wonderful tribute to Chris and his family.

Just before the closing hymn, it was time for two tributes from Chris's brother, Alex, and myself. We were both nervous, but standing together gave us both a bit of assurance. During our speeches there were occasional reassuring touches on the back from each other. I had to avoid looking at El, as that would really have cracked me up. These were my words:

> 'As Chris's Guvnor I have a duty to perform,
> I may not be able to do my duty to the best of my ability,
> but, I will see it through.
> My duty is to honour Chris and try to bring some comfort to his family.
> Anyone who is prepared to risk his life for another is my brother.
> His family is my family and my family belongs to his,
> therefore I have the right to call him brother.

Chris Kirby was a brave, honest and caring young man,
who, in great adversity was determined to enjoy his life.
His family and friends have every right to remember him with
      love and pride.
As a fireman he gave me great joy; he never said no; he never let
      me down.
His attitude and enthusiasm were a breath of fresh air,
there is no reason or justice for Chris being taken away from us,
and we struggle for consolation when a young life is so tragically
      lost.
I find it hard to believe this senseless thing and it makes me
      angry.
It has no value except to realise how fragile this life can be and of
      the emptiness that appears when we leave.
Our grief forms a barrier, which will be hard to get around, but
      we will.
Our good words and memories will help us through to the other,
      better side.
So don't say goodbye, just say goodnight.
Our brother has not wandered far away,
he is not lost or taken,
though unseen to the mortal eye, he is here and loves us.
The dear ones left behind, they do not forget,
our spirits see him, and our hearts grow comforted and calm.
Sometimes on our fevered brow, we feel his touch, a breath of
      balm,
yes, ever near us, though unseen, his dear mortal spirit treads.
For all God's boundless Universe is life – there are no dead.
He was a precious gift that slipped from our hands,
but he will always remain in our hearts.
Chris Kirby. Son, Brother, Friend, Fireman.

My right leg was shaking uncontrollably throughout, but I did feel as
though I had done my duty.

After the church service, we had to get to Kensal Rise Crematorium
where the whole route from the gates to the crematorium was lined with
firemen. The TL was led in by the standard bearer with the White Watch
and Chris's Brigade friends walking behind.

Afterwards, Mr & Mrs Kirby invited us back to the church hall. We didn't stay too long as this was really for the family. It was there that I met the young man who had been driving the car. He had already attended the funeral of his brother. It was quite obvious how distressed he was; he was broken-hearted. Chris had been his best friend; they had been mates since childhood. Later he wrote to the White Watch and me. I keep that letter in my precious file. That poor boy got a prison sentence. I know that a terrible thing had happened but, surely, his life has been ruined already. He will never recover, but I do know that Mr & Mrs Kirby still love him.

From the church hall we went to the pub. The family joined us later and, with the exception of Mrs Kirby, we got slaughtered. El went home with Candy and his wife but I couldn't go home. I stayed with the watch until Graham persuaded me that it was time to go. My memories of that day will stay with me until the end; there was so much emotion. You can never foresee anything like this happening but when it does, not that my loss can in anyway be compared to Chris's family, you feel that that you will be unable to cope. But you do; you have to. When I look at his photograph and that of Colin Townsley, I still can't really get to grips with the truth; that they are dead. I still have this immense feeling of sympathy to Mr & Mrs Kirby and I will always appreciate their benevolence in welcoming the best part of the Fire Brigade into their grief.

## Chapter 36

# A LISTED LONDONER

I continued working until the middle of May. I came home after a night shift and had a sort of breakdown. It was then that El and my daughter Elizabeth demanded that I did not work anymore and to find out what was wrong. After six months of medical tests I was told that I was burnt-out. I didn't know that this was an actual medical condition, and not just an excuse for overworked executives and politicians so that they could spend more time with their families.

This condition crept up on me and should be a warning to anyone whose health deteriorates with no apparent cause. It seems that some of us are not superman; overwork, stress and wrecked sleep patterns do have a permanent effect on the body and a detrimental effect on your wellbeing. Nobody told me that, although you may be enjoying your job, it might make you ill. Some people who may be more robust than I, may have gotten through similar experiences. If you start to feel ill, change your way of life, have a break, or get out of it.

During the year spent away from work I didn't get any better. The damage had been done. My family and friends gave me support and my visits to Welfare and Counselling to see Anne Wilmott made some improvement to my state of mind, but nothing improved the physical effects. The most crucial symptom was that I couldn't sleep for more than about four hours. I would get off quite easily, but I would soon be awake and then my poor old brain wouldn't give me any peace. I got to the stage where everything was a mountain to climb, and even minor problems sent shock waves through my body. Such was my turmoil, I would actually start to tremble at the slightest amount of stress.

Not everything was depressing. There were moments of elation. Grandchildren! What a marvellous invention! Also, the concern shown by the White Watch. The phone went one day. It was Vinnie Stout, one of the two brothers on the watch and an all-round good man. 'Guvnor, do you want to be a 'Listed Londoner?"

I should explain that every day on our local radio station, BBC Radio London, there is a programme hosted by Robert Elms – a mix of good grown-up music and talk. Part of the programme is devoted to listeners' notes and queries about London. Most of the watch was interested in the more obscure topographical and historical London facts and were avid listeners. Each Monday, Robert has an invited guest who he calls his 'Listed Londoner'. I was always moaning about the fact that some of these guests were not even Londoners, or that they didn't take the honour seriously.

Unknown to me, Vinnie and Mick had been harassing Robert by letter and e-mail to get me on. In my fragile state, Vinnie's question sent out the now familiar shock waves. I couldn't let him down, so I agreed. His reply was, 'Well you're on next Monday'. A week away; it was good that I didn't have much time to think about it.

The programme starts with Robert discussing your background and then you have to answer the 'famous 15 questions'. The questions are the same each week and are designed to get his guest's preferences concerning London life.

Vinnie arranged to pick me up from Victoria and take me to the radio station in Marylebone High Street. We were to park at the Square. Red Watch was on duty; this was the watch I had worked with. Although they were mostly strange faces, I had a chat with them. Then, as we had a bit of time to spare, we went to a Starbucks opposite the radio station. As we sat looking out into the High Street, more familiar faces started to walk by. The White Watch was taking breakfast at a café further up the road; we went to see them before we went inside. They had a radio with them so that they could listen to the show. Where? Yes, in the pub!

I was very nervous and I hadn't slept much the night before. I was beset with the dread that when the moment came for me to speak my mouth would cease to function or I might swear! This was live radio.

While we were sitting in reception, we were approached by a producer who wanted us to go on television to talk about the continuing strike action. We both declined, feeling that as everything was so sensitive, it would be detrimental to the firemen's cause.

I was then ushered into the studio. I was introduced to Robert, and the interview started with him reading out Vinnie and Mick's letter. That nearly reduced me to tears. Then I had to speak, on the radio, and my tongue didn't drop out!

I had spoken to Robert before when I had been able to answer a listener's query about the Fire Brigade, and his easy manner soon made me feel at home. Anyone who knows me will say, 'Don't start him off on the Fire Brigade!' The lamp swings and the lips go into overdrive.

There were a lot of errs and umms but Robert did say that it was very good and that I was eloquent and interesting. It was a fantastic experience and another entry into the precious file. I even got some fan mail! Mrs Kirby dropped me a line saying that she listened while on her way to work, and was so involved that she wandered off course!

Of course I recorded it and sent copies to old Fire Brigade chums as far flung as New Zealand. Even now I listen to it to cheer me when I start to miss the job a little too much.

I was upset and aggrieved to miss almost all of my final year. I went into work to walk-out when they went on strike. I went in when the strike days coincided with the White Watch. I felt very guilty; I was off sick and getting paid, although they didn't seem to mind. Nothing was said, but I felt that they understood that I had already done my bit.

## Chapter 37

# THE CROCKER'S FOLLY

Next we had to start thinking about the retirement do. When a fireman retires it's down to his mates to organise a gathering. It's not compulsory. Not every fireman has one; some just disappear into the afterlife. They are noisy, drunken affairs. The establishment makes no contribution. All you get from them is a letter signed by the Chief Officer, which was written by your immediate superior, and if you manage to complete the thirty years, you get a plastic replica of a fire-mark in a cardboard presentation box. I know that it is made of plastic, because when mine arrived it was broken.

There is an admission charge to pay for the venue, the catering and a gift. I had been to many retirements, but I had only had a hand in organising one, Eddie Martin's. It is very hard to estimate the turnout and therefore the size of the venue. In my case there were some suggestions that a telephone box would be big enough!

You would think that there would have been something suitable on Soho's ground, but we couldn't find one. They were either too expensive or too small. It is traditional to put money behind the bar, but after it runs out I didn't want the blokes to get stung with West End prices. We had used the Spice of Life public house on Cambridge Circus. It has the benefit of being near to the station but, not to overestimate my popularity, it was thought to be too small. Where could we choose that would be suitable? We had been to several functions organised by the blokes at Paddington at a pub on their ground called The Crocker's Folly.

This is a big Victorian public house whose interior is subject to a preservation order. William Crocker built it as a hotel on the assumption that it would serve travellers using the Great Midland and Northern Railway. Unfortunately, the railway went straight past the hotel and terminated a couple of miles further on at St Pancras! Mr Crocker, who had invested his entire wealth in the hotel, threw himself off the roof. Hence the Crocker's Folly!

These occasions were memorable, not only for the retirees, but for my misfortunes and excesses. On one occasion, I knew the man who was retiring, but most of the watch didn't know him that well. So I went on my own. It was a hot summer's night so short sleeves were the order of the day. I was sitting outside unaware that I was under a roosting pigeon, which was dropping its stuff on the back of my shirt! When it was brought to my attention, I went to the toilet to wash the shirt. It was pale blue and it sucked-up water like blotting paper!

On another occasion, I must admit, I was very drunk. It got to the end of the evening and the boys wanted to get back to the West End. Like ducks out of water, they were being lured back to O'Neil's in Wardour Street. As usual, they couldn't extract me from a pub full of firemen. It was finally down to the two Micks to get me on the road. 'Come on Guvnor, we're going.' They left the pub with me dying for a pee. Not wanting to be left behind, I followed them. Once outside I realised that I wasn't going to get far and – this really isn't like me, that's why it's so funny – I had to take a pee against a wall. As I'm in full flow, a cab pulls up, and out gets the owner of the wall I'm peeing against. Oh, the shame of it. I'm a grown man with a house of my own, and a respectable member of society. I was ashamed, apologetic and embarrassed.

The Crockers is not on the main road; it was about 2300hrs and we had to find a cab. As we were walking down the road, I spotted a young man sitting in his car. It was a beautiful customised BMW. I don't know what inspired me, probably the drink, but I tapped on his window and asked him if he would give three poor old firemen a lift down to the West End. I know he just wanted to show-off his car but he let us in! Whoosh, this car flew down the Edgware Road with us screaming like girls. I kept telling him how wonderful his car was, but he got wise to the fact that we were taking the piss and would only take us as far as Oxford Street; we had to walk the rest of the way!

The Whites had adopted this O'Neil's as their occasional local for one reason. Up on the first floor there was a sofa that faced a picture window looking out onto the length of Gerrard Street. From there you could watch the rest of the world go by. If anyone was sitting in this seat they were told that it was tradition – to occupy that seat they first had to sing. One night a group of Polish tourists were in the seat. They needed little encouragement and burst into an endless selection of Polish folk songs.

My own retirement was a fabulous night. El and I were booked into the bridal suite at St. Ermine's hotel in Westminster – not just to bring back old Westminster memories, but it was a favourite of mine. Graham excelled making the speech and I will be eternally grateful to Mick who bore the brunt of the organising. I cannot express how wonderful it was to see all my old friends. They came from as far back as the old Battersea days: Ray Firth who went through the aftermath of Kings Cross, all the Soho firemen old and new, and a wonderful turnout from the local stations. The whole thing went by in a flash. There were so many people that I didn't get round to talking to. I didn't want it to end.

My daughter Elizabeth was there. Teresa couldn't make it due to babies, but the son-in-law, who was working in the West End, came along after his performance. Performance? He's a singer and at that time he was starring as the Phantom of the Opera. Teresa met John Owen Jones after Joe had helped to get her a summer job as a dresser at Les Miserables. John had performed several roles in the show and eventually went on to get the lead.

Just as Graham was starting his speech, the doors opened and there was Mr & Mrs Kirby. There is no way to describe what that meant to me. When it came to my turn to speak, I thanked everybody, as most of them had helped me at some time or another. I told a couple of short stories about the White Watch and Soho and then I finished with this:

'Finally, I would like to tell you about my most prized possessions. A tape recording of the 'Listed Londoner' radio show; that is a fantastic memory, and this postcard. (El and I were on holiday in Cyprus and, after a day at the beach, we came back to the hotel to collect our key and I noticed that there was something in my pigeon hole.) It's a picture of Piccadilly Circus. It says, 'Dear Guv. Hope all is well. It's a bit cold here and '2-Bob' wants to know how to switch on your central heating!' (They had prised the holiday details out of Teresa, but worst of all, the two teenage girls were at home alone!)

'Seriously, it's been fantastic. I could talk for a week non-stop. It's been exciting, miserable and horribly sad. I'd swap some of it, but most of it I'd like to hang onto.'

Then the senior fireman, Kingy, presented me with a mounted hand axe. This is the traditional gift for a retiring fireman. Before they took away our personal axes, the retiree's mates would take his axe which had been at his side all the way through his service. It would be polished, varnished, the metal head would be chromed and it would be mounted on a choice hardwood board. Attached to the board would be an engraved plate detailing his service. These days they have to buy a new axe; although not as significant, it is still a magnificent gift.

At the death, there were lots of emotional goodbyes. It was a good job the drink had been flowing, or it would have been the tears.

*Chapter 38*

# THE LAST DETAIL

So that was it. 28th April 2003 came around and my life as a fireman was over. All the experiences would now have to be told in the past tense and all those stories would just be bygone times. I could never be a fireman again. Well, not a proper one.

It was time to make that train journey. Feeling very mixed-up, I left home and caught the train that would take me past Battersea and into Victoria. I was so disappointed not being able to end it on my terms. I had wanted to go through the last year making a point of doing things for the last time, counting-down the paydays. Something that had been a major part of my life for over thirty years had ended, and it was going to be hard to replace.

I got off the train and walked through the station concourse out into Terminus Place where the constant flow of buses and cabs are the start of so many journeys to all parts of London. Nobody is aware of me. No one would ever know how many times I had visited this place after being called to some kind of emergency, from persons injured by trains, to bombs in litter bins and postboxes.

I headed off down Victoria Street; it was my intention to walk to Soho. Left into Buckingham Gate, and then into a narrow pedestrian walkway called Palmer Street. Here there is the shop where I bought my running kit. Cross Caxton Street (where William Caxton started a printing press in 1407), with a quick glance towards the St. Ermine Hotel and Scotland Yard. From there, it is a short walk to Petty France (so called because French wool merchants lived there), past the Home Office, through Queen Anne's Gate, across Birdcage Walk, and into St. James's Park.

With the sun shining, this must be the best part of the City – a place which stirred so many of my memories. Early morning runs before work, sitting in a deck-chair watching the world go by while trying to recover from one night shift and preparing to start another, fires in the early hours when the vandals set light to bins or stacks of deck-chairs, a call to a man on fire who turned out to be a fire-eater rehearsing his act. This was where we used to go begging for plants to brighten up the station.

Through the park and across the Mall. Apart from the famous 'walking race', my best memory of the Mall was in 1977, the night before the Queen's Silver Jubilee. I was driving one of Westminster's trucks and we were returning from a call on Soho's ground. It was a lovely warm night and crowds of good folk were camping out on the Mall. As we drove past, they started waving and cheering; it was infectious. We stopped and chatted until the next call came through and got cheered on our way.

Up Carlton Steps, past The ICA, the cause of so many sleep-disturbed nights. One night we were called to their alarms and there was a lesbian-gay function in progress. Opposite my home lived a couple who bowled around the wicket. They were decent men, good neighbours; they only had one party each year when all these extrovertly dressed people would look completely out of place in my leafy part of Croydon. There they were, outside The ICA, dressed up like the Village People shouting 'Hello Ray!' Did I get some stick? It started as soon as we got back in the truck!

At the top of the steps past the memorial to 'Giro' – the Nazi dog buried in 1934; the faithful hound of the German Ambassador. When we were out testing hydrants, this was a regular resting place. There was always an ice cream van parked there, and if anyone had any money we would mug the driver for non-tourist priced cornets.

Up Waterloo Place and into Lower Regent Street. Past the cinemas where we had cut the chains to release people locked in after the doors had been locked for the night.

Past the Bank of Scotland where a smoky job had caused us to evacuate the cinema next door. This was the same bank where we were called to their alarms at around midnight and found all the doors wide open! Past Fitness First, a health club that had once been the scene of a long drawn-out chemical incident. On towards Piccadilly Circus, HMV, Lilywhites and the Underground; all places where my skills had been called upon. When the Criterion site was being re-developed, we were called to an injured building worker fallen into a basement. We got him out and when the ambulance arrived, one of the paramedics seemed familiar. His daughter was in the same class as my Teresa and I had seen him at parents' nights. We met up a on a few jobs after that; one where we had to remove an injured junkie who, while trying to break-in, had fallen into a basement. That was the first time we had to wear surgical gloves before we touched a bleeding victim.

Piccadilly Circus has its own way of working its magic; a location in so many films and newsreels and the setting for so many celebrations. It's just one of the places I took for granted, which is world famous and visited by people from every part of the globe.

Into the Avenue and past the fast food joints where we used to shout at the cooks and servers. The only time they looked up from their work was when the fire engines gave them a toot and a bit of banter. I remember that part of the avenue when it was a row of shops – no sign of a McDonalds, nothing touristy. There was a wonderful shop called Austins where we Mods could buy imported American button-down collar shirts. Heady days.

Shaftesbury Avenue, the home of the great Lord Shaftesbury; the title inherited by the senior Station Officer at Soho Fire Station. That passed into history with Colin Townsley. It belonged to him; when my turn came I didn't want to live up to that. The Avenue was the scene of too many incidents to recall. It wasn't just the incidents that were important. Just walking out of the station to get a paper could be an event. The people you saw, the locals, the landlady of the Kings Head walking her little dog early in the morning, the lovely lady who ran Patisserie Valerie in Greek Street where you had to buy the cakes on your birthday. All the wonderful people who over the years had taken the time to stop and put a bit of cash in our good-causes collections. Most of them were wonderful, but some were real weirdoes. Nasty, crazy people who, for some reason, wanted to provoke the firemen. I'll always remember the night that Kingy stepped in and saved a girl in a drunken or drugged state being dragged into the darkness by a man with evil intentions.

I opened the front door to the station, still looking to see if it was clean and tidy, if the downstairs visitors' toilet was presentable. Old habits!

Tea in the mess with the boys and give the cook a cuddle – joy. I took a little video of the blokes and the building. One day I'll get up the courage to look at it.

Now for the hard part. Down to the Station Officer's room; it's time to empty my locker.

The last one on the right, next to the window; it had been so much a part of me for 18 years. It may seem strange, but that locker had held not only my belongings, but it was a kind of harbour full of memories and attachments: family photographs pinned inside the door, reminders of events and adventures, Sean Kelly already wearing the Green Jersey sprinting for the line at St. Etienne during the Tour De France, the space where I had pinned Shiner's fiver underwritten with 'Shiner paid-up!', a hand-written list of my annual pay increases (all in chinagraph, naturally). Every time I unlocked it, either it was so good that I had to pinch myself to be sure that I was rightfully standing there in the Station Officer's room at Soho Fire Station, or it was so bad that I was wishing that I could just go home.

It was no good staring at it; it had to be done. There's no point in keeping stuff you will never use again. I gave some away, binned a lot and the rest went home. I did not really comprehend that it was all over, that it wasn't mine anymore. Once when I complained to a senior officer about something he said, 'This is not your station Mr Chilton; it belongs to the Chief Officer.' My reply was, 'Well the next time a drug addict spews up the back doors, perhaps he would like to come and clear it up.' It was mine. I knew all of it; how to re-start the boilers, how to stop the doors banging, everything.

I took them out that night, had too much to drink and much too much emotion. It was not by accident that we ended the night at the Sunset Strip; the place where I went to celebrate the end of my training and had my wallet stolen. They had primed the owner during the day and he laid on my special treat from the ladies. Honestly, El, it was only the second time I had ever been in any such club.

There was no Green Watch Station Officer on duty that night, so after chatting to the lovely Greens and talking even more bollocks to Mick, I was allowed to spend one last night in the Station Officer's room. I didn't have to get up every time the bells went down and I didn't have to get out of bed at 0645hrs to stir the men, although I would have liked to play the music just one more time!

Prior to my forced absence, I had very little to do; it ran itself. The only problems occurred when the Brigade attempted to foul-up paradise with their money-led cuts, although I tried not to let things like that affect the watch. I ran it as though we were the only one in the Brigade. Hardly any senior officers visited the station because of the hassle getting through the traffic. It was like an oasis surrounded, not by sand, but nose-to-nose traffic. If some bit of superfluous administration was not done on time, we always had the excuse that we were too busy – we had the statistics to back us up.

From about 1999 the watch was at its best. It was like one of those moments in time where everything clicked. We just had the right mix of men and officers. Everybody knew what to do on the fireground and back at the station. It was a shame that Eddie had to retire and that 'New Bob' (Bob Edwards) had moved on through promotion. (We had four Bobs on the watch at the same time and we just ran out of suitable nicknames.) In their place I was happy to get the Stout brothers, Vinnie and Colin, plus Peter Moore who got lumbered very quickly with 'Mumbly'. Sorry, Peter, but we couldn't understand a word. Then, just before I went into pre-retirement mode, another new boy came straight from training school. I had little to do with his development and Tony Backhouse was lucky to have Mick to see him through his probation.

They say that you go through a period of grieving when you retire. It is a massive change. I got some consolation from the fact that the job has been altered beyond recognition since the last strike, and the attitude of the men towards the Brigade has worsened. Quite honestly, I would have had great difficulty in dealing with the situation – siding with the men, but having to handle the changes and enforce the rules.

As one generation retires, the next will tell you that you are best out of it. I can honestly say I never really felt that way. I just thought that my time was the best, but now I really do think that they are right.

It has also helped that my White Watch is no longer. All but three have moved on; I suppose the change was a bit too much for them. Now there is a virtually new White Watch with my old friend Steve Colman in charge and I hope he stays there until he retires. I know he will look after it like I did.

Contrary to all my criticisms, all through my illness the Brigade was great. Once they realised that it was serious, the individual departments showed both sympathy and understanding. There really are some people in high positions that still care.

I have been back to Soho a few times and it is wonderful to see any of the firemen from any of the watches, but it's not the same; it's not mine anymore. Eventually there will be no trace of my time except, I hope, that the dedication I gave to *my* Fire Brigade has rubbed off on all the young men and women who ever paid me the compliment of supporting my principles. I'm lucky that my name will stay on the Honours and Awards board in Westminster's watchroom, and I hope that there will always be someone there to pass on what I was about.

All my experiences came accidentally; all my mistakes were honest. I am flattered when I am told that I was thought to be a good man because that was all I ever wanted.

I got some wonderful compliments from some wonderful people; letters that have entered the treasured red lever-arch file. One of the Whites told me that he had modelled his whole life on my standards, and another told me that the 14 years he spent with me at Soho were the best of his life. One more said that he had only transferred so that he could work with me. My heart was touched and maybe it just goes to prove that all the sacrifices were worthwhile.

For me there is no better company than that of firemen and the more I think about it, I realise the uniqueness of my White Watch and of my debt to them. During my service I was honoured to meet some wonderful people, not just firemen but, from all the emergency services: ambulance crews who came to the rescue of our limited first-aid skills, police officers who respected the significance of our work and let us get on with it, and the absolute professionalism of the Helicopter Emergency Medical Service doctors. It was an honour, not only to work with them, but just to stand beside them. To witness that helicopter landing in impossible places and then whisking-away the casualties was something to treasure; and the nurses – oh, the nurses.

As usual, I don't want to leave. Now this is finished, I've got another gap to fill. I have loved writing this; it has given me the chance of reliving a fantastic time. Now I realise there is no way that I will ever get it out of my system, because I don't want to. I suppose that's because in my heart I will always be a fireman, and I sincerely hope that my explanations of what that means is now clear.

Soho Fire Station will carry on until some prat decides that the West End doesn't need the same level of fire cover and yet another fire station can be closed. It has always been my philosophy that fire stations are there for what might happen, not what does happen. If something really nasty is going to happen, it happens in the places where it causes the most destruction and, once the centre becomes gridlocked, all the reinforcements in the world will be of no use; they won't be able to reach the location. World-shattering atrocities do not happen in the leafy lanes of the Home Counties.

There will be young men and young women who will work there seeking excitement. They will love it; if they don't there's something wrong with them. It will be a crying shame if it ever goes. But if ever that day comes, I hope that somebody with more than just economy in mind will look back, appreciate all the good people who have worked there, and all the fantastic work they have done. If they do, they will realise that it is not simply a building which houses fire engines, but an institution with a fantastic history and a tradition that deserves preservation.

Time to say a thank you to a few people. If it were not for certain important people, I would still be slaving away, utterly miserable, mind destroyed, in a factory in Kent. Without their influence at critical times, there would have been no White Watch. It would not have been such a memorable experience, a story worth the telling.

Peter Vallis, who encouraged me to re-join the brigade, is one of those men who was sorely and shamefully overlooked for the lofty heights of the Brigade. ACO Alan Jones, who had faith in me and allowed me my wonderful job. Ron Morris, who has no idea how important he was to my career, my way of thinking, and consequently my life. All the good officers and firemen who taught me, making me realise that they are the *real* Fire Brigade and need to be cherished.

More importantly El, Teresa and Liz who put up with it all – missed me and missed out when I had to work at Christmas and all the other occasions when the other family took me away. They kept out of the way when I needed a sleep during the day and stood by me when things were not going too well.

Most of all, El; for all of the above, her patience and tolerance. She allowed me to keep up the pretence that I was going to work when actually it was simply days and nights out with my mates, charging around the West End in a big red fire engine doing daring deeds and getting big 'eds!

I'll see you in my dreams.

Take care, Ray.

Printed in the United Kingdom
by Lightning Source UK Ltd.
126953UK00001B/11-12/A